Guide to Nonsexist Teaching Activities (K-12)

Guide to Nonsexist Teaching Activities (K-12)

Developed by
Northwest Regional Educational Laboratory
Center for Sex Equity

Karen Stone, Developer
Barbara K. Berard
Lillian Dixson
Janice Druian
Joan Goforth
Ginger Denecke Hackett
Barbara Hutchison, Director

 ORYX PRESS
1983

The rare Arabian Oryx is believed to have inspired the myth of the unicorn. This desert antelope became virtually extinct in the early 1960s. At that time several groups of international conservationists arranged to have 9 animals sent to the Phoenix Zoo to be the nucleus of a captive breeding herd. Today the Oryx population is over 400 and herds have been returned to reserves in Israel, Jordan, and Oman.

Copyright © 1983 by The Oryx Press
2214 North Central at Encanto
Phoenix, AZ 85004

Published simultaneously in Canada

Printed and Bound in the United States of America

Guide to Nonsexist Teaching Activities (K–12) was first published as *BIAS (Building Instruction Around Sex-Equity): Guide to Non-Sexist Teaching Activities (K–12)* by Northwest Regional Educational Laboratory in 1982.

Library of Congress Cataloging in Publication Data
Main entry under title:

Guide to nonsexist teaching activities (K–12)

 Includes bibliographical references and index.
 1. Sex discrimination in education—United States—
Bibliography.   2. Sexism—United States—Bibliography.
3. Sex role—United States—Bibliography.   4. Education
—United States—Curricula—Bibliography.   5. Teaching
—Aids and devices—Bibliography.   I. Northwest
Regional Educational Laboratory. Center for Sex Equity.
Z5814.D5G84   1983   [LC212.8]   016.37019'345   83-42515
ISBN 0-89774-100-5

Contents

Preface

This guide was compiled by the Center for Sex Equity at the Northwest Regional Educational Laboratory to provide K–12 teachers with a descriptive list of nonsexist teaching activity resources. It is not meant to be all-inclusive, but rather to provide a sample of what is available. It can be used to order nonsexist resources helpful in adapting or supplementing biased instructional materials. We believe access to these materials will assist teachers in creating an equitable learning environment for their students.

We suggest teachers use the guide in conjunction with the *Bibliography of Nonsexist Supplementary Books* (published by Oryx Press). Many supplementary books not listed in the guide but found in the bibliography are excellent resources for teachers interested in providing nonbiased instruction.

This work was made possible by a grant from the Women's Educational Equity Act Program of the U.S. Education Department.

Barbara Hutchison, Director

Acknowledgements

The development of this guide has been a collaborative effort requiring the cooperation of many people. The Center for Sex Equity staff would like to thank the following people for their assistance in this effort:

Rene Gentry, Joyce Hollis, and Geri Canfield, Northwest Regional Educational Laboratory, for their cooperation and helpfulness in readying the guide for production.

Patricia Goins and Doris Shakin, our program monitors, Women's Program Staff of the U.S. Education Department, for their advice and support of this work.

We would also like to acknowledge the work of the many persons across the nation who have contributed significantly to the body of knowledge now available in the area of sex equity in education.

Introduction

WHY THE GUIDE WAS COMPILED

Many of the texts and instructional materials used in schools today are

Sex-Biased	They contain a disproportionate number of stories or biographies with males as major characters
and/or	
Sex-Role Stereotyped	They depict males as having a common set of abilities, interests, values and roles that are different from the abilities, interests, values and roles of females

For teachers to teach in an equitable manner and in a way which offers the maximum number of career choices, role models and options for all students, they must have access to activities they can use in the classroom to offset the effect of biased texts and materials. They need lesson plans, teaching activities and information about resources that will enable them to adapt or supplement their biased instructional materials so that student classroom experiences will reflect an equitable and sex-fair environment. This guide has been developed to provide teachers with (1) a description of and (2) ordering information for nonsexist teaching activity resources that will be appropriate for use with K–12 students.

WHO CAN USE THE GUIDE

The guide has been designed for teachers who have direct classroom experiences with students. Curriculum and media specialists, librarians, counselors, coaches, administrators and school district Title IX coordinators may also find the resources listed in this guide helpful when developing courses, materials, programs and strategies that are free of sex bias.

WHAT RESOURCES ARE INCLUDED IN THE GUIDE

The majority of items in the guide focus on the classroom—they include activities teachers can use with their students in a classroom setting. The activities include lesson plans, course outlines, supplementary texts and audiovisual materials. Bibliographies of print and nonprint resources as well as sex equity organizations have also been included so that educators may find additional materials. Anthologies of readings, research, statistics, inservice packages and background information have not been included, unless they seem to be especially adaptable for use with students in the classroom. A sample lesson plan or course outline has been provided for each major subject heading to give users of the guide a feel for the types of activities available.

HOW THE GUIDE IS ORGANIZED

Teaching activities included in the guide are organized according to subject areas frequently found in elementary and secondary schools. Some subjective judgments on the part of the Center for Sex Equity staff were necessary in order to identify the appropriate subject matter area for a particular item since school districts have varying ways of organizing their school curriculum.

The guide is organized into the eight subject areas and subcategories that follow:

General Awareness
- Sex Role Stereotyping
- Women's Educational Equity
- Male Sex Role Stereotyping
- Nonsexist Materials

Counseling and Career Guidance
- Counseling
- Career Guidance

Fine Arts
- Art
- Dance
- Music

Health and Physical Education
- Health
- PE/Sports

Language Arts
- Literature/Children's Books
- Women Writers
- Writing/Language

Math and Science
- Math
- Science

Social Studies
- History
- Social Studies
- Women's Studies

Sex Equity Organizations
- Women's Educational Equity
- Vocational Education
- Publications/Media
- Sex Desegregation Centers

Although attempts were made to avoid unnecessary duplication in compiling the guide, items were included under more than one subject heading in those instances where they covered several topic areas. Items usually appear, however, under one subject heading only. Teachers are therefore encouraged to review all subject areas when looking for a particular item. Many of the general awareness teaching activities can be easily used by career guidance counselors or social studies teachers. Items found in the counseling or health categories may be appropriate for use in social studies classes. Also, many of the career awareness activities and lesson plans can be adapted for use in a variety of subject areas.

Within each subcategory, items are listed alphabetically by title in the following order: lesson plans, course outlines, supplementary texts, periodicals, multimedia programs, audiovisual materials, bibliographies/resource lists.

Information provided for each item includes bibliographic data, ordering procedures, an annotation, footnote reference, and recommended grade level (where available). The availability of an item in microfiche (MF) or hard copy (HC) from the ERIC Document Reproduction Service

(EDRS) also is noted (see Appendix 3 for an explanation of this service).

An index listing all teaching activity resources by title is included to provide easy reference for users of the guide.

HOW THE GUIDE WAS COMPILED

The guide was compiled after staff conducted an ERIC computerized search for nonsexist teaching activities and reviewed brochures, catalogues and bibliographies with an equity emphasis. Materials produced under the auspices of the Women's Educational Equity Act Program also were reviewed.

Many of the materials listed in the guide have not been personally examined by the staff. In many instances the annotations have previously appeared elsewhere and are so indicated with a footnote reference. The guide is not meant to be all-inclusive, but rather to provide a sample of the wealth of nonsexist teaching activity resources available for use by classroom teachers.

FOR MORE DETAILED INFORMATION

Appendixes provide more detailed information about the guide and how to use it.

Appendix 1: Subject Definitions—provides definition of subject categories and descriptors

Appendix 2: Footnote Sources—provides a list of sources in which annotations in this guide first appeared

Appendix 3: How to Obtain Materials Listed in the Guide—provides information on sources for obtaining materials and how to order ERIC documents from EDRS

Appendix 4: Model for Developing Nonsexist Lesson Plans—provides a model for developing nonsexist lesson plans

Appendix 5: Lesson Planning Activity Sheet—provides a structured form to aid in developing lesson plans

Appendix 6: Guidelines for Developing Nonbiased Materials—provides information on how to develop your own nonsexist materials for use in the classroom

For more information about the project, contact Ms. Barbara Hutchison, Director, Center for Sex Equity, Northwest Regional Educational Laboratory, 300 SW Sixth Avenue, Portland, OR 97204, (503) 248-6800.

1.0 General Awareness

EX ROLE STEREOTYPING

esson Plans

1   ASPIRE: Module 1, Sex-Role Socialization. Livonia
Michigan) Public Schools, 1979. 115 p. (Available from:
ducation Development Center, 55 Chapel Street, Newton,
A 02160. $1.50.)

though this model is part of ASPIRE's educator inservice training
ckage, many of the activities are appropriate for use with high
hool students to increase their awareness of the effects of sex role
reotyping. [9–12]

2   Beyond Sex Roles. Alice G. Sargent. St. Paul, MN:
est Publishing Co. $11.50.

fers a variety of individual and small group exercises designed to
p people increase their awareness of those sex role related at-
des and behaviors which limit a person's potential. Also includes
cted readings on sex role socialization, marriage, family rela-
ships and assertiveness training. Useful chapter on teachers as
diators of sex role standards. Each chapter includes a detailed list
eferences.22

Breaking the Mould: Lesson Aid Plans to Explore
Roles, K–8. Margot Smith and Carol Pasternak (eds.).
p. (Available from: The Ontario Institute for Studies in
cation, 252 Bloor Street West, Toronto, Canada M5S
.)

ty-seven class projects and resources for use with K–8 students.
projects, which focus on beginning and advanced conscious-
-raising, work roles, Canadian history, media and texts, are
gned to offer teachers help in combatting sex stereotyping in
entary schools. In addition to the curricular materials, sugges-
for identifying and altering sexist attitudes and behaviors at the
mal level—the "hidden curriculum"—are also included.

A Comparative View of the Roles of Women (Ex-
mental Learning Unit, revised edition). Barbara
er and Jacquelyn Johnson. Center for International Rela-

tions, University of Denver. (Available from: EDRS MF-
$.91—HC-$6.01 plus postage, ED 128 263.)

Twenty-two activities arranged so that students may consider two
questions: (1) What are the appropriate roles of women today, and
(2) What changes could equality bring to students' personal lives,
the community, the nation and the global society? Each activity
provides an introduction, objectives, time required, materials
needed, step-by-step procedures, suggested follow-up and evaluation procedures. Sample activities include asking students to (1)
examine how toys and books promote sex stereotyping for children;
(2) compare attitudes toward childbearing in various cultures; and
(3) examine a reversal of male and female marital roles.

1.5   The Emerging Woman: Quest for Equality. Anita
Wilkes Dore. New York: Globe Books.

Activities and exercises for use in the classroom, using excerpts
from literature to show women's roles in society; a good conscious-
ness-raiser.4 [10–12]

1.6   Focus on the Future. Cleveland State University,
1979. (Available from: Education Development Center, 55
Chapel Street, Newton, MA 02160. $2.00 technical manual,
leader's manual and picture stimulus set, plus 20% handling
charge.)

A three-session module to help adolescents recognize the limiting
effects of sex stereotyping and focus on careers and family relation-
ships.14 [7–12]

1.7   Growing Up Equal: Activities and Resources for
Parents and Teachers of Young Children. Jeanne Kohl
Jenkins and Pam MacDonald. Englewood Cliffs, NJ: Pren-
tice-Hall, Inc., 1979. 214 p. $7.95.

A handbook of practical ideas for exposing young children to a wide
range of activities and helping to keep them from being locked into
stereotypical feminine and masculine roles.44 [K–3]

1.8   Growing Up Human. Unitarian Universalist Wom-
en's Federation. (Available from: Unitarian Universalist
Women's Federation, 25 Beacon Street, Boston, MA 02108.
$3.50.)

A four-session course on sex role stereotyping for grades 8–12.[1] [8–12]

1.9 Maximizing Young Children's Potential: A Non-Sexist Manual for Early Childhood Trainers. Women's Action Alliance. Women's Educational Equity Act Program, 1981. 24 p. (Available from: Education Development Center, 55 Chapel Street, Newton, MA 02160. $3.25.)

A practical guide for developing nonsexist attitudes in young children, this manual details activities and strategies to foster independence and expand the range of children's experiences. Classroom materials, literature, language, and both indoor and outdoor activities are discussed. [K]

1.10 Non-Sexist Learning and Teaching with Young Children. Shiela Morfield. 1978. 54 p. (Available from: EDRS MF-$.91—HC-$3.50 plus postage, ED 154 932.)

A guide to nonsexist lesson plans and teaching activities for K–3 students. Activities focus on five areas: (1) feelings, (2) encouraging nonsexist behavior, (3) body movement, (4) working, and (5) women in history. Also included in the guide is an annotated bibliography of nonsexist books, films and records for young children, and an annotated bibliography of resources for teachers. Activities are appropriate for social studies, career awareness and sex role stereotyping awareness units. [K–3]

1.11 Picture-Pac Activity on Sexism. Council on Interracial Books for Children (CIBC). (Available from: CIBC Resource Center, Room 300, 1841 Broadway, New York, NY 10023. $2.50.)

Stimulating discussion opener. Flexible use for 5th grade through college. Ten photos are examined by small groups who discuss which are, and which are not, sexist. The discussion allows participants to explore their own understanding of sexism at their own level and subsequently arrive at some definitions. These are later redefined by using the materials included in the Activity Packet. The trainer and teacher will also receive a booklet and a detailed lesson plan.[10] [5–12]

1.12 The Role of Men and Women in Our Society: A Consciousness-Raising Group Activity for Use with Grades 10, 11 and 12 Students in Canadian Schools. Phil A. Manuel. University of Toronto. (Available from: EDRS MF-$.91—HC-$1.50 plus postage, ED 095 440.)

A consciousness-raising group experience for 10th- through 12th-grade students to explore issues relating to the role of men and women in our society. A group of 10 to 12 students, with an equal number of male and female participants and a counselor and facilitator, discuss topics introduced on 12 numbered cards, each of which has a short descriptive statement on an issue related to the topic of sex roles. Each of the 12 topics should generate 15–20 minutes of discussion. [10–12]

1.13 Thinking and Doing: Overcoming Sex Role Stereotyping in Education. Dorothy Stein and others. Hawaii Educational Equity Program, 1978. 107 p. (Available from: Education Development Center, 55 Chapel Street, Newton, MA 02160. $5.50.)

Although these materials are designed in workshop format for inservice and preservice training, they will also be a valuable resource when developing classroom activities for elementary and secondary students. The activities, which focus on the general issues of sex roles and the implications of stereotyping in specific content areas, will encourage students as well as others to examine and change their own beliefs, attitudes and behaviors that promote sex stereotyping. [K–12]

1.14 Today's Changing Roles: An Approach to Nonsexist Teaching. Educational Challenges, Inc., 1974. (Available from: Resource Center on Sex Roles in Education, National Foundation for the Improvement of Education, Washington, DC.)

This publication provides a model for dealing with sex role stereotypes in the elementary, intermediate, and secondary classrooms.[8] [K–12]

1.15 Understanding Sex Roles and Moving Beyond: A Learning/Teaching Guide. Joanna Selman and others. University of Tennessee, Model Sex Fair Training Program in Educational Psychology and Guidance, 1979. 194 p. (Available from: Educational Development Center, 55 Chapel Street, Newton, MA 02160.)

These materials were developed to be used in a graduate level course in guidance and counseling. However, all or part of the units could be used for teacher resource materials or in high school classrooms. The three units included are "Formula for Restricted Development: Sex Role Stereotypes in America"; "Examining Sex Roles Across Cultures"; and "Sex Roles in American Institutions: Getting Clear and Moving On." Each unit includes an introduction, objectives, facilitator's directions, learning activities, bibliography and appendix of reading activities, bibliography and appendix of reading and worksheets. Many of the activities are appropriate for language arts, health and social studies classes. [9–12]

1.16 Undoing Sex Stereotyping: Research and Resources for Educators. Marcia Guttentag and Helen Bray. New York: McGraw-Hill, 1976. 342 p. $8.95 hardback, $5.95 paper.

This book is based on an important field survey and intervention program for reducing sex stereotyped attitudes in children. In several school systems at the kindergarten, fifth, and ninth grade levels, the researchers measured children's attitudes about sex roles and then attempted to change them toward nonstereotyped views. The book contains nonsexist curriculum packets for the various grade levels, background materials, resource agencies, bibliographies and guidelines for effective nonsexist intervention.[14] [K–12]

1.17 Woman of Valor, Man of Honor. Beatrice Tainer. New York: Harper & Row, 1975. 39 p.

Exercises on sex roles for high school students.[4] [9–12]

1.18 The Yellow, Blue and Red Book: A Collection of Short-Term Activities Developed by and for Teachers K–6, To Help Expand Students' Awareness of Traditional Sex Role Stereotyping. Project Equality, 1976. 56 p. (Available from: Project Equality, Highline School District, 15675 Ambaum Blvd., SW, Seattle, WA 98166, (206) 433-0111; or EDRS MF-$.91—HC-$4.82 plus postage, ED 028.)

Twenty-nine 10- to 40-minute activities designed to help expand student awareness of sex role stereotyping. Each activity indicates the subject area, suggested grade level and objectives. The activities may be used independently or in sequence and are appropriate for language arts, social studies and career awareness units. [K–6]

Course Outlines

1.19 Roles and Relationships: A Practical Guide to Teaching about Masculinity and Femininity. Barbara Stanford and Gene Stanford. New York: Bantam, 1975. 88 p. $1.75.

Useful collection of ideas for teachers wishing to devise a course for students on sex roles and relationships or for teachers interested in discussing some of these problems in conjunction with other subjects; suggested objectives, reading lists and discussion topics on such subjects as sex and identity, myths, homosexuality, and differences in perception; one flaw—sometimes suggests questions but fails to give information.[3]

Supplementary Texts

1.20 Sex-Role Stereotypes Revisited: Psychological Approaches to Women's Studies. Rhoda Kesler Unger. New York: Harper & Row, 1973. 53 p.

Pamphlet on basics of sex role stereotyping with topics for discussion and writing.[4] [10–12]

1.21 The Social Roles of Women and Men: A Sociological Approach. Helen Mayer Hacker. New York: Harper & Row, 1975. 51 p.

A guide placing women in a sociological perspective; good for stimulating student discussion.[4] [10–12]

1.22 What Are Little Girls Made Of? The Roots of Feminine Stereotypes. Elena Gianini Belotti. New York: Schocken Books, 1976. 158 p. $4.95 p.b.

A book on feminine stereotypes which focuses on the infant and young child who learn so very early the "shoulds" and "should nots" pertaining to sex role stereotypes. Belotti, an Italian Montessori educator, speaks from an Italian point of view, and as Margaret Mead points out in her excellent introduction, she is sometimes biased and strident. Nevertheless, Belotti's points are well taken, and her description of the role teachers play in enforcing stereotypes makes this book a "must" for educators and an excellent resource for secondary students. [11–12]

Games

1.23 When I Grow Up I'm Going to Be Married. California Commission on the Status of Women. (Available from: California Commission on the Status of Women, 1025 Street, Room 340, Sacramento, CA 95814.)

A game which illustrates how time and circumstance affect women. Excellent for use with high school students.[23] [9–12]

Photographs

1.24 Community Helpers. Feminist Resources for Equal Education. (Available from: Feminist Resources for Equal Education, Book 3185, Saxonville Station, Framingham, MA 01701. $2.50.)

Set of nonsexist photographs.[1] [K–3]

Multimedia Programs

1.25 Sex Role Stereotyping: A Multi-Media Program. National Education Association. Multimedia. (Available from: NEA, Room 609, 1201 16th Street, NW, Washington, DC 20036. $3.50.)

For inservice training, parent-teacher groups and students; contains filmstrips, cassette, books, pamphlets and leaflets.[23]

1.26 "Sex Stereotyping in Math Doesn't Add Up"; "Girl, Boy or Person: Beyond Sex Differences"; "Equality in Science: Formula for Changing Sex Bias"; "Exercising Your Rights: Eliminating Sex Bias in Physical Education, Reading, Writing, and Stereotyping"; "Present but Not Accounted for: Women in Educational History"; "We the People: Sex Bias in American History." Patricia B. Campbell and Susan E. Katrin. Multimedia modules. (Available from: Education Development Center, 55 Chapel Street, Newton, MA 02160. $15.60 plus 20% postage, complete set; $2.50 each unit.)

This series of instructional modules on sex role stereotyping in education includes cassette tapes, handouts, transparency masters and a bibliography for each topic area. The modules may be used alone or to complement an instructional unit.[14]

Audiovisual Materials

1.27 American Women: New Opportunities. Butterick Publishing, 1976. Two part, 12-minute, color, sound filmstrips. (Available from: Butterick Publishing Co., 161 Sixth Avenue, New York, NY 10013. $45.00.)

This unit of two sound filmstrips helps high school students explore sex role stereotyping. Part I, "Who Are You?", briefly reviews the traditional roles of women and options for the future. Part II, "Who Can You Be?", confronts the problem that even though new opportunities exist, prejudice—both external and internal—still exists. Five women in nontraditional occupations look at how to shape their lives for the most rewarding and satisfying arrangement.[9] [9–12]

1.28 And Everything Nice. Bailey Film Associates. 20 minutes. (Available from: Bailey Film Associates, 2211 Michigan Avenue, P.O. Box 1795, Santa Monica, CA 90406.)

As a result of changing social conditions, many women find their traditional roles unsatisfying; consequently, they feel exploited and oppressed by the expectations society has placed on them to be "feminine." Film shows the process of consciousness-raising, "CR," during which women develop new expectations for themselves and a sense of self-worth, a new consciousness of what it means to be female.[21] [10–12]

1.29 Anything You Want to Be. New Day Films, 1971. Eight minutes, b/w, sound, 16mm. (Available from: New Day Films, P.O. Box 315, Franklin Lakes, NJ 04717. $115.00; $17.00 rental.)

This is a short, fast-paced film showing how society subtly socializes women into accepted and stereotyped roles. The main character is a bright high school girl who is told she can be anything she wants to be, but receives signals that in reality she can't. This film would be useful with junior high students through adults for discussion about sex stereotypes.[9] [7–12]

1.30   Beyond Black and White. Motivational Media. 28 minutes, color, 16mm. (Available from: Motivational Media, 8271 Melrose Avenue, Los Angeles, CA 90046.)

Deals with the perpetuation of cliches about minorities which have no factual validity; parallels sex stereotyping.[16] [10–12]

1.31   Changes, Changes. Weston Woods. Six minutes, 16mm. (Available from: Weston Woods, Weston, CT 06880.)

In the form of wooden dolls, a husband and wife build their house. Visited by a flood, they reassemble the pieces of their house into an ark. Then another disaster—but again they survive, cleverly transforming the same materials into other shelters and working together as equals.[21] [K–4]

1.32   Do Your Own Thing. McGraw-Hill. 13 minutes, 33mm. (Available from: McGraw-Hill, Department 410, 1221 Avenue of the Americas, New York, NY 10020.)

Demonstrates that boys and girls can enjoy and be successful at the same types of games and activities.[21] [K–6]

1.33   The Fable of He and She. Learning Corporation of America. 13 minutes. (Available from: Learning Corporation of America, 1350 Avenue of the Americas, New York, NY 10019.)

A new film, inspired by women and men's liberation. On an island live two kinds of creatures: the hardybars who hunt and build and the mushamels who cook and take care of the children. Sound familiar? But when the island is split in two by a storm, everyone has to learn to do everything—and when the hardybars and the mushamels are reunited, they are happier with their shared skills. A sophisticated idea carried out in a whimsical way that kids will enjoy.[21] [K–12]

1.34   Happy to Be Me. Arthur Mokin Productions, 1979. 26 minutes, sound, color, 16mm. (Available from: Arthur Mokin Productions, 17 West 60th Street, New York, NY 10023. $425.00; $40.00 rental.)

Students in School District #11, Bronx, New York, reply to questions on sex roles, future expectations in careers and family life. Good for initiating discussion on sex role stereotyping with students, parents and community.[28]

1.35   Hey, What about Us? University of California, 1974. 15 minutes, sound, 16mm. (Available from: University of California, Extension Media Center, 2223 Shattuck Avenue, Berkeley, CA 94720.)

Depicts incidents of stereotyping in physical activities and challenges traditional concepts of what is masculine and feminine.[16] [7–12]

1.36   Hopscotch. Churchill Films. 12 minutes, 16mm. (Available from: Churchill Films, 662 North Robertson Blvd., Los Angeles, CA 90069.)

Attempting to make friends with a boy and a girl playing hopscotch, a boy plays out a succession of roles—from star baseball player to macho bully. He finally is himself, and he's then invited to join the game. Cleverly told and very much to the point.[21] [K–6]

1.37   I Am Me . . . And I Want to Be. Sandler. 12 minutes, 16mm. (Available from: Sandler, 120 West 44th Street, New York, NY 10036.)

Explores the importance of individual differences and diversity in society.[21] [3–6]

1.38   Is Anatomy Destiny? Women in America, A Resource Kit. Multimedia Productions. 53 slides; student and teacher guides. (Available from: Multimedia Productions, Box 3097, Stanford, CA 94305.)

Slides and quotations are provided to create a do-it-yourself audiovisual program on sex roles and the role of women in America. [7–12]

1.39   Katy. Bailey Film Associates. 17 minutes, 16mm. (Available from: Bailey Film Associates, 2211 Michigan Avenue, P.O. Box 1795, Santa Monica, CA 90406.)

Vivacious and energetic Katy wants to be free to ride her horse. When her brother goes away to camp, she takes over his paper route to earn money for riding. Her dreams and aspirations are challenged by the route managers and the boys who are against girls delivering papers.[21] [3–7]

1.40   Male and Female Roles. Coronet Instructional Media, 1975. Nine minutes each, color, sound filmstrips. (Available from: Coronet Instructional Media, 65 East South Water Street, Chicago, IL 60601. $102.00.)

The unit contains six color, sound filmstrips entitled "The Stereotypes," "How Stereotypes Evolved," "How They Are Learned," "Emerging Dissatisfactions," "New Perspectives," and "How Aware Are You?" These can be used as an entire unit or separately to help people from junior high students through adults understand the sociological process of sex stereotyping. A 16-page teacher's guide gives questions for discussion and extra activities.[9] [7–12]

1.41   Male/Female: Changing Lifestyles. Educational Audio-Visual, 1974. Four filmstrips with four cassettes, guide, duplicating masters. (Available from: Educational Audio-Visual, 29 Marble Avenue, Pleasantville, NY 10670.)

Surveys scientific and cultural differences between the sexes which are the basis of sex roles; traces history of sex roles, and how they are changing, and shows the development of the women's movement.[16] [7–12]

1.42   Man and Woman: Myths and Stereotypes. Center for Humanities, 1975. 20 minutes, slide carousels, cassettes or records. (Available from: Center for Humanities, Inc. 2 Holland Avenue, White Plains, NY 10603.)

Using paintings, photography, theater and movie scripts, and popular music, these sets describe how our views of men and women developed in western culture and how these stereotypes are changing today.[16] [9–12]

1.43   Masculine or Feminine: Your Role in Society. Coronet Instructional Films. 18 minutes. (Available from: Coronet Instructional Films, 65 East South Water Street, Chicago, IL 60601.)

Explores the changing attitudes about masculinity and femininity today's society. Interviews with a construction worker, business representative, college professor, woman executive and parent. Give students reveal different, sometimes conflicting, opinions on masculine and feminine roles.[21] [10–12]

1.44 Masculinity and Femininity. Guidance Associates, 1969. Two filmstrips with cassettes. (Available from: Guidance Associates, 757 Third Avenue, New York, NY 10017.)

Part I presents a case history of a couple who have reversed roles—she is a worker outside the home, he is a homemaker—in order to discuss sex roles and stereotypes. Part II deals with traditional sex roles and sex-assigned tasks in other cultures with emphasis on cultural and biological influences.[16] [9–12]

1.45 Ranchgirl. AIC Films. 26 minutes, 16mm. (Available from: AIC Films [Paramount Oxford], 5451 Marathon Street, Hollywood, CA 90038 or 35 West 45th Street, New York, NY 10036.)

A young girl saddles her horse and goes for a ride. She tells us about what she sees—from wildflowers to the skeleton of an animal killed by a mountain lion. During a rainstorm, she competently takes care of herself.[21] [4–6]

1.46 Re-Education of Women and Men: Creating New Relationships. Center for Humanities, Inc., 1976. Two carousels and records or tapes. (Available from: Center for Humanities, Inc., 2 Holland Avenue, White Plains, NY 10603.)

Each carousel investigates different areas of sex role differences, dating, success, and achievement; psychological studies concerning sex roles.[16] [8–12]

1.47 Stardust. McGraw-Hill. 8 minutes, 16mm. (Available from: McGraw-Hill, Department 410, 1221 Avenue of the Americas, New York, NY 10020.)

Is the astronaut navigating through space in this lovely film a boy or girl? I think it's a girl. She attempts to land her spacecraft on a cold blue planet that rebuffs her. When she succeeds, she kisses the planet's surface which responds by pulsating with glowing colors.[21] [4–6]

1.48 Sugar and Spice. Bailey Film Associates. 32 minutes. (Available from: Bailey Film Associates, 2211 Michigan Avenue, P.O. Box 1795, Santa Monica, CA 90406.)

Children learn what is "appropriate" behavior for boys and girls at an early age. Today, more and more parents and educators feel that these stereotypes stunt children's growth and limit their capacity to deal with a changing society. Film is about what people are doing to eliminate sex role stereotypes.[21] [7–12]

1.49 A Tale of O: On Being Different. Goodmeasure, Inc., 1980. Synchronized slide-tape (available in other formats, including videotape). 27 minutes. (Available from: Goodmeasure, Inc., 6 Channing Place, Cambridge, MA 02138. $425.00 purchase; $150.00 plus shipping for three-day rental.)

Tale of O explores the consequences of being different. It focuses on a group of people in which there are "the many," referred to as "X's," and "the few," referred to as the "O's." Used as a training tool for managing diversity, it is appropriate for affirmative action awareness sessions; management development programs; supervisory skills training; and support groups for women and minorities.

1.50 To Be a Woman. Billy Budd Film Co. 25 minutes. (Available from: Billy Budd Film Co., 235 East 57th Street, New York, NY 10022.)

Several young women discuss stereotypes about females and their feelings on the meaning of femininity and womanhood; accompanied by Peter Max-type cartoons. Recommended for counselors, teachers and young girls.[21] [10–12]

1.51 Waterwheel Village. Filmfair Communications. Sound, color, 16mm, plus guide. (Available from: Filmfair Communications, 10900 Ventura Blvd., P.O. Box 1728, Studio City, CA 91604.)

A model village built by a girl produces strong reactions in two brothers who are torn between a desire to play with the village and a stereotyped attitude toward girls. Useful for initiating discussion on sex roles.[28] [K–6]

1.52 Women Today. Guidance Associates, 1974. (Available from: Guidance Associates, 757 Third Avenue, New York, NY 10017. $59.50.)

By exploring the changes that have affected society's view of women's roles, this sound filmstrip helps students examine themselves as people rather than as males or females whose destinies are determined by their biological sex. It also helps students examine their own sex prejudices and stereotypes.[22] [9–12]

1.53. Yes Baby, She's My Sir! Feminist Productions, 1978. Two filmstrips with a cassette and guide. (Available from: Feminist Productions, 23 Whalers Cove, Babylon, NY 11702.)

This animated cartoon filmstrip dramatizes the sexist world of language which excludes women; remedial exercises and use of alternative words and phrases are included in discussion guide.[16] [9–12]

Bibliographies/Resource Lists

1.54 Sex Role Socialization and Sex Discrimination: A Synthesis and Critique of the Literature. Constantina Safilios-Rothschild. National Institute of Education, October 1979. 120 p. (Available from: Social Processes/Women's Research Team, National Institute of Education, Washington, DC 20208 or EDRS MF-$.91—HC-$10.82 plus postage, ED 175 797.)

A comprehensive rather than selective bibliography providing a synthesis of the literature on sex role socialization and sex discrimination in education between 1960 and 1978. The bibliography covers a wide spectrum of disciplines, from history and literature to sociology, psychology, economics and anthropology.

WOMEN'S EDUCATIONAL EQUITY

Lesson Plans

1.55 Materials for Sex Equality Education for Use by Teachers, Parents and Young People. National Organization for Women, 1974. 214 p. (Available from: NOW,

Greater Champaign Area Chapter, 809 South Fifth Street, Champaign, IL 61820. $3.00 or EDRS MF-$.91—HC-$1.85 plus postage, ED 099 894.)

Interdisciplinary materials compiled to help teachers overcome sex role stereotyping in their classrooms. Materials include classroom activities; lesson plans; a list of feminist resources; annotated bibliographies of nonsexist readers, sex education references and counseling materials; and a survey of media on the women's movement. [7–12]

1.56 Maximizing Young Children's Potential: A Non-Sexist Manual for Early Childhood Trainees. Women's Action Alliance, Non-Sexist Child Development Project. 124 p. (Available from: Education Development Center, 55 Chapel Street, Newton, MA 02160. $2.00.)

By creating nonsexist environments for young children, educators can help to transcend sex role stereotyping that so often limits aspirations and achievements. This training manual, *Maximizing Young Children's Potential,* was developed for use with staff, support personnel and parents involved in preschool programs. The activities and exercises encourage independence and expose all children to a range of experiences. One section of the manual provides step-by-step directions for conducting workshops on nonsexist curricula, children's literature and sexism in language. Another section contains practical strategies for integrating a nonsexist approach into all areas of the classroom, including the housekeeping corner, blocks and outdoor play. The resource section lists sources for classroom materials, an annotated bibliography of nonsexist books and suggestions for further reading. [K–3]

1.57 Non-Sexist Education for Young Children: A Practical Guide. Barbara Sprung. New York: Citation Press. $3.25.

Written by the Project Director of the Women's Action Alliance, this is a nonsexist education guide for parents and educators. Included are pointers for parents to help bring up children in a nonsexist manner and a guide for teachers suggesting classroom activities to promote sex equity.[22]

1.58 Promoting Educational Equity through School Libraries. Arizona State University, Women's Educational Equity Act Program. (Available from: Education Development Center, 55 Chapel Street, Newton, MA 02160. $4.75 plus 20% postage.)

Multimodule series for teachers and librarians sensitizing them to sex role and bias problems and what they can do about them; also includes materials to use in the classroom.[14] [9–12]

Supplementary Texts

1.59 Changing Sexist Practices in the Classroom. Marjorie Ster. American Federation of Teachers. (Available from: American Federation of Teachers, AFL-CIO, 1012 Fourteenth Street, NW, Washington, DC 20025. Item No. 600. $1.00 for 10 or more copies.)

These materials for teachers and classroom use include statistics on working women and feminists in history, independent study project suggestions, teaching activities, course outlines, resources for women's studies, and criteria and guidelines for evaluating and improv-

ing the image of women in instructional materials. The guide also contains two bibliographies.[14] [9–12]

1.60 Eliminating Sexism: Rewriting the Scripts. Rose M. Etheridge and Eric Rice. 1977. 203 p. (Available from: System Sciences, Inc., P.O. Box 2345, Chapel Hill, NC 27514. $20.00.)

This is a self-instruction package designed for all students with eighth grade reading level or above. It requires 5 to 20 class sessions. Topics include sex stereotyping and the work force, minority groups, schools and the law. The package contains preassessment and postassessment instruments, self-check questions and teacher materials.[2] [8–12]

1.61 Sex Equality in Schools. Sex Equality in Educational Administration. Sex Equality in Instructional Materials. American Association for School Administrators, 1975. 18–25 p. each. (Available from: AASA Publications Division, 1801 North Moore Street, Arlington, VA 22209. $1.00 each; $2.50 set.)

Three well-written handbooks for school administrators which contrast traditional sex stereotyping with the needs of individuals and changes in society. Action suggestions.[26]

1.62 Sexism in Education. Emma Willard Task Force on Education. (Available from: Emma Willard Task Force on Education, Box 14229, University Station, Minneapolis, MN 55408. $6.00.)

Classic resource book on sexism in education; includes units for classroom use and staff inservice.[4]

1.63 A Student Guide to Title IX. Myra Sadker. 1977. 45 p. (Available from: The Resource Center on Sex Roles in Education, The National Foundation for the Improvement of Education, 1201 Sixteenth Street, NW, Room 701, Washington, DC 20036.)

Guide to rights and responsibilities of students, emphasizing right to nonsexist education.[4] [9–12]

Periodicals

1.64 Created Equal. Southeastern Public Education Project (SEPEP), American Friends Service Committee. (Available from: SEPEP, Box 22652, Jackson, MS 39205.)

Reports on sex equity problems and progress in southern schools. Free as of this writing. Citizens in Alabama, Arkansas, Georgia, Louisiana, Mississippi and South Carolina can call on the project for help in combatting sex discrimination in local schools.

1.65 PEER Perspective. Project on Equal Education Rights (PEER). (Available from: PEER, 1112 13th Street, NW, Washington, DC 20005. Free.)

An informative, quarterly newsletter that focuses on Title IX and school desegregation efforts in schools across the nation. Includes legal information and a resources section.[44] [K–12]

1.66 TABS: Aids for Ending Sexism in Schools. Lucy Picco Simpson (ed.). (Available from: TABS, 744 Carroll Street, Brooklyn, NY 11215.)

A quarterly journal for ending sexism in schools, which contains articles, posters, lesson plans, biographies and school programs for nonsexist education.[8] [K–8]

1.67 Women's Studies Newsletters. (Available from: The Feminist Press, Box 334, Old Westbury, NY 11568.)

A quarterly published by The Feminist Press and the National Women's Studies Association. Contains articles on women's studies at all levels of education: new programs, innovative courses, teaching techniques, curricular materials, book reviews, conference reports, bibliographies and job information.

Multimedia Programs

1.68 Toward Equality. Betsy Wesner (ed.). Dallas Independent School District. (Available from: Dr. Joe M. Pitts, Dallas Independent School District, Box 12, Dallas, TX 75204. Limited copies.)

This collection of already existing materials and strategies may be used by classroom teachers and staff development planners interested in implementing educational change relating to sexism and racism. The materials included are geared for upper elementary and secondary levels as well as adults. A nine-page annotated reading list is also included.[14]

Audiovisual Materials

1.69 Edupak on Sex Role Stereotyping. Multimedia package. (Available from: NEA Order Department, Academic Building, Sawmill Road, West Haven, CT 06516. $79.50.)

This package contains the two filmstrip units, "Cinderella Is Dead" and "The Labels and Reinforcement of Sex Role Stereotyping"; three books dealing with nonsexist education, sex stereotyping in schools, and women's studies; four cassette tapes including discussions on sexism, racism and classism in schools, and a four-part tape on women's rights and multicultural equity; and two research reports and pamphlets. Each item can also be ordered separately. A publication list is available.[2] [6–12]

1.70 We Are Women. Motivational Media. 16 minutes. (Available from: Motivational Media, 8271 Melrose Avenue, Suite 204, Los Angeles, CA 90046.)

"We Are Women" makes a strong case for individual rights for women and an equally strong case for what this means for men. Designed to depolarize men and women regarding women's nontraditional concept of themselves.[21] [6–12]

Bibliographies/Resource Lists

1.71 Alternatives in Print: An Index and Listing of the Publications Reflecting Today's Social Change Activities. Special Responsibilities Round Table Task Force of the American Library Association. (Available from: Publications Committee, Ohio State University Library, 1858 Neil Avenue, Room 322A, Columbus, OH 43210. $4.00.)

Multimedia sourcebook of information on women.[1]

1.72 An Annotated Selected Bibliography of Bibliographies on Women. Margaret Eichler (ed.). Pittsburgh: KNOW, Inc., 1976. 33 p. $3.00.

Ninety annotated listings of readily accessible bibliographies on women. The annotations reflect the table of contents or the authors' subdivisions and/or statements about the intent and the limitations of their bibliographies. Sponsored by American Sociological Association's Section on Sex Roles.[20]

1.73 Directory. Women's Educational Equity Communications Network. (Available from: Women's Educational Equity Act Program, U.S. Department of Education, Donahoe Building, Room 1105, 400 Maryland Avenue, SW, Washington, DC 20202. $5.00.)

Lists national organizations and programs involved in furthering women's educational equity; some national and state directories and organizations; and for each state, the Commission on the Status of Women, vocational education, sex equity and Title IX coordinators, and the National Organization of Women state coordinator.[17]

1.74 Feminist Resources for Elementary and Secondary Schools. Task Force on Sexism in Schools. (Available from: Task Force on Sexism in Schools, Valley Women's Center, 200 Main Street, Northhampton, MA 01060.)

A compilation of references for readings on sex role socialization and stereotyping and for resources, such as books, films, slides, graphics and articles for elementary and secondary schools.[23] [K–12]

1.75 Hispanic Women and Education: Annotated Selected References and Resources. Women's Educational Equity Communications Network. (Available from: Women's Educational Equity Act Program, U.S. Department of Education, Donahoe Building, Room 1105, 400 Maryland Avenue, SW, Washington, DC 20202. $2.50.)

Cites bibliographies, curricula, journal articles, research studies, and other resources that relate to education, economic status and counseling of Hispanic women.[17]

1.76 Resources for Ending Sex Bias in the Schools. Project on Equal Education Rights (PEER). (Available from: PEER, 1112 13th Street, NW, Washington, DC 20005. Free.)

This listing of books and other resources aims to help educators, parents and community groups recognize sex bias in educational settings, understand how it harms children and suggests how to take effective action to promote a sex fair school environment. Covers kindergarten through high school.[22] [K–12]

1.77 Resources for Ending Sex Bias in the Schools. PEER. 6 p. (Available from: PEER, 1029 Vermont Avenue, NW, Washington, DC 20005. Single copies and small orders free; $6.00 per 100.)

Six-page annotated bibliography of useful materials.[26]

1.78 Resources in Women's Educational Equity. Women's Educational Equity Communications Network. 341 p. (Available from: Superintendent of Documents, U.S. Government Printing Office, Washington, DC 20402. Order No. 017-080-02014-9. $6.50 prepaid.)

More than 1,600 citations on "girls and women in education" from 13 major data bases such as ERIC and MEDLARS. Most documents, articles, dissertations and other materials cited are annotated. The work features author, subject and institution indexes.

1.79   Toward Equity: Effective Title IX Strategies, K-Postsecondary. California Coalition for Sex Equity in Education. 316 p. (Available from: Education Development Center, 55 Chapel Street, Newton, MA 02160. $6.75.)

Title IX compliance is but a first step toward the important task of achieving gender equity for all students and staff in educational programs and activities. *Toward Equity: Effective Title IX Strategies, K-Postsecondary* addresses the practical, philosophic and theoretical questions raised by the federal law intended to prohibit sex discrimination in education. The book provides specific information about the law, monitoring practices and evaluation procedures. It presents strategies for overcoming resistance to change and provides detailed suggestions for working within a political climate on issues of educational decision making. The book presents a unique format of systematic planning and problem solving. Worksheets outline change strategies and action steps for resolving specific issues of gender equity. An extensive bibliography of organizations, agencies and other equity resources is included. [K–12]

1.80   WEECN Resource Roundup: Asian/Pacific Women in America. Women's Educational Equity Communications Network, 1980. 8 p. (Available from: Women's Educational Equity Act Program, U.S. Department of Education, Donahoe Building, Room 1105, 400 Maryland Avenue, SW, Washington, DC 20202. Single copies free by sending a self-addressed, stamped envelope.)

This bibliography is one of a series of Resource Roundups published by the Women's Educational Equity Communications Network. It represents a selective sampling of resources focusing on Asian/Pacific women in America. Entries are divided into seven categories: general resources on Asian/Pacific American women, historical resources, education and employment resources, other contemporary issues and problems, research and psychological studies, nonprint resources, and organizations and projects.

1.81   WEECN Resource Roundup: Black Women and Education. Women's Educational Equity Communications Network, 1979. 6 p. (Available from: Women's Educational Equity Act Program, U.S. Department of Education, Donahoe Building, Room 1105, 400 Maryland Avenue, SW, Washington, DC 20202. Single copies free by sending a self-addressed, stamped envelope.)

This bibliography is one in a series of Resource Roundups published by the Women's Educational Equity Communications Network. The resources were chosen for their usefulness to black women, administrators, researchers, instructors, counselors and others interested in helping black women gain educational equity. Entries are listed under six categories, including general resources, elementary and secondary schools, higher education, educational administration, careers and counseling resources, and national organizations and projects.

1.82   WEECN Resource Roundup: Disabled Women and Equal Opportunity. Women's Educational Equity Communications Network, 1979. 6 p. (Available from: Women's Educational Equity Act Program, U.S. Department of Education, Donahoe Building, Room 1105, 400 Maryland Avenue, SW, Washington, DC 20202. Single copies free by sending a self-addressed, stamped envelope.)

This bibliography is one of a series of Resource Roundups compiled by the Women's Educational Equity Communications Network. The resources should be of interest to physically disabled people and to teachers, counselors, administrators and others responsible for providing accessible services. Items are listed under the following categories: general resources, elementary and secondary resources, vocational and higher education, occupational resources, health education and sex counseling, nonprint media, media services, and organization and resource sources.

1.83   Womanhood Media: Current Resources about Women. Helen Rippier Wheeler. Metuchen, NJ: Scarecrow Press. $8.50.

A combination of source material and information relating to the contemporary women's movement. This annotated bibliography of more than 350 currently available books is broad in scope and contains both liberating and sexist materials. Audiovisual aids and a directory of sources are also included.[22]

1.84   Womanhood Media Supplement: Additional Current Resources about Women. Helen Rippier Wheeler. Metuchen, NJ: Scarecrow Press, 1975. 489 p. $16.50.

This supplement brings the basic annotated collection of available books to 826 titles and describes more than 1,000 additional audiovisuals of many types, with full purchase and borrowing information provided. Pamphlets are now organized within 25 subject areas, with more coverage of Canadian and Latina resources, and such areas as affirmative action and women's studies. An additional 250 periodicals and a directory of 1,500 additional sources are included. The extensive list of women's groups, centers and studies programs, caucuses and task forces makes *Womanhood Media* and its supplement well-suited to active support of implementation of affirmative action employment, equal educational opportunity and women's studies.[45]

1.85   Women's Educational Equity: Annotated Selected References and Resources. Women's Educational Equity Communications Network. (Available from: Women's Educational Equity Act Program, U.S. Department of Education, Donahoe Building, Room 1105, 400 Maryland Avenue, SW, Washington, DC 20202. $2.50.)

Includes information on books, reports, bibliographies, journals, newsletters and resource publications and library collections.[17]

1.86   Women's Movement Media: A Source Guide. Cynthia Ellen Harrison. New York: R.R. Bowker, 1975. 269 p.

Resource lists of organizations, government agencies, publishers, etc., which produce information and materials on women and feminism.[4]

MALE SEX ROLE STEREOTYPING

Lesson Plans

1.87 Being a Man: A Unit of Instructional Activities on Male Role Stereotyping. David Sadker. Resource Center on Sex Equity. (Available from: Superintendent of Documents, U.S. Government Printing Office, Washington, DC 20402. Stock No. 017-080-01777-6. $2.00.)

This instructional package provides classroom activities for use in exploring masculinity and sex stereotypes. Directions are given for each activity, defining teacher and student roles.[2]

Supplementary Texts

1.88 Boys Have Feelings Too: Growing Up Male for Boys. Dale Carson. New York: Atheneum, 1980. 165 p. $8.95.

This book emphasizes the idea that men are human beings first; men second. It urges young men not to fall into the "hero" or "macho" role often assigned to the male sex, but to learn who they are and what they really want rather than being defined by others. [9–12]

Audiovisual Materials

1.89 American Man: Tradition and Change. Butterick Publishing, 1976. (Available from: Butterick Publishing, 161 Sixth Avenue, New York, NY 10013. $45.00.)

This unit of two 12-minute, color, sound filmstrips introduces the concept of sex role stereotyping to high school students. Part I, "Traditions in Question," explores some of the traditional qualities expected in men. Part II, "Living with Change," uses interviews with both males and females, adults and students to examine some of the problems confronting men because of their role training. A 6-page teacher's guide accompanies the unit.[9] [9–12]

1.90 Beyond Masculinity. Warren Farrell. 1974. 28 minutes, cassette. (Available from: Center for Cassette Studies, 110 Webb Avenue, North Hollywood, CA 91605.)

Warren Farrell discusses the effect of the feminist movement on men and the status of "men's liberation." [16] [9–12]

1.91 Masculinity. Schloat Productions. 1976. Four filmstrips with three cassettes. (Available from: Schloat Productions, 150 White Plains Road, Tarrytown, NY 10591.)

This set of filmstrips explores concepts of masculinity and femininity through a general discussion, an enactment of a situation concerning sex roles and a silent filmstrip of images.[16] [8–12]

1.92 Men's Lives: A Documentary Film about Masculinity in America. New Day Films. 43 minutes, color, sound, 16mm. (Available from: New Day Films, P.O. Box 315, Franklin Lakes, NJ. $500.00; $56.00 rental plus $4.00 handling.)

This academy award-winning film (Best Student Documentary) examines how men are conditioned to aggressively compete, win and strive for material success at the expense of intimacy and communication. The filmmakers present interviews with men, boys, women, workers, teachers, coaches, athletes and students, interspersed with film clips of movie heroes, football games, and comic strip heroes to represent with insight and humor a microcosm of masculine attitudes.[2]

Bibliographies/Resource Lists

1.93 Men's Studies Bibliography. Massachusetts Institute of Technology (MIT). (Available from: MIT Humanities Library, Room 14S-200, Cambridge, MA 02139. $3.00.)

A list of part of the collection of the Humanities Studies Collection at MIT, including newspaper and journal articles, unpublished theses and papers and ephemera of the men's movement.[1]

NONSEXIST MATERIALS

Lesson Plans

1.94 Sexism, Racism and Other Isms: Hidden Messages in Childrens' Stories ("The Princess and the Pea"). Council on Interracial Books for Children (CIBC). (Available from: CIBC Resource Center, Room 300, 1941 Broadway, New York, NY 10023. $1.50.)

A "fun" lesson plan for 5th grade through college. "The Princess and the Pea" opens a discussion of subtle ways in which sexism, racism, materialism and elitism permeate the simplest of stories. The level of discussion will vary with age, but participants learn how to spot hidden messages while enjoying a lively discussion.[10] [5–12]

Bibliographies/Resource Lists

1.95 Advisory List for Instructional Media for Reduction of Sex Bias. North Carolina State Department of Public Instruction, 1977. 27 p. (Available from: North Carolina State Department of Public Instruction, Division of Educational Media, Raleigh, NC or EDRS MF-$.91—HC-$2.06 plus postage, ED 149 755.)

An annotated bibliography of instructional media to aid in the reduction of sex bias in elementary and senior high school classrooms. Items reviewed include books, films, posters, slide sets and film strips arranged in three categories: biographies; history, sociology and biology of sex roles; and curriculum materials illustrating balanced sex roles. [K–12]

1.96 An Annotated Bibliography of Non-Stereotyped Picture Books. Jeanne Bracken and Sharon Wigutoff. Old Westbury, NY: The Feminist Press, 42 p. $2.00.

A critically annotated list of 200 recent picture books in such categories as working mothers, handicaps, multiracial and adoption.[39] [K–12]

1.97 Bibliography of Materials on Sexism and Sex-Role Stereotyping in Children's Books. Kathleen Gallagher and Alice Peery. Chapel Hill, NC: Lollipop Power, Inc., 1976. 9 p.

An unannotated bibliography of journal articles, newsletters, monographs, reports and resources focusing on sexism and sex role stereotyping in children's books. Although many of the references cited focus on primary and intermediate grade education, the bibliography should prove useful to the junior high school teacher. [7–9]

1.98   Fair Play: A Bibliography of Non-Stereotyped Materials (Volume I). Olin Ferris. June 1976. 68 p. (Available from: Training Institute for Sex Desegregation of the Public Schools, Rutgers University, Federation Hall-Douglass Campus, New Brunswick, NJ 08903. $3.00.)

An annotated bibliography of nonsexist, nonracist resources for educators. The bibliography includes both student materials and teacher resources and is organized by grade level and subdivided into subject areas. [K–12]

1.99   Fair Play: A Bibliography of Non-Stereotyped Materials (Volume II). Marilyn A. Hulme. September 1977. 82 p. (Available from: Training Institute for Sex Desegregation of the Public Schools, Rutgers University, Federation Hall-Douglass Campus, New Brunswick, NJ 08903. $3.00.)

An annotated bibliography of nonsexist, nonracist resources for educators. The bibliography includes both student materials and teacher resources and is organized by grade level and subdivided into subject areas. Also included is a list of publishers. [K–12]

1.100   Fair Textbooks: A Resource Guide. United States Commission on Civil Rights, December 1979. 430 p. (Available from: Superintendent of Documents, U.S. Government Printing Office, Washington, DC 20402. Stock No. 005-00224-9.)

A comprehensive, unannotated bibliography of bias-free educational materials and resources, organized into four major categories: material resources, procedural resources, directories and organizational resources. Within each of these larger categories, the resources have been organized into smaller sections by type of material, subject area applicability, and grade and age level.

1.101   Feminist Resources for Schools and Colleges: A Guide to Curricular Materials. Merle Froschl and Jane Williamson. Old Westbury, NY: The Feminist Press, $2.95.

A newly revised and expanded feminist resource which has more than 500 listings of nonsexist books, pamphlets, articles, audio-visual resources and other materials.[8]

1.102   Films for, by and about Women. Kaye Sullivan. Metuchen, NJ: Scarecrow Press, 1980. 560 p. $25.00.

Films for, by and about Women developed out of a recognized need for easy access to media sources in all areas of women's studies. It offers a comprehensive listing of films (features, documentaries and shorts) by women since the beginning of filmmaking, along with films on topics of special interest to women today, dealing with such subjects as aging, day care, childbirth, family life, health and hygiene, housing, nutrition, sex roles, human sexuality, management and supervisory training, women in other countries, the women's movement and feminism. The author's aim is to assist both women and men in exploring the changing and diverse roles women assume in society and to present women filmmakers and identify the genre of films made by each one. The main index is an alphabetical listing of approximately 2,800 film titles, with the following information provided for each: running time, black and white or color,

production or release date, format identification, and a brief description, including director and producer, and sales and rental sources throughout the U.S. A comprehensive subject index and an index of women filmmakers with their films are also included in the volume, along with a directory of film sources and filmmakers, a bibliography and a list of symbols used. Sullivan compiled this work with women and women's studies in mind, but the subject matter mirrors the concerns of both women and men. It is a must for educational institutions, libraries, churches, organizations and all others who are trying to raise the level of people's consciousness about the problems of living today. It is an important tool for filmmakers, film researchers and film educators as well.[45]

1.103   Films on the Women's Movement. Janice Mendenhall. (Available from: Office for Civil Rights, General Services Administration, Washington, DC 20405. Single copies free.)

This is a very comprehensive list of films dealing with various aspects of women's lives or the women's movement. Provides a wide selection for a variety of audiences. This list is updated twice a year.[1]

1.104   A Guide to Non-Sexist Children's Books. Judith Adell and Hilary Dole Klein. Chicago: Academy Press 1976. $3.95.

An annotated bibliography of nonsexist children's books. Titles are divided into the broad categories of fiction and nonfiction within the three major categories of preschool through third grade, third grade through seventh grade, and seventh grade through twelfth grade. The bibliography provides a wealth of titles and includes the publisher, copyright date, recommended grade level and price; however, no criteria for determining reading level or nonsexist content has been provided. [K–12]

1.105   Images of Women: A Bibliography of Feminist Materials and New Perspectives and **A Bibliography of Racial Ethnic and Feminist Resources.** (Available from Elizabeth Haller, Bureau of Curriculum Services, Department of Education, Box 911, Harrisburg, PA 17126.)

These guides will refer you to not only recommended readings for elementary and secondary students, but also to audiovisual resources, curriculum kits and organizations. If you order nothing else, order these two resource guides.[24] [K–12]

1.106   Images of Women: Curriculum Resources for Teachers and Students. Media Monitor, *Informedia* Vol. No. 2–3 (Winter 1978). (Available from: Media Monitor, Informedia, Box 1020, Pearl River, NY 10965.)

The entries in this briefly annotated list cite current filmstrips, slides, records, cassettes, simulation games, study prints and other software. One hundred forty-seven of the listings are for the secondary level, 28 for elementary use and the remaining 53 are professional readings covering curriculum guides, bibliographies and other teaching aids.[14] [K–12]

1.107   The Liberty Cap: A Catalogue of Non-Sexist Materials for Children. Enid Davis (ed.). Chicago: Academy Press, 1977. 236 p. $4.95.

Unusual format and refreshing personal style. Discussions and special lists, as well as reviews. Well indexed. For librarians, teachers and parents.[26]

1. 108 List of Games about Sexism, Sex-Role Stereotyping, and Related Women's Issues. (Available from: University of Michigan Extension Service, 412 Maynard Street, Ann Arbor, MI 48109.)

This is an excellent guide to 25 games. Almost all of the games listed are unevaluated, but basic information is provided about developers, cost, time, rules and number of players.[24] [7–12]

1. 109 List of Media (October, 1979). Training Institute for Sex Desegregation, 1979. 26 p. (Available from: Training Institute for Sex Desegregation, Rutgers University, Federation Hall-Douglass Campus, New Brunswick, NJ 08903.)

Annotated bibliography of print and nonprint materials available to districts associated with the Institute.

1. 110 Multicultural Resources for Children: A Bibliography of Materials for Preschool through Elementary School in the Areas of Black, Spanish Speaking, Asian American, Native American and Pacific Island Cultures. Margaret S. Nichols and Peggy O'Neill. Multicultural Resources, 1977. 205 p. (Available from: Multicultural Resources, Box 2945, Stanford, CA 94305. $4.00.)

An extensive bibliography with resources on folk tales, poetry, art and music, social studies materials, pictures, maps and materials from foreign publishers.[44] [K–12]

1. 111 New Day Films: Films about Women and Men. (Available from New Day Films, P.O. Box 315, Franklin Lakes, NJ 07417.)

A catalogue of films available from New Day Films, a distribution cooperative for feminist films organized in 1972.

1. 112 New Feminist Scholarship: A Guide to Bibliographies. Jane Williamson. Old Westbury, NY: The Feminist Press, $15.00.

This new annotated bibliography brings together nearly 400 bibliographies on every aspect of women's lives and history in one indispensable volume. The most comprehensive such volume to date, *New Feminist Scholarship* is organized into 30 subject headings which include anthropology and sociology, art and music, child care, history, lesbians, psychology, third world countries and work. An essential research tool for student, teacher and general reader.[19] [K–12]

1. 113 1980 Annotated Bibliography. Resource Library, Midwest Sex Desegregation Assistance Center, January 1980. 36 p. (Available from: Midwest Sex Desegregation Assistance Center, 1627 Anderson Avenue, Manhattan, KS 66506.)

An annotated bibliography of school, community and student resources, with level of use and the group of people most likely to find the materials useful. This bibliography includes books, films, filmstrips, readings and booklets to promote sex-fair education.

1. 114 Non-Print Resources in Women's Educational Equity. Women's Educational Equity Communications Network, February 1978. 245 p. (Available from: Women's Educational Equity Act Program, U.S. Department of Education, Donahoe Building, Room 1105, 400 Maryland Avenue, SW, Washington, DC 20202, or Superintendent of Documents, Government Printing Office, Washington, DC 20402. Stock No. 017-080-01836-5. $4.25.)

A catalog of information about films, filmstrips, transparencies, audiotapes, videotapes, records and other instructional materials that deal with women's educational equity. Preprimary through adult, as well as teacher training materials, are included.[17] [K–12]

1. 115 Positive Images: A Guide to Non-Sexist Films for Young People. Linda Artel and Susan Wengraf. San Francisco: Booklegger Press, 1976. 168 p. $5.50.

This media guide contains evaluative annotations of over 400 films, videotapes, slides and filmstrips. Entries include recommended age level (preprimary through high school) and also indicate whether the item is appropriate for adults.[14] [K–12]

1. 116 A Resource List for Non-Sexist Education. Judy Cusick. Resource Center on Sex Roles in Education. (Available from: Resource Center on Sex Roles in Education, Room 804E, 1201 16th Street, NW, Washington, DC 20036. Free.)

A list of games, books, pictures, and posters to promote sex fair-education. The three main sections are: (1) Understanding the Problem: The Need for Non-Sexist Education; (2) Developing Non-Sexist Education; and (3) Reference Materials.[22] [K–12]

1. 117 A Selected-Annotated Bibliography on Sexism. St. Cloud State University, Equity in Education Institute. (Available from: St. Cloud State University, Equity in Education Institute, St. Cloud, MN.)

Annotated bibliography of nonsexist and nonracist articles and media for use in schools.[4]

1. 118 Sourcebook for Sex Equality: Small Presses. Marilyn A. Hulme. Training Institute for Sex Desegregation of the Public Schools, 1977. (Available from: Training Institute for Sex Desegregation of the Public Schools, Rutgers University, Federation Hall-Douglass Campus, New Brunswick, NJ 08903.)

This listing of lesser-known resources for nonsexist materials includes small presses and nonprofit educational firms; women's sections of professional and trade organizations; task forces in state education departments; and feminist publishers, bookstores and distributors. [K–12]

1. 119 Strong Women: An Annotated Bibliography of Literature for the High School Classroom. Deborah Silverton Rosenfelt. Old Westbury, NY: The Feminist Press, 1976. $1.95.

A selective, annotated bibliography for high school teachers and students who want inexpensive supplementary readings by women, which emphasize the strengths and accomplishments of women. The bibliography has organized the materials according to anthologies, autobiography and biography, drama, novels, short stories and poetry. A cross topical index with the following categories also is provided: adolescence, female sexuality, women in the arts and professions, women and political commitment, third-world women and working class women. [9–12]

1. 120 200 Plus: A Framework for Non-Stereotyped Human Roles in Elementary Media Center Materials.

Kalamazoo Public Schools, September 1977. 25 p. (Available from: Media Services, Kalamazoo Public Schools, 1220 Harvard Street, Kalamazoo, MI 49008.)

200 Plus lists elementary materials, indicating grade use and reading level for each item. Over 80 percent of the 206 books are in the first three categories—picture books, fiction, and social studies; other categories are language arts, miscellaneous and audiovisuals. The Kalamazoo bibliographies are updated every year. Orders are filled with the latest editions, which include all items that were listed in previous editions. [12] [K–8]

1. 121   Women's Film Co-op: Catalogue. Northhampton, MA: Mother Jones Press, 1974. 43 p.

Listing of films by and about women, with introductory essay on women and film. [4]

1. 122   Women's Films in Print: An Annotated Guide to 800 Films by Women. Bonnie Dawson. San Francisco: Booklegger Press, 1975. 165 p. $4.00.

Women's Films in Print is an excellent guide to films made by women. In it, Bonnie Dawson, a librarian and freelance consultant on women's films, makes a valuable contribution to the field of filmmaking and women's history by identifying over 370 female filmmakers and providing access to 800 of their films. All of the films included in the guide were produced or directed by women, individually, in collaboration with other women or men, or as a part of a collective group. All are 16mm and are not necessarily feminist, about women, or new (the oldest is "Salome," produced in 1922). Entries include full-length features, documentaries, shorts and animated cartoons. [27]

1. 123   Women's Studies Film List. University of Michigan Audio-Visual Education Center. (Available from: University of Michigan Audio-Visual Education Center, 416 Fourth Street, Ann Arbor, MI.)

A listing of films available through the center which are appropriate for women's studies courses at all grade levels. [1]

SAMPLE LESSON PLAN: GENERAL AWARENESS
Examining Stereotypes: Personal Decisions

AUDIENCE:

Students grades 6–12

OBJECTIVES:

- To identify instances of sex role stereotyping in one's own life, with friends, at school, and at home.
- To identify alternatives for reducing sex role stereotyping in one's own life.
- To clarify one's values regarding sex roles and to make decisions regarding the alternatives identified.

LEARNING CONCEPTS:

1. Each of us experiences sex role stereotyping in various aspects of our lives.
2. Each of us has a range of alternatives possible for reducing sex role stereotyping.
3. Each of us has the right to choose from a wide range of both traditional and nontraditional options for males and females.

MATERIALS:

Ditto copies of "Examining Stereotypes: Personal Decisions."

HOW TO USE:

1. Distribute the "Personal Decisions" worksheet to every student.
2. Explain to students that every person has the right to make his or her own decisions about roles and about sex role stereotyping. It is important to emphasize that it is understanding that there are

choices which is the important thing, not choosing in a particular way. The worksheet can be used by all students in thinking about their own choices.
3. Ask students to fill out the worksheets. Remind them that they can think about examples and actions that they have identified and discussed earlier in the unit.
4. Ask volunteers to share their answers with the class. Remind them that every student has the right to decide to make changes or not to make changes.
5. Ask students to discuss whether there are any changes they would like to make as a class or in the class to reduce sex role stereotyping. If they decide to take actions but need some help with ideas, some of the following suggestions might get them started:
   - Reading a book about sexism
   - Writing a letter to a television station protesting sex role stereotyping in a program or commercial
   - Writing a letter to the editor protesting sex role stereotyping in an advertisement or elsewhere in a magazine or newspaper
   - Making a bulletin board of nonsexist photographs or articles
   - Constructing a slide, tape, or other presentation about sex role stereotyping in popular music
   - Studying a textbook for sex role stereotyping and writing a report of the findings
   - Making a class contract that males and females will share all classroom duties equally (e.g., watering plants, carrying books, running audiovisual equipment, etc.)

These are only examples; students will be able to generate many others, some of which may be quite different from those listed here.

Examining Stereotypes: Personal Decisions

I can identify the following examples of sex role stereotyping	I would/would not like to change these because:	Actions I would take to make any changes I have chosen:	Actions I plan to take: (place an asterisk in this column next to any action you plan to take)
With my friends:			
At school:			
At home:			

From: *Being A Man: A Unit of Instructional Activities on Male Role Stereotyping,* developed by David Sadker for the Resource Center on Sex Roles in Education under funds from the Women's Educational Equity Act Program of the Office of Education, U.S. Department of Health, Education and Welfare.

2.0 Counseling and Career Guidance

COUNSELING*

Lesson Plans

2.1 Assertion Skill Training: A Group Procedure for High School Women. Catherine M. Steel and Janice M. Hochman. American Personnel and Guidance Association. 63 p. (Available from: Order Services, American Personnel and Guidance Association, 2 Skyline Place, Suite 400, 5203 Leesburg Pike, Falls Church, VA 22041. Order No. 72053.)

Intended for high school counselors and those in related helping professions. A straightforward description of how to facilitate a high school assertion group. Includes an assertion behavior scale, assessment sheet and outlines of 14 sessions.[46] [9–12]

2.2 How to Decide: A Guide for Women. Helle Tumlin Scholz and others. New York: College Entrance Examination Board, 1975. 121 p. $5.95.

Exercises and activities for women of all ages which will make it easier for them to make decisions.[49] [7–12]

2.3 Strategies for Equality: Volume I, Guidance, Social Studies, Physical Education. Training Institute for Sex Desegregation. (Available from: Training Institute for Sex Desegregation, Rutgers University, Federation Hall-Douglass Campus, New Brunswick, NJ 08903. $3.50.)

Compendium of curricular projects devised and tested by educators in their own classrooms. For teachers, coaches, counselors and administrators.[16]

2.4 Women as Winners: Transactional Analysis for Personal Growth. Dorothy Jongeward. Reading, MA: Addison-Wesley, 1978.

A practical and positive book for women and men who are ready to better understand the dynamic and perplexing changes facing women. Since women are coping with rapid change, this book advocates meaningful choices of lifestyle so that women can achieve their fullest potential. It contains numerous exercises, photographs, case histories and techniques for producing positive changes.[34] [9–12]

2.5 Your Parenting Decision Values. National Alliance for Optional Parenthood, 1978. (Available from: National Alliance for Optional Parenthood, 2010 Massachusetts Avenue, NW, Washington, DC 20036.)

A quiz for teens to help them examine their attitude about having a child.[37] [8–12]

Supplementary Texts

2.6 About Dying. Sara Bonnett Skin. New York: Walker and Company, 1974. 47 p. $7.95.

This unique presentation creates a shared experience for adult and child by offering two texts. The author enables children to explore their feelings about death and prepares adults for questions children might ask. The presentation is well done and includes pictures of children of mixed races. [K–3]

2.7 Are You Kidding Yourself. National Alliance for Optional Parenthood, 1978. (Available from: National Alliance for Optional Parenthood, 2010 Massachusetts Avenue, NW, Washington, DC 20036.)

A cartoon leaflet for teens on teenage pregnancy.[37] [8–12]

2.8ᵃ Leaving Home. Arlen Kramer Richards and Irene Willis. New York: Atheneum, 1980. 163 p. $8.95.

Written for both girls and boys in senior high school and/or college, this book is about the task of becoming an independent person. Using many examples, both male and female, the authors discuss the conflict young people feel between the desire to be on their own and the difficulty they experience in separating themselves psychologically from parents. The case histories effectively clarify the

---

*Subcategories of ''Counseling,'' indicated by superscript letters following entry numbers, are designated as follows: a=Counseling (Families); b=Counseling (Assertiveness); c=Counseling (Abortion); d=Counseling (Pregnancy); e=Counseling (Rape).

motivations behind varying parental attitudes as well as the internal conflicts of the young people. The ingredients for true independence are explained in a commonsense, nonjudgmental manner, and the message is that truly "leaving home" is a long process rather than a magical and abrupt change. [11–12]

2.9 Life with Working Parents. Esther Hautzig. New York: Macmillan, 1976. 124 p. $7.95.

A cheerful informative guide written particularly for boys and girls who live in households with a single parent, two working parents, or just simply where no one person assumes 100 percent responsibility for housekeeping. Young persons reading this book will be delighted and encouraged to realize all the things they can do to make a household run smoothly. Caring for younger children, plants and pets; cooking; organizing; cleaning; and doing simple repairs all help develop a sense of responsibility and pride for looking out for oneself. The author avoids sex role stereotypes in both parent careers and family responsibilities. Practical suggestions for meals, crafts and family entertainment make this very enjoyable reading.

2.10[b] Liking Myself. Pat Palmer. San Luis Obispo, CA: IMPACT, 1977. Paperback.

A child-size introduction to concepts of feelings, self-esteem and assertiveness, designed for young readers ages 5–9. Although the illustrations tend toward stereotypes in the portrayed roles, they are racially mixed. [K–5]

2.11[a] A Look at Divorce. Margaret Sanford Pursell. Minneapolis: Lerner Publications, 1977. 30 p.

With black and white photographs and simple text, this book reassures children of their continuing relationships with their parents despite the problems a family faces when a divorce occurs. A mix of races are represented in the illustrations. [K–3]

2.12 The Mouse, the Monster, and Me: Assertiveness for Young People. Patricia Palmer. 1977. (Available from IMPACT Publishers, P.O. Box 1094, San Luis Obispo, CA, 805-543-5911. $3.95.)

Dedicated to children who wish to be free and to the adults who will help them. The book is divided into eight parts and contains numerous descriptive illustrations. This book is full of ideas about how children can grow up to be assertive, make good decisions and stand up for themselves. Outlines games which help children learn about themselves and encourages new ways of thinking and self-expression. Practice of assertiveness is encouraged through parental or teacher friendship interaction.[22] [3–9]

2.13 Single and Pregnant. Ruth I. Pierce. Boston: Beacon Press, 1970. 214 p. $5.95.

Without traditional moralizing, this book answers questions and provides information for the single, pregnant girl, on abortion, adoption, marriage and single parenthood. A wealth of information is offered, including facts on contraceptives, conception, the physical changes during pregnancy, relationships with family and friends, maternity homes, community resources, medical care, and counseling and therapy. The appendix includes abortion referrals, planned parenthood affiliates, and maternity and infant care projects. However, some of the information is out-of-date, particularly regarding the legality of abortion and the treatment of minors. It is also geared toward white, middle class girls, and some of the careers are stereotyped. With these cautions in mind, this book should provide an acceptable resource for young women.

2.14 Why Am I So Miserable If These Are the Best Years of My Life. Andrea Boroff Eagan. Philadelphia: J.B. Lippincott, 1976. 241 p. $7.95.

A positive, helpful guide for young women to learn how to have more control over their lives, to enjoy their school years and to make good choices for the future. The author frankly discusses sex and birth control in a clear, concise and objective way. Physiological, emotional and social aspects of sex are thoroughly discussed in regard to both girls and boys. The book emphasizes throughout the need to develop good decision-making skills that will affect future career plans, interpersonal relationships and one's overall happiness. The author has a good sense of humor and enormous respect for young women's potential for growth.

Audiovisual Materials

2.15[a] And They Lived Happily Ever After. National Film Board of Canada, 1974. 13 minutes, 16mm. (Available from: National Film Board of Canada, 150 Kent Street, Ottawa, Ontario, Canada.)

Discussion of some of the consequences of marriage, such as lack of privacy, children, possibilities of divorce and separation.[16] [7–12]

2.16 Assertive Training for Women: Part I. American Personnel and Guidance Association. 17 minutes, sound, color, 16mm. (Available from: Order Services, American Personnel and Guidance Association, 2 Skyline Place, Suite 400, 5203 Leesburg Pike, Falls Church, VA 22041. Order No. 77538.)

Especially appropriate for high school and college students. Ten vignettes deal with simple interpersonal situations: borrowing class notes; refusing dates; dealing with friends, a physician, a pushy waitress, and a job interview; as well as more complex situations involving parents who are overly protective and controlling or critical of friends and grades in school.[46] [9–12]

2.17 Counseling Women. American Personnel and Guidance Association, 1971. 75 minutes, cassette tape. (Available from: Order Services, American Personnel and Guidance Association, 2 Skyline Place, Suite 400, 5203 Leesburg Pike, Falls Church, VA 22041. Order No. 72906.)

No annotation available.

2.18[a] Different Folks. Agency for Instructional Television, 1975. 15 minutes, color, sound, 16mm. (Available from: Agency for Instructional Television, 1111 West 17th Street, Bloomington, IN 47401. $180.00.)

This film is one of a series of 15 films aimed at helping 11- to 13-year-olds cope with emotional and social problems. "Different Folks" deals with sex role identification in a changing world from a boy's point of view. The story explores what happens in a family where the mother works outside the home as a veterinarian, the father works at home as an illustrator, and the children share in the housework. A teacher's guide outlines questions for discussion and follow-up activities.[9] [6–8]

2.19[a] Divorce/Separation: Marriages in Trouble. Guidance Associates, 1977. Two filmstrips with cassettes, teachers' guide. (Available from: Guidance Associates, A/V Subsidiary, 757 Third Avenue, New York, NY 10017.)

This two-part filmstrip is designed for use in high school classrooms and focuses on divorce as an emotional process. Taped interviews provide students with personal views of the divorce process from other young people.[16] [7–12]

2.20ª   The Family in Transition: Program 3 of the Family Life Series. Butterick Publishing, 1976. Six, 10-minute filmstrips and cassettes. (Available from: Butterick Publishing, 161 Sixth Avenue, New York, NY 10013.)

Three segments with lessons and teacher's guide on divorce, aging and new lifestyles. An excellent exploration of new lifestyles, the role of women and problems of aging.[16] [8–12]

2.21ª   The Future of the Family. Guidance Associates. Two filmstrips with discs or cassettes, discussion guide. (Available from: Guidance Associates, A/V Subsidiary, 757 Third Avenue, New York, NY 10017. $48.50.)

Examines past and present trends in family living and projects into the future—communes, nuclear family, women's liberation, urban vs. suburban life.[1] [10–12]

2.22ª   Getting Married. Bailey Film Associates. 16 minutes. (Available from: Bailey Film Associates, 2211 Michigan Avenue, P.O. Box 1795, Santa Monica, CA 80604.)

Examines reasons people marry in a serious review of strengths and weaknesses of institution of marriage. Real-life interviews, dramatic scenes and silent film clips illustrate practical reasons compelling people in the past to marry, which are now giving way to changing views toward marriage and single life. Stresses runaway divorce rate in a look at wrong reasons for marrying and has multiracial appeal. At times dramatic scenes are somewhat stereotyped and predictable—or maybe it just seems that way because such domestic problems actually are rampant. Useful especially to stimulate discussion in guidance programs and marriage and family living.[21] [11–12]

2.23   Improving Personal Relationships: Assertion Issues for High School Women, Part I. American Personnel and Guidance Association. 15 minutes, sound, color, 16mm. (Available from: Order Services, American Personnel and Guidance Association, 2 Skyline Place, Suite 400, 5203 Leesburg Pike, Falls Church, VA 22041. Order No. 77559. $265.00; $25.00 rental per day of use.)

The aim of this film is to help young women (and men) to stand up for their legitimate rights and to express feelings in a direct and honest fashion without violating the basic rights of others. Part I is a general introduction to assertion issues for high school women. The vignettes focus on relations with parents, friends, school personnel and employers. This film can be used by junior and senior high school counselors and allied helping professionals who wish to assist young people in improving their ability to deal with a changing world. (Leader's Guide included.)[46]

2.24   Improving Personal Relationships: Assertion Issues for High School Women in Relating to Men, Part II. American Personnel and Guidance Association. 15 minutes, sound, color, 16mm. (Available from: Order Services, American Personnel and Guidance Association, 2 Skyline Place, Suite 400, 5203 Leesburg Pike, Falls Church, VA 22041. Order No. 77560. $265.00; $25.00 rental per day of use.)

While this film is intended for use in an assertive training framework, it may also serve to stimulate discussion about improving human relationships regardless of theoretical framework. Part II deals with the problems of high school women in relating to men, especially those situations in which assertive behavior will help women maintain their dignity and equality. The film also examines the dating culture as a particularly important facet of high school life. Intended especially for counselors of junior and senior high school women, *Assertion Issues for High School Women* can be invaluable to any woman who has less than an ideal rapport with men in her life. (Leader's Guide included.)[46] [7–12]

2.25   An Introduction to Assertive Training Procedures for Women. Patricia Jakubowski. American Personnel and Guidance Association, 1973. 32 p. (Available from: Order Services, American Personnel and Guidance Association, 2 Skyline Place, Suite 400, 5203 Leesburg Pike, Falls Church, VA 22041. Order No. 72049. $3.50.)

This introduction to the Assertive Training film series is required reading for counselors, psychologists, social workers and all those in the helping professions who deal with women. The booklet lays out the methods which will enable girls and women to stand up for their basic human rights. Such is the essence of assertive training: developing the ability to maintain one's own rights without violating the rights of others.[46]

2.26ᶜ   It Happens to Us. New Day Films. (Available from: New Day Films, P.O. Box 315, Franklin Lakes, NJ 07417, $30.00 rental.)

A documentary of women of different ages, classes and races, talking about their abortion experiences.[1] [10–12]

2.27ª   Love and Marriage. Guidance Associates. Two filmstrips with two 12″ LPs or two cassettes, discussion guide. (Available from: Guidance Associates, A/V Subsidiary, 757 Third Avenue, New York, NY 10017.)

A teenage couple, engaged couple, married couple, divorced couple and a couple living together discuss adjustments and concepts. [10–12]

2.28ᵈ   Lucy. Picture Films Distribution Corporation, 1971. 13 minutes, b/w. (Available from: Picture Films Distribution Corporation, 43 North 16th Street, New York, NY 10020.)

Lucy is the story of an unwed, pregnant teenager. The brief narrative presents her romantic relationship with her boyfriend, the tensions the pregnancy causes in the family and the alternatives Lucy faces as an expectant mother. The film has an urban setting, and the central character is a Puerto Rican girl. This nonmoralistic film is designed to stimulate discussion and lead to an understanding of the problem of teenage pregnancy. It is outdated in relation to the topic of abortion. The film was produced in 1971, before abortion was legalized, but class discussion can compensate for that deficiency.[3]

2.29ª   Male/Female: Changing Lifestyles. Educational Audio-Visual. Four filmstrips, four discs or cassettes, teachers' notes. (Available from: Educational Audio-Visual, 29 Marble Avenue, Pleasantville, NY 10670. $60.00, discs; $68.00, cassettes.)

This set of filmstrips begins by presenting facts about sexual development. There is a two-part history of sex roles, including development of the women's movement from the 19th century to today. The final part offers comments by grade and high school students on issues, such as the family, social pressures, work and relationships.[1] [10–12]

2.30 Parenthood: A Series, Preparing for Parenthood. Guidance Associates, 1971. 17 minutes, two filmstrips with cassettes. (Available from: Guidance Associates, A/V Subsidiary, 757 Third Avenue, New York, NY 10017.)

This program discusses the changes children make in parents' lives and the responsibilities, as well as the joys, involved in parenthood.[16] [7–12]

2.31 People—Different but Alike. Aims. 10 minutes, 16mm. (Available from: Aims, 621 Justin Avenue, Glendale, CA 91201.)

People are superficially different (tall-short, fat-thin, black-white, rich-poor, some wear glasses, others stutter, etc.). But what's inside a person—that's what counts. Don't prejudge people merely because they're different from you. A fun approach to sensitive problems via pantomime, music and rhyme.[21] [K–6]

2.32 Proactive Counseling for Women. American Personnel and Guidance Association, 1971. 75 minutes, cassette tape. (Available from: Order Services, American Personnel and Guidance Association, 2 Skyline Place, Suite 400, 5203 Leesburg Pike, Falls Church, VA 22041. Order No. 72905. $8.00; 3 for $23.00.)

No annotation available.

2.33[e] Rape: Some Facts and Myths. Center for Cassette Studies, 1974. 41 minute cassette. (Available from: Center for Cassette Studies, 8110 Webb Avenue, North Hollywood, CA 91605.)

Two rape victims describe their personal experiences with rapists and a defense expert recommends ways to counterattack.[16] [11–12]

2.34[e] Rape: The Savage Crime. Audio Visual Narrative Arts, 1975. Two filmstrips and cassettes, teacher's guide. (Available from: Audio Visual Narrative Arts, Box 9, Pleasantville, NY 10570.)

The first filmstrip focuses on the rapist—the reasons for rape and the laws and social views concerning rape. The second looks at the victim and where the crime occurs, how fear of rape affects women, and how women are acting to change the situation.[16] [7–12]

2.35 A Whole New Ball Game. Bailey Film Associates. Nine minutes. (Available from: Bailey Film Associates, 2211 Michigan Avenue, P.O. Box 1795, Santa Monica, CA 90406.)

A preadolescent girl is first discouraged by adults from playing football and then treated as the object in a kissing game by the boys who have just been her teammates. An open-ended film, valuable for discussion.[21] [7–12]

Bibliographies/Resource Lists

2.36 Sex-Discrimination in Guidance and Counseling (Volume 2). Michele Harway, et al. 1976. 177 p. Higher Education Research Institute, Inc. (Available from: EDRS MF-$.91—HC-$10.03 plus postage, ED 132 500.)

This unindexed, extensively annotated bibliography contains 167 references arranged by author. Citations include books, journals, articles, dissertations and experimental studies with detailed reporting of results.[2]

2.37[d] Teenage Pregnancy: A Selected Bibliography. National Alliance for Optional Parenthood, 1978. 21 p. (Available from: National Alliance for Optional Parenthood, 2010 Massachusetts Avenue, NW, Washington, DC 20036. $1.00.)

An annotated resource list of printed materials available on teenage pregnancy.[37] [8–12]

2.38 Women: Sexuality, Psychology and Psychotherapy: A Bibliography. Emily A. Cary. Boston, MA: Womanspace, 1976.

Includes bibliographies on Counseling Women (1975) and Issues in the Psychology and Counseling of Women (1976).[4]

CAREER GUIDANCE*

Lesson Plans

2.39 Assembling: A Saleable Work Skill. Project Equality. (Available from: Project Equality, Highline School District, 15675 Ambaum Boulevard, SW, Seattle, WA 98166, (206) 433-0111.)

An occupation simulation packet designed as a hands-on career education activity based on the "isolated skill concept." This is the singling out of a saleable skill required for a wide variety of jobs and already possessed, in some measure, by the student. The student identifies and uses the skill in a hands-on simulated work experience. As students apply their skills, it becomes clear that a skill is not dependent on sex and that a skill required for one type of work is often transferable to another. Discussion questions emphasize these two points. Lesson plans and many required materials are included with the packets. Materials are sensitive to many kinds of discrimination; illustrations show a mix of races as well as sexes. [3–4]

2.40 Beating the Numbers: A Math Careers Program Handbook. Boston Community School Board and Boston University. Women's Educational Equity Act Program, 1981. (Available from: Education Development Center, 55 Chapel Street, Newton, MA: 02160. $8.00.)

An increasing number of jobs require strong math skills. This handbook describes a successful Boston-based program that combines math instruction and counseling to help undereducated and underemployed women develop basic math skills, broaden their career aspirations and overcome barriers to job advancement. Designed as a short-term continuing education or tutorial program for women with high school or general equivalency diplomas, the

---

*Subcategories of "Career Guidance," indicated by superscript letters following entry numbers, are designated as follows: a=Career Guidance (Nontraditional Careers); b=Career Guidance (Vocational Education); c=Career Guidance (Home Economics).

handbook can also be used in high schools. It includes a bibliography of mathematics, counseling and career information; a 16-week lesson plan model; eight counseling workshops; and occupational math modules for traditional and nontraditional careers. [9–12]

2.41   Career Education Activity Manual: 4th, 5th and 6th. Janet Atwood. Cleveland Heights—University Heights (Ohio) City School. 94 p. (Available from: EDRS MF-$.91—HC- $4.67 plus postage, ED 156 869.)

An activity manual designed to stand alone or supplement a career education classroom program. Ten lesson plans are provided for each of the following seven units: (1) general information activities, (2) career education activities, (3) resource people contact lessons, (4) research activities, (5) value activities for awareness of self, (6) sexism awareness activities and (7) role playing activities. [4–6]

2.42   Career for Peers. Wider Opportunities for Women, 1975. (Available from: Wider Opportunities for Women, 1649 K Street NW, Washington, DC 20006. $10.00; additional sets of student booklets $2.00 each.)

A manual for training high school students as career center information specialists. It presents interviewing techniques, employment information, sex role stereotyping information and guidelines on planning an activity program. Set of four student booklets and a facilitator's manual; four booklets address self-assessment, occupational field, career decisions, and job-finding techniques.[44] [9–12]

2.43   Choices and Careers. Women's Educational Resources. (Available from: Women's Educational Resources, 610 Langdon Street, 423 Lowell Hall, Madison, WI 53706. $2.00 per unit.)

Written by Wisconsin Indian women, this package offers more than 20 curriculum units that include materials for girls 9–11, 12–14, and 15–18 and for parents and educators.[36] [4–12]

2.44   Color Discrimination: A Saleable Work Skill. Kris Ripley. Project Equality. 35 p. (Available from: Project Equality, Highline School District, 15675 Ambaum Blvd., SW, Seattle, WA 98166, (206) 433-0111; or EDRS MF-$.91 plus postage, ED 172 011.)

This occupation packet is designed to provide K–2 students with a simulated work experience using the "isolated skill concept." Students will learn how color discrimination is a saleable work skill necessary for a wide variety of jobs and a student's sex should not expand or limit his or her potential. Students will explore how color discrimination is used by telephone factory wire sorters, store clerks and interior decorators. Included in the packet are objectives, evaluation procedures, sequence of activities, materials needed, time required, and pre- and posttests. [K–2]

2.45   Crawling and/or Squatting: A Saleable Work Skill. Margery Montgomery. Project Equality. 38 p. (Available from: Project Equality, Highline School District, 15675 Ambaum Blvd., SW, Seattle, WA 98166, (206) 433-0111; or EDRS MF-$.91 plus postage, ED 172 010.)

This occupation simulation packet is designed to provide K–2 students with a simulated work experience using the "isolated skill concept." Students will learn how crawling and/or squatting is a saleable work skill necessary for a wide variety of jobs, and a student's sex should not expand or limit his or her potential. Students

will explore how crawling and/or squatting is used by store checks, plumbers and carpenters. Included in the packet are objectives, evaluation procedures, sequence of activities, materials needed, time required, and pre- and posttests. [K–2]

2.46   Creativity: A Saleable Work Skill. Project Equality. (Available from: Project Equality, Highline School District, 15675 Ambaum Blvd., SW, Seattle, WA 98166, (206) 433-0111.)

An occupation simulation packet is designed as a hands-on career education activity based on the "isolated skill concept." This is the singling out of a saleable skill required for a wide variety of jobs and already possessed, in some measure, by the student. The student identifies and uses the skill in a hands-on simulated work experience. As students apply their skills, it becomes clear that a skill is not dependent on sex and that a skill required for one type of work is often transferable to another. Discussion questions emphasize these two points. Lesson plans and many required materials are included with the packets. Materials are sensitive to many kinds of discrimination; illustrations show a mix of races as well as sexes.[36] [3–4]

2.47   Curriculum Guide: Reducing Sex-Role Stereotyping through Career Education. Kathy Quinn. Bristol, CT: Career Education Program. 47 p. (Available from: EDRS MF-$.91—HC- $2.06 plus postage, ED 130 058.)

Fifteen lesson plans developed by teachers to increase awareness of sex role stereotyping and its relationship to career education. The lesson plans have intended grade level, subject area, goals, career education objectives, procedures, expected results and follow-up activities. They vary widely, however, in the quality and quantity of activities and directions provided. There are lesson plans for biology, clothing, community studies, distributive education, Spanish, special education, springmaking, typing, women in literature, and world history classes. Perhaps more useful are the bibliographies of recommended nonsexist references for the numerous subject areas.

2.48   Dreams to Reality. Girl Scouts of the U.S.A., 1978. (Available from: Girl Scouts of U.S.A., National Equipment Services, 830 Third Avenue, New York, NY 10022 or Girl Scout departments in retail stores. Activity book, $2.00; career cards, $2.25; leader's guide, $1.00.)

Activities and cards are designed to expose young women to career options. Cards have photographs and descriptions and are designed to make career exploration a fun game.[44] [7–12]

2.49   Expanding Career Horizons. Department of Adult Vocational and Technical Education, Illinois Office of Education, 1978. (Available from: Curriculum Publication Clearinghouse, Western Illinois University, 76B Horrabin Hall, Macomb, IL 61455. $25.00. For information on inservice workshops: Program Information Office, The National Center for Research in Vocational Education, The Ohio State University, 1960 Kenny Road, Columbus, OH 43210.)

These materials are designed for both sexes in grades 7 through 14. They include five 50-minute activity oriented lessons designed to create awareness and help eliminate sex role stereotyping. Each lesson can stand alone and be used in a variety of classroom situations, both vocational and nonvocational. A 46-page teacher's guide contains performance based objectives for students. Materials are packaged in kit form with each kit containing one teacher's guide and 30 sets of student materials.[2] [7–14]

2.50 Exploring Nonconventional Careers for Women. Jane Morris. *The School Counselor*, Vol. 23, No. 2 (November 1975), pp. 127–32.

Three sessions which can be easily incorporated into the regular classroom, designed to allow 9th and 10th grade girls to explore nonconventional careers. Activities include job analysis, self-analysis, group feedback, roleplaying, game simulation and fantasy. Each session has two to three parts with the purpose, time required, preparation and procedures. [7–12]

2.51 The Female Experience in America: Development, Counseling and Career Issues. University of Tennessee, Model Sex Fair Training Program in Educational Psychology and Guidance, 1979. 208 p. (Available from: Education Development Center, 55 Chapel Street, Newton, MA 02160.)

These materials were developed to be used as a graduate level course in guidance and counseling. However, all or some of the units could be used for teacher inservice or in the high school classroom. The four units include: ''Female Development''; ''Women's Career Patterns-Life Styles''; ''Women Growing and Changing: Counseling Approaches''; ''Critical Incidents in Female Development: Counseling Issues.'' Each unit includes an introduction, objectives, directions for facilitator preparation, suggested learning activities, a bibliography, and an appendix of readings and worksheets. Materials are attractively presented and very current. [9–12]

2.52 Focus on the Future. Cleveland State University, 1979. Technical manual; leader's manual; picture stimulus sets. (Available from: Education Development Center, 55 Chapel Street, Newton, MA 02160. $2.00 plus 20% handling charge.)

This is a career-guidance activity for secondary school students. It is designed to stimulate discussion of sex stereotyping and its implications for planning for the future. [9–12]

2.53a The House that Jill and Jack Built. Phyllis Kopelman. Berkeley United School District, Berkeley, CA, 1976. (Available from: EDRS MF-$.91—HC-$3.50 plus postage, ED 149 013.)

A guide to developing a career education program using carpentry as a vehicle. Included are lesson plans, information on supplies and equipment and supplementary resources. The guide focuses on hammering, sawing and drilling procedures. Although the activities are appropriate for K–12 students, the emphasis is on delivering specific information about tools to K–3 students. [K–12]

2.54 How Women Find Jobs: A Guide for Workshop Leaders. Vera Norwood (ed.). New Mexico Commission on the Status of Women, 1979. 279 p. (Available from: Education Development Center, 55 Chapel Street, Newton, MA 02160. $5.50.)

This manual serves as a guide for organizing and conducting workshops or classes intended to provide job finding techniques. Detailed guidelines are provided for conducting group discussions and lead activities which focus on identifying job skills, writing a resume, applying for a job, interviewing, and coping with both work and home life. A Spanish translation of the activity sheets is included. [9–12]

2.55 In Search of a Job: A Simulated Activity in Occupational Decision Making. Eric Rice, et al. 1977. 82 p. (Available from: System Sciences, Inc., P.O. Box 2345, Chapel Hill, NC 27514. $10.00.)

This group process simulation is designed for students, eighth grade reading level and above. It requires 6 to 15 sessions. The topics include constraints on individual choices and sex bias in the world of work, family and employer roleplays, groups' decision making processes and the analysis of sex bias in job seeking activities. The package includes want ads, applications, job descriptions, family and employer descriptions, a simulation activity, an interview guide and day-by-day instructions.[2] [8–12]

2.56 Many Thousand Words—Work Pictures. Project Equality. (Available from: Project Equality, Highline School District, 15675 Ambaum Blvd., SW, Seattle, WA 98166, (206) 433-0111.)

This looseleaf book contains a set of pictures of women and men, girls and boys, in a variety of nonstereotyped work settings at home, school, and in the community, depicting various skills and abilities. Discussion questions focus on the job skills needed and on whether persons of either sex might have those skills.[36] [1–6]

2.57 Measuring: A Saleable Work Skill. Project Equality. (Available from: Project Equality, Highline School District, 15675 Ambaum Blvd., SW, Seattle, WA 98166, (206) 433-0111.)

An occupation simulation packet designed as a hands-on career education activity based on the ''isolated skill concept.'' This is the singling out of a saleable skill required for a wide variety of jobs and already possessed, in some measure, by the student. The student identifies and uses the skill in a hands-on simulated work experience. As students apply their skills, it becomes clear that a skill is not dependent on sex and that a skill required for one type of work is often transferable to another. Discussion questions emphasize these two points. Lesson plans and many required materials are included with the packets. Materials are sensitive to many kinds of discrimination; illustrations show a mix of races as well as sexes.[36] [5–6]

2.58b New Career Realizations. Michigan State University. (Available from: Michigan State University, Career Education Resources, 301D Erickson Hall, East Lansing, MI 48824. $3.90.)

This five-lesson module explores sex role stereotyping as it pertains to vocational planning and the family role. It includes teacher's decision making skills and pre- and posttests. [7–9]

2.59 New Directions for Rural Women: A Workshop Leader's Manual. The Grail, 1979. 40 p. (Available from: Education Development Center, 55 Chapel Street, Newton, MA 02160. $2.25.)

Although geared to adult women who need to know about local job resources and identify individual occupational needs, the exercises included in this workshop manual could be used with high school students. The contents include activities to assess personal work values, assertiveness training exercises, information on jobs and education, a bibliography and sample workshop formats. [9–12]

2.60c New Faces and Places for Home Economics: Human Roles Examining Choices through Education. *Illinois Teacher of Home Economics*, Vol. 18, No. 5, pp. 269–349.

Materials, activities and exercises on sex roles for home economics teachers.[4]

2.61   Non-Sexist Community Careers. The Instructo Corporation. (Available from: The Instructo Corporation, Cedar Hollow Road, Paoli, PA 19301.)

Flannel board cutouts, showing women and men in equal roles—27 people dressed to fit hundreds of occupational roles with appropriate tools and props. Multiethnic.[1] [K–6]

2.62   Options: A Career Development Curriculum for Rural High School Students. Dartmouth College Education Department, 1980. (Available from: Education Development Center, 55 Chapel Street, Newton, MA 02160. $21.00 Unit I; $6.00 Unit II; $55.00 Unit III; $35.00 Unit IV; $3.50 regional adaptation packet.)

A curriculum to equip rural students with information and problem solving skills and to enable them to practice responding to career choice dilemmas through simulated but realistic situations. The curriculum is divided into four units, each of which can be used separately. Each unit is organized as day-by-day lessons, complete with instructions for classroom activities, homework, student worksheets, list of materials and supplemental resources. *Unit I: Understanding People in Our Area* involves students in defining situations and problems faced by people in their own community and exploring decisions they will make if they remain at home. In *Unit II: Decision Making,* students learn and practice skills needed to cope with problems defined in the first unit. *Unit III: Life Planning* uses a simulation game as one technique for students to consider the consequences of decisions they may make as young adults. *Unit IV: The Juggling Act: Lives and Careers* provides case studies to explore complex family and work situations typical of modern life. [9–12]

2.63ᵃ   People at Work: A Non-Sexist Approach. The Instructo Corporation. (Available from: The Instructo Corporation, Cedar Hollow Road, Paoli, PA 19301. $6.00.)

A multiethnic unit with 24 pictures of people at various jobs and nontraditional roles. Good for early career education, language development and learning about our society. Has complete teaching guide.[1] [K–6]

2.64ᶜ   Planning for Free Lives: Curriculum Materials for Combatting Sex Stereotyping in Home Economics, Family Living and Career Awareness Courses. Feminists Northwest, 1975. 41 p. (Available from: Feminists Northwest, 5038 Nicklas Place, NE, Seattle, WA 98105 or EDRS MF-$.91, ED 128 236.)

A variety of classroom activities focusing on general awareness, foods, sewing, family lifestyles and options, individual growth vs. stereotyping, parenting and child development, unpaid work and paid work. Although designed for high school home economics classes, many of the activities are appropriate for use in social studies units and with junior high students. Instructions for teachers and student self-assessment questionnaires, sample activity sheets and a bibliography of resource materials are included. One sample activity has students interview housewives and prepare a sample time pattern of "unpaid" work for comparison with a person who works a 40-hour, paid work week. Another activity suggests boys sew articles such as backpacks if they are feeling inhibited about learning to sew. [7–12]

2.65   Professional Women. Feminist Resources for Equal Education. (Available from: Feminist Resources for Equal Education, Box 3185, Saxonville Station, Framingham, MA 01701. $2.50.)

A set of good role models for women and girls.[1]

2.66   A Qualitative Incremental Improvement to Reduce Sex Role Stereotyping in the Career Choices of Junior High Students. (Available from: Jefferson County Public Schools, 1209 Quail Street, Lakewood, CO 80215, (303) 234-7000.)

Program materials entitled *The Now and the Future* were developed for career exploration activities in junior high grades during the 1976–1977 school year. Emphasis is placed on career exploration and eliminating sex stereotyping of occupations.[9] [7–9]

2.67   A Resource Guide for Career Development in the Junior High School. Arland Benson. 1973. 161 p. (Available from: Minnesota Department of Education, Division of Instruction, Capitol Square Building, St. Paul, MN 55101.)

Learning activities, games, etc., to enhance career education.[4] [7–9]

2.68   See and Sew: Menswear. Butterick Fashion Marketing, 1973. (Available from: Butterick Fashion Marketing, Butterick Pattern Service, 161 Sixth Avenue, New York, NY 10013.)

Kit with step-by-step approach to men's clothing construction.[4][9] [7–12]

2.69   Sex Equity in Career Education (K–8): Resource Guide. Southeastern Massachusetts University, July 1979. 20 p. (Available from: EDRS MF-$.91—HC-$1.82 plus postage, ED 179 723.)

Twenty-eight lesson plans for K–8 students, designed to meet career education and sex equity objectives to expand awareness of career choices and options. Each activity includes objectives, procedure and materials needed. A brief resource list of sex equity organizations, alternative publishers, and print and nonprint materials are included. [K–8]

2.70   Sex Fairness in Career Guidance: A Learning Kit. Linda B. Stebbins, et al. 1975. 265 p. Multimedia kit (Available from: Abt Publications, 55 Wheeler Street, Cambridge, MA 02138. $15.00 plus $1.50 shipping.)

This self-administered curriculum for counselors, teachers, and students is organized into four chapters dealing with orientation to sex fairness, recommendations for sex fair career guidance programs, sex fair use and interpretation of interest inventories, and resource guide. Included in the kit are seven spirit masters, eight roleplay cards, and one audiocassette entitled "Supplementary Exercises."[2] [8–12]

2.71   Sex-Stereotyping, Bias and Discrimination in the World of Work: A Student Handbook. Eric Rice, et al. 1977. 159 p. (Available from: Systems Science, Inc., P.O. Box 2345, Chapel Hill, NC 27514. $15.00.)

This workbook uses discovery learning materials for students eighth grade reading level and above to discuss what is work, belie about working women and men, looking for a job and being on the job. Teacher materials include an introduction and instructions for specific activities. It can be used in 5- to 45-minute classroom sessions.[2] [8–12]

2.72   Sexism in Education. Emma Willard Task Force on Education, 1972. (Available from: Emma Willard Task Force on Education, Box 14229, University Station, Minneapolis, MN 55408. $3.50.)

A book of materials used by this group in its work against sexism; includes bibliographies, consciousness-raising exercises for teachers and students, a checklist for evaluating sexism in instructional materials and a game for counselors to use with students about career aspirations and sex roles.[25] [9–12]

2.73   Strategies for Equality: Volume II, Vocational Education. Training Institute for Sex Desegregation. (Available from: Training Institute for Sex Desegregation, Rutgers University, Federation Hall-Douglass Campus, New Brunswick, NJ 08903.)

Compendium of curricular projects devised and tested by educators in their own classroom. For teachers, coaches, counselors and administrators.[16] [9–12]

2.74   Teaching Module for Expanding Occupational Awareness of Preschool, Second and Fourth Grade Children. Ramond Marotz-Badeu and Pamela Riley. 1979. 157 p. (Available from: EDRS MF-$.91—HC-$10.82 plus postage, ED 183 859.)

Three modular units, each ranging from six to nine weeks, designed to facilitate career education by reducing sex role stereotypes of various occupations. Each unit provides an outline of each week's activities and includes objectives, materials needed and procedures. [K–4]

2.75   The Whole Person Book: Toward Self-Discovery and Life Options. Nebraska Commission on the Status of Women, 1979. 245 p. (Available from: Education Development Center, 55 Chapel Street, Newton, MA 02160. $5.25.)

Provides curriculum materials for increasing awareness of sex bias and promoting more positive attitudes and participation in sex fair career education and counseling. This manual is designed to supplement other materials or to serve as a basis when planning programs. The student activities are organized around three major areas related to career exploration. "Self-Exploration" provides activities to help students explore personal values, interests and talents influencing career choices. "Decision Making" provides opportunities for making simulated and actual decisions as participants examine various decision making methods and their resulting outcomes. In "Life Planning," learners are encouraged to match personal qualities with occupational skills, identify educational alternatives and examine potential lifestyles relevant to career interests. Other sections of the book include "Facilitator's Guide," "Learner Materials," and "Resources." All major sections are color coded for easy reference. [9–12]

2.76   Women and the World of Work: A Career Education Resource Guide (Minnesota Guidance Series, Learning Opportunities Package G). Richard J. Thoni, et al. University of Minnesota, 1972. 36 p. (Available from: EDRS MF-$.91—HC-$2.06 plus postage, ED 128 550.)

This package is one of a series developed for use at the high school level constituting a career development curriculum. There is a variety of class and small group activities focusing on women and the world of work, which teachers can implement through traditional subject areas or as a self-contained mini-course. The enabling objectives and learning experiences are designed to move the student from basic to more complex concepts and include: (1) discovering elements within our culture which have contributed to the continuance of the traditional view of women; (2) investigating the opinions that contemporary women hold of themselves and their place in the world of work; (3) reading and discussing relevant literature dealing with women, their traditional roles and their place in the world of work; (4) participating in and observing situations in which women are found in roles other than traditional ones; (5) citing examples of change within the modern work society which have affected the traditional division of labor by sex; (6) identifying several life patterns which might be followed by women and the significance of each in regard to the personal development and family life of a woman; and (7) gathering information concerning vocational opportunities for women in various areas of work. Teachers are provided with discussion questions, student questionnaires, fact sheets and other background information. Sample activities include debates, roleplaying and examining popular songs. [9–12]

2.77   Women Workers. Childcraft Education Corporation. (Available from: Childcraft Education Corporation, 20 Kilmer Road, Edison, NJ 08817. $6.50.)

A kit consisting of six painted, wooden figurines showing a woman as a doctor, carpenter, school crossing guard, dairy worker, mail carrier and sanitary engineer.[4] [K–3]

Course Outlines

2.78[a]   Fortune Telling: A Program for Girls about Women, Work, and Nontraditional Occupations. YWCA. (Available from: Fortune Telling Coordinator, Boston YWCA, 140 Clearedon Street, Boston, MA 02116. $8.50.)

Involves five conversations and participatory activities to learn about women's work prospects, importance of marketable skills, "female" and "male" jobs (disadvantages and advantages), women's ability to handle nontraditional jobs and school opportunities in preparing for nontraditional jobs.[14] [10–12]

2.79[c]   Home Economics Unlimited. Training Institute for Sex Desegregation. (Available from: Training Institute for Sex Desegregation, Rutgers University, Federation Hall-Douglass Campus, New Brunswick, NJ 08903. $3.50.)

How to develop an integrated and innovative home economics program, K–12.[16] [K–12]

2.80[c]   Outline for Single Living. Renee Fishman. Dumont High School, 1974. (Available from: Dumont High School, New Milford Avenue, Dumont, NJ 07628.)

A course outline for a unit in a family living or related course.[4] [10–12]

Supplementary Texts

2.81[c]   Accent on Home Economics. Nancy B. Greenspan and Elaine P. Davis. New York: Julian Messner, 1978. 255 p.

Surveys the various fields within home economics and shows diversity of careers available to both women and men.[49] [7–12]

2.82   Apprenticeship and Other Blue Collar Job Opportunities for Women. Valerie Wheat and Christie Niebel. Women's Educational Equity Communications Network, 1978. (Available from: Women's Educational Equity Act Program, U.S. Department of Education, Donahoe Building, Room 1105, 400 Maryland Avenue, SW, Washington, DC 20202.)

Offers a guide to the apprenticeship process and general information on blue collar jobs. Includes profiles and photographs of women on the job, resource list and bibliography.[41]

2.83   Blue Collar Jobs for Women. Muriel Lederer. New York: E. P. Dutton, 1979. 257 p. $7.95 p.b.

The main part of this book consists of descriptions of a myriad of jobs in the trades. The descriptions often include personal reports of women in the field and always cover the requirements, substance, working conditions, pay ranges, opportunities for employment and further sources of information. This well-written, comprehensive book also aids the reader in evaluating chances for success. Appendices include a glossary, many addresses and a chart of salary averages.[44] [9–12]

2.84   Changing Learning, Changing Lives: A High School Women's Studies Curriculum from the Group School. Barbara Gates, Susan Klaw, and Adra Reich. Old Westbury, NY: The Feminist Press, 1978. 256 p.

This material was developed for young working class women at an alternative high school in Cambridge, Massachusetts. The curriculum is divided into nine areas, including "Messages from Society," "Growing Up Female," "Women and Work," and "Women Organizing Themselves." The units can be used as supplements to English, history, psychology, anthropology, career education or health courses. Throughout the packet recommendations are made on how to teach as well as what to teach.[14]

2.85   Chemistry Careers. L.B. Taylor. New York: Franklin Watts, 1978. 62 p.

Excellent introduction for junior and senior high school students to careers available in the field of chemistry from chemists and chemical engineers to technical writers and patent agents. Included are salary information and required educational preparation. Book is exemplary in its use of nonsexist language, and women and ethnic minorities are represented in the photographs. [11–12]

2.86   Community Careering: A Career Education Gamebook. Moravia, NY: Chronical Guidance Publications, 1974. 60 p.

A children's workbook on career awareness.[49] [K–6]

2.87[c]   Concepts in Clothing. Judy Lynn Graef and Joan Buescher Strom. New York: McGraw-Hill, 1976.

Textbook for new coeducational courses in sewing.[4] [10–12]

2.88[a]   Conversations: Working Women Talk about Doing a Man's Job. Terry Wetherby. Millbrae, CA: Les Femmes, 1977. 269 p. $6.95.

Fascinating interviews in question and answer format with 22 women in nontraditional jobs. Includes professional careers and some

trades as well as unusual careers such as stuntperson and dragster. [9–12]

2.89[a]   Country Women: A Handbook for the New Farmer. Sherry Thomas and Jeanne Tetrault. Garden City, NY: Doubleday. $6.95.

A how-to book for those farming or living in the country who wish to work with minimum reliance on outside or professional help.[4] [7–12]

2.90   Deadline. Kathleen A. Begley. New York: Dell, 1977. 169 p. $1.50 p.b.

Kathleen Begley's story of her experiences as a newspaper reporter is a fascinating behind-the-scenes look at a large daily newspaper. It also is an example of the hard work and determination it takes to become a good reporter. Begley obviously loves her work but does not try to glamorize it. [8–12]

2.91   Dentistry: The Career of Choice for Women. (Available from: Council on Dental Education, American Dental Association, 311 E. Chicago Avenue, Chicago, IL 60611. Free.)

Career pamphlet.[47]

2.92   Doctors for the People. Elizabeth Levy and Mara Miller. New York: Dell, 1979. 111 p. $1.25 p.b.

Profiles of two female and three male doctors. All not only care for, but care about their patients since they have placed commitment to patient care above anything else. One of the women is a black surgeon and legislator; the other is a feminist gynecologist. The men include a geneticist, a family practitioner, and a general practitioner who works with migrant farm workers. In addition to the individual profiles, the book describes a unique clinic for teenagers which provides a wide range of medical, psychological and vocational services. [7–9]

2.93   Equity for Black Female Students in Suburban Schools. National Council of Negro Women, 1979. (Available from: National Council of Negro Women, Montgomery City Section, P.O. Box 1625, Silver Springs, MD 20802.)

A manual and a series of pamphlets which illustrate how to help black students set career goals, strengthen academic skills, improve self images and understand sex and race stereotyping.[44]

2.94[b]   Expanding Adolescent Role Expectations: Information, Activities, Resources for Vocational Educators. Community Service Education Department, New York State College of Human Ecology, Cornell University. (Available from: Media Services Printing, New York State College of Human Ecology, B-10, Martha Van Rensselaer Hall, Cornell University, Ithaca, NY 14853. $3.00.)

Includes background information, fact sheets, checklists, guidelines and resources on women and work, negative aspects of stereotyping, sex stereotyping in textbooks and activities for the classroom.

2.95[b]   Exploring the Construction Industry. M. Roger Betts and others. Bloomington, IL: McKnight, 1976. 582

Textbook for vocational education—construction—showing both girls and boys working on projects in its illustrations and written in neutral style. [7–12]

2.96 Facilitating Career Development for Girls and Women. American Personnel and Guidance Association, 1975. (Available from: Order Services, American Personnel and Guidance Association, 2 Skyline Place, Suite 400, 5203 Leesburg Pike, Falls Church, VA 22041. Order No. 72211. $4.00.)

Selections from papers presented at a workshop, held at Appalachian State University, Boone, North Carolina in July, 1973. Among the topics were "Career Barriers: Are They Falling Down?" by S. Norman Feingold; "Young Children's Perceptions of Occupational Roles" by Nancy Schlossberg; and "Women in Politics" by Lura Talley. This book will serve as a text in any modern career development curriculum, and it will also make a worthwhile addition to the library of any socially conscious counselor.[46]

2.97 Free to Be . . . You and Me. Marlo Thomas, et al. (eds.). New York: McGraw-Hill, 1974. 143 p. $6.95 p.b.

A delightful, nonsexist collection of songs, stories, poems and pictures designed to expand young children's personal horizons and dispel myths and limiting stereotypes. Children, parents and teachers will find it both entertaining and thought-provoking. [K–6]

2.98 Free to Choose: Decision-Making for Young Men. Joyce Slayton Mitchell. New York: Dell, 1977. 261 p. $1.75 p.b. (Originally published by Delacorte, 1976.)

An anthology of brief essays offering young men—and women—a wealth of information and advice on matters of personal, social, educational and career development. The selections provide a discussion of the variety of choices men and women must make, including sexual, relationship, liberation, turning-on, spiritual, athletic and educational choices. This book would be particularly appropriate for use in health, career guidance and social studies classes, as well as for free reading. Although the book is aimed primarily toward college-bound students, some information is also provided on military and occupational trades.

2.99 The Gender Trap: A Closer Look at Sex Roles Book 1: Education and Work). Carol Adams and Rae Laurikietis. London: Academy Press, 1977. 116 p. $4.50 p.b. (Originally published by Quartet Books Limited, 1976).

Designed for high school-aged young people, this book deals with basic issues of women and work. It discusses how parents and the educational system mold and perpetuate stereotyped behaviors and career expectations for girls and boys. It provides statistics, quotes, cartoons, interviews and stories focusing on the world of work from a feminist perspective. Although adapted for American audiences, this book was written by two English authors and provides an English outlook. [8–12]

2.100 He Bear She Bear. Stan and Jan Berenstain. New York: Random House, 1974. 36 p. $2.25.

Careers open to both sexes are portrayed in this easy reader.[1] [K–3]

2.101[c] Home Economics for Young Men: A Teaching Guide. Eleanore L. Kohlmann. Iowa State University Press, 1975. 214 p. (Available from: Iowa State University Press, Ames, IA.)

Excellent nonsexist guide to such topics as family life, personal economics, textiles, food and nutrition, housing.[49] [7–12]

2.102 I Can Be Anything: Careers and College for Young Women. Joyce Slayton Mitchell. New York: College Entrance Examination Board, 1978. 294 p. Paperback.

This guide to 108 careers provides a candid look at what each career is like, including on-the-job interviews with women from every part of the country. Includes required educational background, present employment opportunities, lists of colleges, and sources for additional information. Readers should note that the book was published in 1978, making salary information inaccurate. Looks at many nontraditional careers for women in a positive manner. [10–12]

2.103 Law and the New Woman. Mary McHugh. New York: Franklin Watts, 1975. 107 p.

This book is part of an exciting new series designed to help young women choose lifestyles and careers best suited to their interests and talents. The author encourages young women to pursue a law career if they have the fundamental qualifications: good LSAT scores, high grade-point average and a sincere interest in investing the time and energy in a legal education. She describes law school and the many kinds of job opportunities open to law graduates. The author further explains that law is a good career to choose if one is interested in women's issues because it touches so many different areas such as education, politics and business.

2.104 Lawyers for the People: A New Breed of Defenders and Their Work. Elizabeth Levy. New York: Dell, 1974. 128 p. $1.25 p.b.

Nine profiles of women and men who are a growing minority in the legal profession: public interest lawyers. Using a variety of approaches in various organizations, they represent people who have traditionally been too poor or unorganized to obtain legal services. This book shows that a career in law and a desire to change society are not incompatible. [9–12]

2.105 Looking Forward to a Career: Veterinary Medicine. Helen L. Gillum. Minneapolis: Dillon Press, 1976. 107 p.

This book explains what a veterinarian does and what preparation is needed for the career of veterinary medicine as well as related careers. Print size and use of photographs make this book appropriate for junior high readers. [6–8]

2.106[c] The Masculine Focus in Home Economics. Judy H. Dowell and Bonnie B. Greenwood. Home Economics Association, 1975. 31 p. (Available from: EDRS MF-$.91—HC-$2.06 plus postage, ED 116 002.)

This booklet suggests strategies for recruiting and teaching young men in home economics classes. There is an analysis of the "masculine image" and existing barriers, including teachers' attitudes.[9] [10–12]

2.107 Math Equals: Biographies of Women Mathematicians and Related Activities. Teri Perl. Reading, MA: Addison-Wesley, 1978.

Biographies of nine women mathematicians, with related math activities. The women range from Hypatia of Greece (370-415 A.D.) to Emmy Noether (1882–1935). The relatively brief biographies are fascinating. Each one notes the particular problems which the female mathematician faced by virtue of her sex. The mathematical activities are related to the work of the mathematicians covered in the book and are presented in original and thought-provoking ways. Appendices and solutions to the problems are included, and the book is well illustrated. [7–12]

2.108   Medicine—A Woman's Career. American Medical Women's Association. (Available from: American Medical Women's Association, 1740 Broadway, New York, NY 10019.)

Career pamphlet.[47]

2.109   Mothers Can Do Anything. Joe Lasker. Chicago: Albert Whitman, 1976. 35 p. $4.75.

A picture book depicting women in various occupations.[1] [K–3]

2.110   Ms. Attorney. D. X. Fenton. Philadelphia: Westminster Press, 1974. 159 p. $5.50.

This is a comprehensive book for students contemplating a career in the legal profession. It not only describes the career role of an attorney, it also reviews coursework and tests that are required before entering the field. Book also discusses the realities of discrimination against women and explodes the fallacy about the appropriateness of "lady-lawyers."

2.111   My Doctor Bag Book. Kathleen Daly. Racine, WI: Golden Press, 1977. 24 p.

Cathy takes her doctor bag everywhere to cure the ills of her friends, their pets and dolls. She is treated by her physician, a woman. [K–3]

2.112   Other Choices for Becoming A Woman. Joyce Slayton Mitchell. New York: Dell, 1975. 267 p. $1.25 p.b. (Originally published by KNOW, Inc., 1974).

This anthology of brief essays provides a wealth of information designed to help young women—and men—realize their potential in today's world and to encourage them to explore the wide range of careers and lifestyles from which they can choose. The information provided is organized around sexual, relationship, beauty, turning-on, spiritual and educational choices and is geared for college-bound young women. Its companion book, "Free to Choose: Decision-Making for Young Men," offers additional information on military and nonprofessional career choices.

2.113   People and Places, U.S.A. Women's Educational Equity Act Program, 1981. (Available from: Education Development Center, 55 Chapel Street, Newton, MA 02160. $11.50.)

Educational and fun for girls and boys in grades three to five, *People and Places, U.S.A.,* includes 30 episodes describing the adventures of six youngsters. The stories contribute to the development of a positive self-image and encourage career exploration based on interest and competence. A reference and skill index as well as suggestions for follow-up activities are included for the teacher. [3–5]

2.114   Project Choice: Creating Her Options in Career Exploration. Case Western Reserve University, 1979. 580 p. (Available from: Education Development Center, 55 Chapel Street, Newton, MA 02160. $11.25.)

A diagnostic and prescriptive model for use by career counselors to assist high school females in broadening their career options and increasing positive self awareness. [9–12]

2.115   Pscyhology and the New Woman. Mary McHugh. New York: Franklin Watts, 1976. 114 p.

This book is part of a series designed to help young women choose lifestyles and careers suited to their interests and abilities. This volume contains a comprehensive study of the field of psychology from graduate training to the many specialty areas of psychology: clinical, environmental, developmental, educational, experimental, counseling and the psychology of women. The author frankly discusses salaries and how this type of career can be coordinated with having a family. A very good book for a young person looking at career choices.

2.116   Saturday's Child. Suzanne Seed. Chicago: J. Philip O'Hara, Inc., 1973. 158 p. $4.95 p.b.

Interviews with women representing 37 careers in four areas: arts and communications; science and medicine; trades, services and businesses; and commerce and government. Women who work as sportswriters, oceanographers, carpenters and city planners tell how they got started, what they do on the job and why they enjoy their chosen careers. The book is illustrated with photographs and contains a section on where to write for more information. This is an excellent idea generator for students who are uncertain about a career. [7–12]

2.117   Science Career Exploration for Women. Walter Smith and Karla Stroup. National Science Teachers Association. (Available from: National Science Teachers Association, 2742 Connecticut Avenue, NW, Washington, DC 20009. Stock No. 471-14748. $2.50.)

Junior high and high school level materials for teachers and others influential in science education. Includes curriculum suggestions, resource lists and background material on females at adolescence regarding careers, etc.[14] [K–12]

2.118   Space for Women. American Astronomical Society. (Available from: American Astronomical Society, 21 Fitz Randolph Road, Princeton, NJ 08540. Free.)

Career pamphlet.[47]

2.119[b]   STEREO (Strategies, Techniques, and Effectiv Resources for Equalizing Opportunities): A Handbook t Assist in Overcoming Sex Bias and Sex Stereotyping i Vocational Education. Arizona Department of Education (Available from: Arizona Department of Education, Div sion of Career and Vocational Education, 1535 West Je ferson, Phoenix, AZ 85007.)

Notebook of resources for teachers and students regarding activitie classroom suggestions, questionnaires, statistics and legislation a fecting sex discrimination.[14] [9–12]

2.120[b]   Try It, You'll Like It! A Student's Introductio to Nonsexist Vocational Education. Resource Center Sex Roles in Education, National Foundation for the In provement of Education. (Available from: Superintendent Documents, U.S. GPO, Stock No 017-080-01864-1.)

Workbook collection of thoughts, information and questions to he students think about new alternatives in vocational education [9–12]

2.121   What Can She Be? (An Architect; A Comput Scientist; A Geologist; A Lawyer; A Legislator; A Mu

tapes. (Available from: Scholastic Book Service, 906 Sylvan Avenue, Englewood Cliffs, NJ 07632.)

Career and life descriptions of the following people: female Puerto Rican doctor working in a large urban hospital; male baker who lives in a small town in Vermont; woman quilt maker in the Smoky Mountains who lives on a farm; male park ranger at the Cape Cod National Seashore; and manufacturer of toys in New England. All show family life, as well as work life; all emphasize the role of wife, husband and children within family unit.[28] [K–6]

2.149   Career Decision-Making: Examining Your Interests. McKnight, 1977. Filmstrip with cassette. (Available from: McKnight Publishing, Bloomington, IL 61701.)

Three young people examine their personal interests to discover how these interests can play a significant part in career decision making.[16] [10–12]

2.150   Career Decision-Making: Social Influences. McKnight, 1977. Filmstrip with cassette. (Available from: McKnight Publishing, Bloomington, IL 61701.)

Three youths from different backgrounds discuss decisions they must make on their careers and how their families and social backgrounds influence them.[16] [9–12]

2.151   Careers and Lifestyles. Guidance Associates. 70 minutes, sound filmstrips, LP or cassette, with discussion guide. (Available from: Guidance Associates, A/V Subsidiary, 757 Third Avenue, New York, NY 10017. $147.50.)

Spotlights interesting individuals in different occupations and lifestyles.[1]

2.152   Careers: Business and Office. Guidance Associates, 1978. Two filmstrips with cassette, guide. (Available from: Guidance Associates, A/V Subsidiary, 757 Third Avenue, New York, NY 10017.)

Job opportunities in the field of business are described, from banking and insurance to small businesses and government offices. Portrays women and men but lacks adequate minority representations.[28] [7–12]

2.153   Careers in Energy. Pathescope Educational Media, Inc., 1977. Two filmstrips with cassette, (13 and 12 minutes), guide. (Available from: Pathescope Educational Media, Inc., 71 Weyman Avenue, New Rochelle, NY 10802.)

Shows the great diversity of careers in the energy field and discusses the requirements for a variety of jobs, from professional engineer to coal miner and offshore rig operator.[28] [7–12]

2.154   Careers: Marketing and Distribution. Guidance Associates, 1978. (Available from: Guidance Associates, A/V Subsidiary, 757 Third Avenue, New York, NY 10017.)

Job opportunities are described in marketing, which include research, product manager, stock worker and copywriter. Portrays women, men, and minorities.[28] [7–12]

2.155   Careers Related to Science. Denoyer-Geppert Audio-Visuals, 1977. Three filmstrips with cassette, guide. (Available from: Denoyer-Geppert Audio-Visuals, 5235 Ravenswood Avenue, Chicago, IL 60640.)

Based on interviews with women and men working in science, this program shows how they started, what they think about their work and how they work. Part I includes: meteorology, tool and die machining, chemical technology. Part II includes: drafting, nursing, gardening and National Park Service. Part III includes: pharmaceutical industry, dentistry, chemical engineering and medical illustration.[28] [7–12]

2.156   Count Me In: Educating Women for Science and Math. Mills College Department of Mathematics. Videotape cassettes. (Available from: Education Development Center, 55 Chapel Street, Newton, MA 02160. $34.00; $5.00 rental.)

Documents successful curricular career program to interest women in entering scientific and technical fields. For high school students, math and science faculty, guidance people, administrators and others.[14] [7–12]

2.157   The Fascinating World of Work: Career Awareness Series. National Career Consultants, 1977. Six cassettes, filmstrips with guides and evaluation forms. (Available from: National Career Consultants, 1300 East Arapaho, Richardson, TX 75248.)

Explores different types of jobs, both professional and skilled trades and enables the student to rate them according to lifestyle, home life, security, job content and satisfaction.[47] [7–12]

2.158   Free to Be—You and Me. McGraw-Hill. 42 minutes. (Available from: McGraw-Hill, Department 410, 1221 Avenue of the Americas, New York, NY 10020.)

Free to Be—You and Me is designed to examine life goals and social roles from the point of view of individual fulfillment and not in terms of traditional sex role stereotyping—hence the theme "Expectations."[21]

2.159   Free to Choose. Filmfair Communications, 1974. 16 minutes, color, sound, 16mm. (Available from: Filmfair Communications, 10900 Ventura Blvd., Studio City, CA 91604. $220.00; $20.00 rental.)

This film was produced for junior high to adult audiences. It begins with a brief history of women's rights and social legislation, then focuses on a man in early childhood education, a women who is head of an architectural urban planning division, a female homemaker, and a working couple with a small child who share household duties and decision making. The purpose of this film is to encourage choice of work and lifestyle based on interests and skills rather than on traditional male and female roles.[9] [K–12]

2.160   Freestyle. Community Television of Southern California, 1978. 13 videotapes, with guide and calendar. (Available from: Science Research Associates, Palo Alto, CA 94305. $425.00.)

This career awareness program is designed to encourage children, grades 4–8, to explore their interests, develop their skills and consider career options, with an emphasis on reducing effects of sex and race stereotyping. Magazine with follow-up activities also available. [4–8]

2.161[a]   Great Opportunities. Michigan State University. 15 minutes, sound filmstrip. (Available from: Michigan State University, Career Education Resources, 301D Erickson Hall, East Lansing, MI 48824. $10.00.)

A 15-minute sound filmstrip show for junior high students using upbeat illustrations and music to present vocational education in a sex-fair and affirmative manner. Useful for recruiting students into nontraditional training and careers. [7–9]

2.162   I'm Going to Be. . . . University of California. Sound, color, 16mm. (Available from: University of California, Extension Media Center, 2223 Shattuck Avenue, Berkeley, CA 94720.)

With a little bit of magic, a girl and boy find out all about the different types of engineers. Useful for career education and elementary classes and staff development.[47] [K–6]

2.163[a]   Increasing Job Options for Women. National Audio Visual Center. 74 slides with cassette and script. (Available from: National Audio Visual Center, General Services Administration, Washington, DC 20409. $26.25.)

Shows women working in nontraditional jobs and encourages women to consider these occupations. Reviews equal employment opportunity regulations against sex discrimination in employment and contract compliance requirements for affirmative action.[22] [9–12]

2.164   Intern: A Long Year. Encyclopedia Britannica Educational Corporation Films, 1972. 20 minutes, sound, color, 16mm. (Available from: Encyclopedia Britannica Educational Corporation Films, 425 North Michigan Avenue, Chicago, IL 60611.)

Shows a woman intern rotating through different departments and experiencing day-to-day occurrences in an inner city hospital; includes her home and social life. (Note: some scenes are not for the faint-hearted.)[47] [7–12]

2.165[a]   It's Her Future. Pennsylvania Commission for Women, 1979. 17 minutes, color, 16mm or ¾" videotape cassette, with discussion guide. (Available from: Education Development Center, 55 Chapel Street, Newton, MA 02160. Film $100.00, $8.00 rental; videotape $31.00, $5.00 rental; booklet $.45.)

A media program designed to provide information about and insight into the world of work, including current occupational training opportunities and the benefits and concerns of females pursuing nontraditional careers. [10–12]

2.166[a]   Jobs and Gender. Guidance Associates, 1971. 18 minutes, color, sound, 16mm. (Available from: Guidance Associates, 757 Third Avenue, New York, NY 10017. $48.00.)

This two-filmstrip unit presents people who have crossed the sex role work barrier, such as a female carpenter, a male nurse, a female reporter, and a male kindergarten teacher. The program challenges junior and senior high school students to examine their own biases and encourages them to explore what they really would like to be. A 29-page discussion guide accompanies the unit.[9] [7–12]

2.167   Jobs in the City: Women at Work. Centron Educational Films. 11 minutes, 16mm. (Available from: Centron Educational Films, 1621 West 9th, Lawrence, KS 66044.)

Some of the women at work portrayed in this film include newspaper printer, physician, computer key punch operator, bank teller, pilot,

mathematician, aircraft executive, realtor, television commentator and fashion artist.[21] [K–6]

2.168   Joyce at 34. New Day Films, 1973. 28 minutes, color, sound, 16mm. (Available from: New Day Films, P.O. Box 315, Franklin Lakes, NJ 07417. $350.00, $35.00 rental plus $4.00 handling.)

This award-winning film explores the changes and adjustments made by a career woman and her husband as they start a family. It explores the conflict of work versus family and how it is handled by two generations of working women. Televised nationally on PBS, this film can be used with high school and adult groups.[2] [7–12]

2.169   The Kingdom of Could Be You. Encyclopedia Britannica Educational Corporation Films. Five to six minutes each, 16mm. (Available from: Encyclopedia Britannica Educational Corporation Films, 425 North Michigan Avenue, Chicago, IL 60611.)

A series of sixteen career guidance films for young children, in which a clear attempt has been made to show that girls and boys can do the same work and have the same choices ahead of them.[21] [3–7]

2.170[a]   Looking at Tomorrow . . . What Will You Choose? Churchill Films. 20 minutes, color, sound, 16mm. (Available from: Churchill Films, 662 North Robertson Boulevard, Los Angeles, CA 90069. $210.00.)

This film is targeted to elementary, junior high and senior high students and gives a documentary treatment of seven young women at their jobs: lawyer/congressperson, bricklayer, violin maker, telephone lineperson, employment representative, self-employed artist/business owner, air traffic controller and animal nutritionist. The dialogue focuses on choice, preparation and satisfaction. A teacher's guide presents questions for discussion.[9] [5–12]

2.171   The Math/Science Connection: Educating Young Women for Today. Mills College, 1979. 18 minutes, sound, color, 16mm or videotape cassette ¾". (Available from: Education Development Center, 55 Chapel Street, Newton, MA 02160. 16mm $115.00, $8.00 rental; video tape cassette $32.00, $5.00 rental.)

Excellent film depicts strategies in mathematics and science to encourage girls and women to learn and enjoy these subjects.[4] [7–12]

2.172   My Mother Works. Eye Gate House, 1975. Six filmstrips with three cassettes. (Available from: Eye Gate House, 146-01 Archer Avenue, Jamaica, NY 11435. $58.25.)

Insight into the reasons why some mothers work and some stay home. Covers mother as a home-manager, in self-directed "home" jobs, in offices, in a store, in professions, and in a variety of surprising occupations. Job details and work satisfactions are shown in each.[42] [4–6]

2.173   Never Underestimate the Power of a Woman. University of Wisconsin. 15 minutes, 16mm. (Available from: Bureau of Audio-Visual Instruction, University of Wisconsin Extension, Photo-Cinema Lab, 45 North Charter Street, Madison, WI 53706.)

This film brings attention to nontraditional jobs, especially those the factory and craft worker. Shows women's participation in training for various craft jobs.[49] [7–12]

2.174 New Horizons for Women. Pathescope Educational Media, Inc., 1975. One filmstrip with record or cassette, teacher's guide. (Available from: Pathescope Educational Media, Inc., 71 Weyman Avenue, New Rochelle, NY 10802. $25.00.)

To develop awareness of women's role in the working world: human needs, historical events, current trends and future prospects.[42] [4–6]

2.175[a] Non-Traditional Careers for Women. Pathescope Educational Media, Inc., 1974. Two filmstrips with cassette tapes. (Available from: Pathescope Educational Media, Inc., 71 Weyman Avenue, New Rochelle, NY 10802.)

Descriptions of interviews with women in nontraditional careers, ranging from chef and architect to line repairer and engineer.[16] [6–12]

2.176[a] Other Women, Other Work. Churchill Films. 20 minutes. (Available from: Churchill Films. 662 North Robertson Boulevard, Los Angeles, CA 90069.)

A valuable documentary showing a variety of women in a variety of jobs: pilot, truck driver, construction worker and reporter. The film is somewhat disjointed, but each woman speaks with authority and expertise.[21] [10–12]

2.177[a] People at Work: New Horizons for Women. Pathescope Educational Media, Inc., 1975. One filmstrip with cassette, guide, duplicating masters. (Available from: Pathescope Educational Media, Inc., 41 Weyman Avenue, New Rochelle, NY 10802.)

A young black girl questions the participation of women in nontraditional jobs, and is shown how options and opportunities in a variety of occupations are opening up for women.[28] [3–6]

2.178 People Who Help: Careers in Aviation. Bailey Film Associates. 16 minutes. (Available from: Bailey Film Associates, 2211 Michigan Avenue, P.O. Box 1795, Santa Monica, CA 90406.)

Reviews careers available in three major areas of aviation: commercial, general and aerospace. Among specific jobs touched on are commercial pilot, flight attendant, crop duster, weather forecaster, airplane repairer and aeronautical engineer. Excellent onsite footage of aviation careers in action and interviews with men and women on the job vitalize message. Good color, well-paced and nice general summary of aviation careers, which gives special emphasis to women working in the field.[21] [9–12]

2.179 Project Women in a Man's World of Work. American Personnel and Guidance Association, 1972. 75 minutes, cassette tape. (Available from: Order Services, American Personnel and Guidance Association, 2 Skyline Place, Suite 400, 5203 Leesburg Pike, Falls Church, VA 22041. Order No. 72904. $8.00; three for $23.00.)

No annotation available.

2.180[a] Sandra, Zella, Dee and Claire: Four Women in Science. 19 minutes, sound, color, 16mm. (Available from:

Education Development Center, 55 Chapel Street, Newton, MA 02160.)

An astronomer, a veterinarian, a physicist and an engineer discuss their work and family life. Excellent portrayal of women working in nontraditional jobs.[28] [7–12]

2.181 Take This Woman. Films Incorporated. 25 minutes, color, 16mm. (Available from: Films Incorporated, 440 Park Avenue South, New York, NY 10016. $325.00; $23.00 rental.)

A study of equal employment opportunity as it relates to women.[1] [10–12]

2.182[a] Why Not a Woman. Pennsylvania Department of Education, 1976. 16 minutes, color, sound, 16mm. (Available from: Pennsylvania Department of Education, Harrisburg, PA.)

Examination of women's work in the skilled trades, the reasons why women are entering such fields in greater numbers, and myths and stereotypes vs. the reality of women in the skilled trades world.[16] [9–12]

2.183[b] Women and Work. Training Institute for Sex Desegregation of the Public Schools, 1977. 46 slides in carousel with script. (Available from: Training Institute for Sex Desegregation, Rutgers University, Federation Hall-Douglass Campus, New Brunswick, NJ 08903.)

Surveys the position of the working woman and how she is discriminated against in terms of career choice, pay and status. Includes statistics on the working woman.[16] [9–12]

2.184[a] Women at Work: Change, Choice, Challenge. Encyclopedia Britannica, Educational Corporation Films, 1977. 19 minutes, sound, color, 16mm. (Available from: Encyclopedia Britannica, Educational Corporation Films, 425 North Michigan Avenue, Chicago, IL 60611.)

Women in nontraditional jobs describe their work, their attitudes and the barriers to success. Jobs shown include refinery worker, judge, surgeon, line repairer. Includes minority women.[28] [7–12]

2.185 Women at Work: Choice. Guidance Associates, 1975. 18 minutes, color, sound filmstrips. (Available from: Guidance Associates, A/V Subsidiary, 757 Third Avenue, New York, NY 10017. $48.50.)

This unit contains two color, sound filmstrips designed for high school students and adults, to explore the changing role of women in the labor force and alternate lifestyles available to women. Part I summarizes the development of women's work roles throughout important periods in United States history. Part 2 provides interpersonal insights into the effects of work on women. A 40-page discussion guide accompanies the units.[9] [9–12]

2.186 Women in Science: Illustrated Interviews. American Association of Physics Teachers, 1975. Slides and three cassettes. (Available from: American Association of Physics Teachers, Graduate Physics Building, State University of New York, Stonybrook, NY 11794.)

This package presents interviews with six successful women scientists. Each woman talks about her background, how she became interested in science, her training and career specialty, and what it is like to be a woman in traditionally male fields.[16] [7–9]

2.187 Women's Work: Engineering. 26 minutes, sound, color, 16mm. (Available from: Education Development Center, 55 Chapel Street, Newton, MA 02160.)

Interviews with women engineers (civil, materials and chemical) who discuss education and training necessary to become engineers. This film shows women at work and at home, providing excellent role models.[47] [7–12]

Bibliographies/Resource Lists

2.188[b] Equal Access and Opportunity in Vocational Education: An Annotated Bibliography of Articles, Reports and Projects. National Center for Research in Vocational Education. (Available from: The National Center for Research in Vocational Education, The Ohio State University, 1960 Kenny Road, Columbus, OH 43210. Order No. BB 36. $2.80.)

Includes resumes of relevant documents in ERIC and AIM/ARM systems, citations of journals articles and descriptions of projects in progress.[18]

2.189 Every Woman's Guide to College. Eileen Gray. Millbrae, CA: Les Femmes. $3.95.

Lists colleges and resource centers; includes how to finance your college education.[4]

2.190[b] Implications of Women's Work Patterns for Vocational and Technical Education: An Annotated Bibliography. Sylvia L. Lee, et al. 1967. (Available from: The National Center for Research in Vocational Education, The Ohio State University, 1960 Kenny Road, Columbus, OH 43210.)

Identifies references related to the needs of girls and women for vocational and technical education and the labor force participation of women.[15]

2.191 Keys to Careers in Science and Technology. National Science Teacher's Association, 1973. 74p. (Available from: National Science Teacher's Association, 1742 Connecticut Avenue, NW, Washington, DC 20009.)

Lists resources for information on different careers in science and technology; includes lists of societies and associations.[4]

2.192 New Career Options for Women. Helen S. Farmer and Thomas E. Becker. Human Interaction Research Institute. (Available from: Human Sciences Press, 72 Fifth Avenue, New York, NY 10011 or Human Interaction Institute, Kirkely Center, Suite 1120, 10889 Wilshire Blvd., Los Angeles, CA 90024. $25.48 a set.)

This publication contains three parts. A *Counselor's Sourcebook* (400 p., hardbound, $16.95) addresses counselors in educational institutions, public service agencies, and counselor educators. It lists resources, counseling strategies and ways to change stereotyped attitudes. A *Women's Guide* (96 p., paperback, $4.95; bulk rate of ten or more, $3.95) summarizes major topics covered in the sourcebook and contains materials for women returning to work. It may be used independently or as part of counseling material. A *Selected Annotated Bibliography* (138 p., hardbound, $9.95) contains 240 citations of books, journals, articles, and reports from the fields of economics, sociology, anthropology and psychology pertaining to women and work.[2] [9–12]

2.193 Nonsexist Career Counseling for Women: Annotated Selected References and Resources, Part I. Women's Educational Equity Communications Network. (Available from: Women's Educational Equity Act Program, U.S. Department of Education, Donahoe Building, Room 1105, 400 Maryland Avenue, SW, Washington, DC 20202. $2.50.)

Provides resources on counselor training and professional development, counseling resources, career interest measurements and minority women.[17] [8–12]

2.194 Nonsexist Career Counseling for Women: Annotated Selected References and Resources, Part II. Women's Educational Equity Communications Network. 31 p. (Available from: Women's Educational Equity Act Program, U.S. Department of Education, Donahoe Building, Room 1105, 400 Maryland Avenue, SW, Washington, DC 20202.)

One of five in a series of annotated bibliographies compiled for educators, researchers, students, librarians and others concerned with women's educational equity. Part II provides resources on women and work and women in specific occupations and professions, including management and business, math and science, the skilled trades and other fields. This publication also describes programs related to women's career preparation, curriculum materials development and staff training.

2.195 People Working . . . Especially Women. Sharon Valiant. Training Institute for Sex Desegregation of the Public Schools, 1976. 22 p. (Available from: Training Institute for Sex Desegregation of the Public Schools, Rutgers University, Douglass Campus-Federation Hall, New Brunswick, NJ 08903. $2.50.)

A bibliography which also contains some activities and ideas for the classroom about women working, past and present.[44] [9–12]

2.196[b] Resource Update: 1979—Sex Equity in Vocational Education. Faith L. Justice. The National Center for Research in Vocational Education. (Available from: The National Center for Research in Vocational Education, The Ohio State University, 1960 Kenny Road, Columbus, OH 43210. Limited supply available free from the Program Information Office.)

Lists resources for educators, counselors, administrators and parents for use in achieving sex fairness in program planning, preservice and inservice activities, classroom activities and program monitoring.

2.197[b] Resources on Eliminating Sex Role Stereotyping in Vocational Education. National Center for Research in Vocational Education. (Available from: The National Center for Research in Vocational Education: The Ohio State University, 1960 Kenny Road, Columbus, OH 43210, (6) 486-3655. Free.)

Provides an annotated listing of resources, including sections state and local projects, secondary vocational education programs and referrals and references.[18]

2.198 Science and Engineering Careers: A Bibliography. Eleanor Babco. Scientific Manpower Commission, 1974. (Available from: Scientific Manpower Commission, 1776 Massachusetts Avenue, NW, Washington, DC 2002. $2.00.)

A bibliography of guidance literature published by various organizations interested in science and engineering education.[44]

2.199[b] Secondary Students' Views on Occupational Sex Stereotyping and **Sex Equity Resources for Vocational Education and Counselors.** Vocational Education Information Services, Indiana University, January 1979. 84 p. (Available from: Vocational Education Information Services, Indiana University Library, W501, Bloomington, IN 47405. $2.00.)

This combined report and bibliography has an annotated listing of resources incorporating sex equity concerns for vocational educators and counselors.

2.200[b] Sex Equity in Vocational Education: A Chance for Educators to Expand Opportunities for Students. Barbara G. Schonborn and Mary L. O'Neil. Women's Educational Equity Communications Network, 1978. 33 p. (Available from: Women's Educational Equity Act Program, U.S. Department of Education, Donahoe Building, Room 1105, 400 Maryland Avenue, SW, Washington, DC 20202.)

A resource booklet containing definitions of terms in the area of sex equality in vocational education; an overview of the problems created by sex discrimination; a description of the laws and activities that are helping to eliminate sex discrimination; information about teacher and counselor training and about curriculum materials and methods that teachers may use in vocational education programs; and lists of print, nonprint and human resources that are accessible to teachers and administrators. [7–12]

2.201 Women and Health Careers: A Guide for Career Exploration. Sheryl B. Ruzek. Northwestern University, 1974. 19 p. (Available from: Northwestern University, Program on Women, 1902 Sheridan Road, Evanston, IL 60201. $7.50.)

This manual describes over 100 professional and paraprofessional careers. It was developed during a two-year study at the University of California, San Francisco, and funded by the U.S. Office of Health Resources.[43]

2.202[b] Women and Vocational Education: An Information Packet. Jean Marzone. Women's Educational Equity Communications Network, 1978. (Available from: Women's Educational Equity Act Program, U.S. Department of Education, Donahoe Building, Room 1105, 400 Maryland Avenue, SW, Washington, DC 20202.)

A newly updated compendium of materials including a summary of the final regulations implementing the Vocational Education Amendments of 1976, a list of groups working on vocational education reform, a list of state vocational education and sex equity coordinators, and a listing of resources.[41]

2.203 Women and Work—New Options: A Guide to Nonprint Media. Linda Artel and Valerie Wheat. Women's Educational Equity Communications Network, 1979. (Available from: Women's Educational Equity Act Program, U.S. Department of Education, Donahoe Building, Room 1105, 400 Maryland Avenue, SW, Washington, DC 20202.)

Lists more than 100 nonprint media pieces dealing with new career options for women. Full citations, ordering information and brief descriptions for each piece are included.[41]

2.204 Women at Work: An Annotated Bibliography. Mei Liang Bickner. 1974. (Available from: Manpower Research Center, Institute of Industrial Relations, University of California at Los Angeles, Los Angeles, CA. $6.50.)

Six hundred entries of articles dealing with working women, both professional and nonprofessional.[1]

2.205 Women in Medicine. Sandra L. Chaff, Ruth Haimbach, Carol Fenichel and Nina Woodside. Metuchen, NJ: Scarecrow Press, 1977. 1,136 p. $37.50.

This annotated bibliography comprehensively covers the published literature about women physicians. International in scope, it provides over 4,000 citations to material which documents the lives of specific women physicians and groups of women physicians, as well as the history of women physicians and healers and the institutions and issues related to that history. Complete bibliographic citations are provided, along with carefully written annotations which convey the flavor as well as the content of the items. The bibliography provides citations to literature which documents the increasing involvement of women in medicine and examines the causes and future course of this trend. It includes materials that help provide insight into how the careers of most women physicians have differed from their male colleagues. The work should prove useful to persons representing a wide range of interests and information needs: researchers, guidance counselors, and people and agencies in general wishing to know woman's heritage.[45]

SAMPLE LESSON PLAN: CAREER GUIDANCE AND COUNSELING
Nontraditional Career Exploration

AUDIENCE:

Students grades 10–12

OBJECTIVE:

Students will become aware of some specific nontraditional career opportunities.

MATERIALS:

1. *Nontraditional Careers for Women*, Sarah Splaver (Julian Messner, 1973).
2. Bias-free brochures and pamphlets on nontraditional careers.
3. Bureau of Labor statistics.

TIMING:

Several large group guidance or class sessions; may be offered as an all day career awareness program, with preparation and follow-up activities.

LEARNING ACTIVITIES:

1. Provide students with Bureau of Labor statistics on salaries currently offered for a variety of careers and comparative forecasts of job availability.
2. Develop and administer a short interest questionnaire to determine what nontraditional career areas students are interested in learning about.
3. Have students bring in newspaper articles about women and men in nontraditional careers. Post articles on bulletin board and devote a class period to discussion of what articles reveal about these people and their pursuits.
4. Using results from the survey, invite several people to talk about their experiences in nontraditional careers.
5. Have students write about what they have learned from the people they heard speak.
6. Have students form small groups and interview a person in the nontraditional career in which they are interested, and report back to the large class.
7. Through the administration of the General Aptitude Test Battery (GATB), have students compare nontraditional career interests with their aptitudes.
8. Have students write an essay about how they see themselves in relation to their work 20 years from now.

3.0 Fine Arts

ART*

Lesson Plans

3.1ᵃ Becoming Sex Fair: The Tredyffrin/Easttown Program (A Comprehensive Model for Public School Districts). Tredyffrin/Easttown (Pennsylvania) School District, 1979. (Available from: Education Development Center, 55 Chapel Street, Newton, MA 02160. $17.75.)

This program provides a model for assessing sex bias within a school district and specific materials and processes for moving toward the goal of sex fairness in all areas of school life. Designed to be carried out in three stages under the leadership of a coordinator and a coordinating committee, the program systematically and gradually involves more and more people within the district for increased support and commitment. Of particular interest to the classroom teacher will be the *Stage Three Manual: Revising the Curriculum* (108p. $8.50). It outlines a process for revising curricula at the elementary and secondary level. Numerous sample materials and resources for use or adaptation within major subject matter areas are provided. [K–12]

3.2 In Praise of Diversity: Multicultural Classroom Applications. Gloria Grant. 1977. 318 p. (Available from: Teacher Corps, Center for Urban Education, The University of Nebraska at Omaha, 3805 North 16th Street, Omaha, NE 68110 or EDRS MF-$.91—HC-$16.73 plus postage, ED 144 854.)

Fifty-one activity units written for the classroom teacher who is interested in implementing multicultural and nonsexist education in the areas of social studies, language arts, science, math and art. Each activity unit offers a rationale, desired learning experiences, suggestions for implementation, supplementary activities and instructional and background resources for teachers. The wealth of activities may be modified and adapted by teachers so that they are relevant to a particular grade level and to the needs of students.

---

*Subcategories of "Art," indicated by superscript letters following entry numbers, are designated as follows: a=Art/Music; b=Art/Dance; c=Art/Photography; d=Art/Film.

Many of the activities were designed to incorporate ideas and materials from the companion document: *In Praise of Diversity: A Resource Book for Multicultural Education.* [K–8]

Course Outlines

3.3 Women's Art and Culture (Nancy Fire Conklin and Vivian M. Patraka); **New Women, New World: The American Experience** (Carlene Bagnall, et al.); **A Cross-Cultural Study of Women** (Margot Morrow, et al.); **Women and Identity** (Ann Coleman, et al.). 1977. (Available from: Women's Studies Curriculum Series, Women's Studies Program, 1058 LS & A Building, University of Michigan, Ann Arbor, MI 48109. $10.00 total set, plus $2.00 handling; $2.50 each.)

These four interdisciplinary course outlines offer conceptual frameworks and resource materials. The books include themes to be developed, lectures outlines, bibliographies and discussion questions. They may be used as the basis of a women's studies course or may be used as supplementary materials for other courses. Although designed for junior college and university level, they would be suitable for older high school students also. [14] [10–12]

Supplementary Texts

3.4 Black Artists of the New Generation. Elton C. Fax. New York: Dodd, Mead, 1977. 361 p. $9.95.

In this follow-up to *Seventeen Black Artists*, Elton Fax (a black artist himself) profiles nine women and eleven men, black artists of a new generation. The artists come from virtually every section of the country, with widely divergent backgrounds and different modes of artistic expression. In every case, however, they share the experience of being black in America and a determination to follow a dream. Readers of all races will be inspired by their stories. [7–12]

3.5ᵇ In Her Own Image: Women Working in the Arts. Elaine Hedges and Ingrid Wendt. Old Westbury, NY: The Feminist Press, 1980. 301 p. Paperback.

Excellent anthology of works of Western women in the arts, represented by selections from their poetry, fiction, autobiographies, essays, journals and letters, and photographs; their sculpture, painting, graphics, photography, ceramics, needlework, music and dance. In all these forms, the women are making statements about their view of themselves as women. The book is organized in a way that shows the relationship between women's art and the condition of women's lives. Each section is introduced with an essay which explores and connects the book's themes; each artist is introduced with a brief biography. [8–12]

3.6   Kathe Kollwitz: Life in Art. Mina C. Klein and H. Arthur Klein. New York: Schocken Books, 1976. 182 p. $6.95. (Originally published by Holt, Rinehart & Winston, 1972.)

This is the life of Kathe Kollwitz (1867–1945) told through her art. The title of the book is apt, as the artist's life and art were so completely intertwined. Kathe Kollwitz worked in a number of media, including drawing, etching, lithographing, sculpting and woodcutting. Her work expressed her personal concern with Germany's social ills of her time. Probably the most intense experience in Kollwitz's life that was reflected in her art was the death of one of her sons in WWI. Her priorities, she claimed, were her children, her companion-husband and her work. The story of the last years of Kollwitz's life and art give a devastating perspective on the repression of art in Hitler's Germany. The book is a valuable lesson in art, feelings and history. [K–12]

3.7   Our Hidden Heritage: Five Centuries of Women Artists. Eleanor Tufts. New York: Paddington Press, 1974. 156 p. $7.95.

This collection of short biographies of 22 women artists from the Renaissance to the 20th century provides fascinating portrayals and new insights into the lives and works, the frustrations and successes of these talented women. This book is highly commendable for redressing the collective and rather recent cultural neglect of women artists in basic art survey books used today. The author makes plain that in the past women were appointed as court painters, accepted as professionals and unstintingly appreciated by their contemporaries. More than 125 black and white reproductions are included in this work. [K–12]

3.8   Popcorn Venus. Marjorie Rosen. New York: Avon, 1974. 447 p. $1.95 p.b. (Originally published by Coward, McCann & Geoghegan, 1973).

In this fascinating and somewhat ''gossipy'' retrospective on women in films—on camera and off—the author asks the question of whether ''art'' (pop culture) reflects life or life reflects ''art.'' Although that judgment is left to the reader, the author suggests it is time to reinterpret the American Dream and the fantasy roles movies define for women as part of that dream. This book provides an excellent resource for a student or class studying the sociology of women and American pop culture by contrasting the lives of women as they were and are in reality versus the lives of women portrayed on the silver screen. Especially commendable is the emphasis placed on labor statistics and the variety of careers and jobs performed by women in ''real life'' since the turn of the century. [K–12]

3.9   Women Artists: Recognition and Reappraisal from the Early Middle Ages to the Twentieth Century. Karen Petersen and J. J. Wilson. New York: Harper Colophon, 1976. 212 p. $5.95 p.b.

A chronological history of women's art, beginning with the fifth century A.D. and continuing through to the present. Its focus is on art that women have created rather than the form women took in other people's art. The book is very complete with numerous black and white reproductions. It is specific, detailed and an excellent resource for references on women artists. [K–12]

3.10   Women in Television. Anita Klever. Philadelphia: Westminster Press, 1975. 142 p. $5.95.

Thirty-seven women—each with a different job—talk about their careers in television, off camera and on. In brief, first-person interviews, each woman talks about what she does, how she got to her position, and the ''rocky road of making it.'' Because this book offers a look at personal job histories, it is less dry than many ''career'' books for girls. It provides a fascinating look at a fast-paced, competitive and often glamorous industry with a wide variety of career possibilities for young women. [K–12]

Periodicals

3.11[d]   Film Library Quarterly: Women in Film. Film Library Information Council. (Available from: Film Library Information Council, Room 720, 17 West 60th Street, New York, NY 10023.)

This is one of the best collections of information about women in film; contains analyses and reviews.[1]

3.12   Heresies: A Feminist Publication on Art and Politics. (Available from: *Heresies*, P.O. Box 766, Canal Street Station, New York, NY 10013. $11.00, one year/four issues for individuals; $18.00 for institutions.)

Heresies is an idea-oriented journal devoted to examining art and politics from a feminist perspective. Each issue has both a different theme and a different editorial staff made up of women from the community who want to work on that issue. An open meeting is held both to form the issue collective and to evaluate the issue after it is published. *Heresies* seeks the participation and involvement of all feminists, in this country and abroad.[7]

Audiovisual Materials

3.13   Black Art Kit. Scholastic Book Service. Filmstrip, record or cassette. (Available from: Scholastic Book Service, 906 Sylvan Avenue, Englewood Cliffs, NJ 07632. $19.00.)

A discussion of the influence of African art on Western art and black artists in America; accompanied by African and modern jazz sound track.[1] [7–12]

3.14   Four American Artists. Educational Dimensions Corporation, 1976. 18 minutes, two filmstrips and cassettes. (Available from: Educational Dimensions Corporation, Box 126, Stamford, CT 06904. $45.00.)

This set examines the work of four, 20th century women artists: Georgia O'Keefe, Helen Frankenthaler, Louise Nevelson and Marisol.[16] [7–12]

3.15   Mary Cassatt: An American Impressionist. Educational Dimensions Corporation. Filmstrip, with disc or cassette, teacher's guide. (Available from: Educational Dimensions Corporation, Box 126, Stamford, CT 06904. $22.50

Description of the life and the development of the work of Mary Cassatt, an American impressionist. The influence of Degas in her work is discussed and her technique is described in detail.[1] [10–12]

3.16c Profiles of Black Achievement: Margaret Walker Alexander/James Van Der Zee. Guidance Associates. Two filmstrips with two 12" LPs or two cassettes, discussion guide. (Available from: Guidance Associates, A/V Subsidiary, 757 Third Avenue, New York, NY 10017. $48.00.)

Part I: Alexander recalls her southern childhood, northern college years, and her teaching novel *Jubilee*; reads from her poem. Part II: Van Der Zee's life as photographer of black experience.[1] [10–12]

3.17 Profiles of Black Achievement: Sterling Brown/ Alma Thomas. Guidance Associates. Two filmstrips with two 12" LPs or two cassettes, discussion guide. (Available from: Guidance Associates, A/V Subsidiary, 757 Third Avenue, New York, NY 10017. $48.00.)

Part I: Brown's life as poet and university educator. Part II: Thomas discusses her 35-year career as an art teacher and artist.[1] [10–12]

3.18 Women Artists: Four Slide Collections. (1) Women Artists: A Historical Survey; (2) Women Artists: The Twentieth Century; (3) Women Artists: Third World; (4) Women Artists: Images, Themes and Dreams. Available from: Harper & Row, Audiovisual Department, 10 East 53rd Street, New York, NY 10022.)

No annotation available. [10–12]

Bibliographies/Resource Lists

3.19 American Black Women in the Arts and Social Sciences: A Bibliographic Survey. Ora Williams. Metuchen, NJ: Scarecrow Press, 1973. 141 p.

A book containing over 1200 entries of works by American black women including movies, tapes and recordings, as well as printed materials.[1] [K–12]

3.20c Women and Film: A Bibliography. Rosemary Ribich Kowalski. Metuchen, NJ: Scarecrow Press, 1976. 87 p. $12.50.

The story of women in film has been lost amidst the history of the entire industry. This annotated bibliography attempts to separate the contributions of women from those of men. It is designed to aid scholars in the fields of film history, film criticism and women's studies and to help film buffs or filmmakers locate articles or books of particular interest. The bibliography is divided into four major sections: women as performers, women as filmmakers, images of women presented on the screen, and women as columnists and critics. Annotations are provided for most of the 2,302 entries listed. A subject and name index is included in the work.[45]

DANCE

Supplementary Texts

3.21 African Rhythm—American Dance: A Biography of Katherine Dunham. Terry Harman. New York: Alfred Knopf, 1974. 213 p.

Biography of the versatile and multitalented Katherine Dunham, a black dancer and choreographer noted for her dances drawn from African and Caribbean sources. After studying anthropology, she went to the Caribbean where she lived in isolated villages and used anthropological field techniques to trace the African sources in the people's dances and customs. The story of how she incorporated their dances into her choreography, the subsequent impact of her work on the theatrical and dance world, her efforts to help other black dancers and students, her involvement with Haiti and the Haitians, as well as her ensuing writing career, make fascinating reading of an outstanding woman and her times. [K–12]

3.22 Frontiers of Dance: The Life of Martha Graham. Walter Terry. New York: Thomas Y. Crowell, 1975. 157 p.

The story of Martha Graham's dance career is told by Walter Terry, a dance critic, editor and lecturer. He begins with the childhood influences that steered Martha Graham toward dancing. Much of the chronology deals with Graham's relationships with her teachers in her early dancing years, and with her contemporaries in dance throughout her lifetime. The reader is shown how Graham's growth and changes surface in her personality and the dances she creates. Graham rejects ballet and looks to deep emotions and social issues as themes for her pioneering dance form. Terry emphasizes Graham's strengths—her conviction to dance in a radically new way and her almost super human physical power as a dancer. [K–12]

3.23 The Language of Show Dancing. Jacqueline Lower and Charles Selber. New York: Charles Scribner's Sons, 1980. 35 p. $9.95.

This book is an exciting visual interpretation of some of the more colorful show dancing terms. Martha Swope's photographs are delightful. [9–12]

Audiovisual Materials

3.24 Black Dance Kit. Scholastic Book Service. Filmstrip with record or cassette. (Available from: Scholastic Book Service, 906 Sylvan Avenue, Englewood Cliffs, NJ 07632. $19.00.)

Important and little-known black dances and dancers, including Josephine Baker, Pearl Primus and Katherine Dunham.[1] [7–12]

3.25 Dance on a May Day. Learning Corporation of America, 1977. 11 minutes, sound, color, 16mm. (Available from: Learning Corporation of America, 1350 Avenue of the Americas, New York, NY 10019. $175.00; $20.00 rental.)

Freestyle dance sequence choreographed and produced by Jacques D'Amboise with a group of 8- to 14-year-old boys.[28] [3–10]

MUSIC

Supplementary Texts

3.26 Lady Sings the Blues. Billie Holiday. New York: Avon, 1976. 192 p. $2.25 p.b.

Billie Holiday vividly describes her struggles as a black woman, singer, wife and drug addict. Her style of writing quickly moves the reader through her life—years crowded with tragic disappointment and bitter sorrow, the exultation of a gifted artist sharing her talent with a devoted audience and the sting of racial prejudice. There are a variety of interesting anecdotes about famous singers, musicians and actors who were part of Billie's life. The book's realism may make it more appropriate for mature readers. [K–12]

3.27   New Women in Entertainment. Kathleen Bowman. Mankato, MN: Creative Educational Society, 1976. 47 p.

Short biographies of seven women who have been highly successful in various fields of entertainment: Lily Tomlin, Buffy Sainte-Marie, Judy Collins, Cicely Tyson, Valerie Harper, Diana Ross and Malvina Reynolds. The women presented are strong, positive role models who have contributed much to society as well as to art. [7–9]

3.28   Somebody's Angel Child: The Story of Bessie Smith. Carman Moore. New York: Dell, 1969. 126 p. $.95 p.b. (Originally published by Thomas Y. Crowell, 1969).

This biography of Bessie Smith provides an easy-to-read portrait of the woman. It shows how "Mr. Blues" shadowed her life and how she expressed in her music the misery of being poor and black in the early 1900s. [K–12]

3.29   Working Women's Music: The Songs and Struggles in the Cotton Mills, Textile Plants, and Needle Trades. Evelyn Alloy. Sommerville, MA: New England Free Press, 1976, 44 p. $2.50.

History of the words and music of working women of the 19th century.[4] [10–12]

Photographs

3.30   Women in Music. Barbara Stanford and Felicia Diamond. Portland, ME: J. Weston Walch, 1974. 19 p. $4.00.

A series of photographs of famous women in music, from Clara Schuman to Joni Mitchell. Includes short biographical notes.[1] [K–3]

Audiovisual Materials

3.31   Antonia: A Portrait of the Woman. Phoenix Film. 58 minutes. (Available from: Phoenix Film, 470 Park Avenue, South, New York, NY 10016.)

A deeply warm and affectionate portrait of Antonia Brico, who in the 1930s established an international reputation as an accomplished orchestra conductor. Today she teaches conducting and piano in Denver, Colorado, while leading the Brico Symphony, a community orchestra which she founded. *Antonia* is the story of a person who, as a 73-year-old woman, seeks in the face of adversity and discrimination, the opportunity to lead a major symphony orchestra in a field dominated by men in the Western world. Antonia's love of music, joy of life, spirit and determination have been captured by Judy Collins and Jill Godmilow in this truly powerful film.[21] [7–12]

3.32   Aunt Molly Jackson. Rounder Records. (Available from: Rounder Records, 727 Somerville Avenue, Somerville, MA 02143. $4.00.)

Songs from the 1930s in Kentucky are sung by a union organizer and a storyteller.[1] [7–12]

3.33   Black Music Kit. Scholastic Book Service. Two filmstrips, with records or cassettes. (Available from: Scholastic Book Service, 906 Sylvan Avenue, Englewood Cliffs, NJ 07632. $42.00.)

African music, blues, spirituals, ragtime, jazz. Includes Ella Fitzgerald and Louis Armstrong.[1] [7–12]

3.34   Lady in the Lincoln Memorial. Sterling Educational Films. (Available from: Sterling Educational Films, Division of Walter Reade Organization, 241 East 34th Street, New York, NY 10016.)

Marian Anderson expressed her commitment for change through her art. This film follows her early career of singing in churches through concert tours of Europe and America to a historic concert at the Lincoln Memorial after being denied use of Constitution Hall.[21] [10–12]

3.35   Songs of the Suffragettes. Folkways Records, 1978. Records and cassettes, guide. (Available from: Folkways Records, 701 7th Avenue, New York, NY 10036. $6.98.)

Songs from the late 19th and early 20th centuries on suffrage and prohibition; guide includes texts of the songs and a brief history of the women's suffrage movement.[16] [7–12]

3.36   Woman's Work: Works by Famous Women Composers. Gemini Hall Records, 1975. Two records, guide (Available from: Gemini Hall Records, P.O. Box 124, New York, NY 10019.)

Anthology of music written by neglected women composers, performed by women musicians.[16] [9–12]

3.37   The Work of the Women. Educational Activities 1975. Record and guide. (Available from: Educational Activities, 1937 Grand Avenue, Baldwin, NY 11510.)

Songs about the work of women, including a slave lullaby, the housewife's lament and Union Maid. Texts and discussion guide included.[16] [9–12]

3.38   The Working Girl: Women's Songs from Mountains, Mines and Mills. Voyager Recordings. (Available from: Voyager Recordings, 424 35th Avenue, Seattle, WA 98122.)

Lively and traditional Appalachian songs, all about women, featuring Kathy Kahn and the Cut Cane Fiddle Band.[1] [7–12]

Bibliographies/Resource Lists

3.39   Women Composers: A Handbook. Susan Stern. Metuchen, NJ: Scarecrow Press, 1978. 199 p. $9.00.

Women Composers: A Handbook is a bibliography of women composers of classical music from nine Western countries (United States, Canada, England, Belgium, France, West Germany, Austria, Switzerland and Italy) from the 17th century onward. The more than 1,500 composer entries provide brief biographical data, note major contributions and cite sources of biographical information in music reference books, journal and periodical articles. A handy reference source for those who wish to perform or study works by women.[45]

3.40　Women in American Music: A Bibliography.
JoAnn Skowronski. Metuchen, NJ: Scarecrow Press, 1978.
191 p. $9.00.

Skowronski has compiled an annotated bibliography of writings
about women in American music, 1776–1976. A total of 1,305
books and pertinent articles are cited by author and arranged within
time periods marked by significant events in the history of women,
with additional categories for general history and bibliographies,
dictionaries and indexes. Descriptive annotations are provided for
most entries; an index of authors and names appearing in the titles or
annotations provides easy access for the user. *Women in American
Music* should be of special interest to the researcher examining the
place of women in music, from the birth of the United States until the
present. Since many black women played a significant role in

America's music, it should interest researchers with black studies
interests as well.[45]

3.41　Women in Music: A Bibliography. Don L. Hixon
and Don Hennessee. Metuchen, NJ: Scarecrow Press, 1975.
358 p. $14.00.

More than 4,000 women musicians of all periods and countries are
identified in *Women in Music,* a handy tool for locating biographical
information in a representative selection of significant dictionaries
and encyclopedias. The volume also serves as a brief biographical
dictionary, since it provides a relatively detailed entry for each
musician, and it can be used independently even if a library owns
none of the volumes indexed. Only classical musicians are treated in
the work, which includes a significant number of foreign musicians.[45]

SAMPLE LESSON PLAN: FINE ARTS
Women in Songs

AUDIENCE:

Junior high and secondary students

OBJECTIVE:

To identify stereotypes in musical selections from the
50s, 60s and 70s.

MATERIALS:

Records from the 50s, 60s and 70s and songbooks
with songs of the 50s, 60s and 70s, e.g., "Look at
That Stupid Girl" (Rolling Stones), "Just Like a
Woman" (Bob Dylan).

TIMING:

30 minutes

HOW TO USE:

1. Listen to records from each of the three decades.
   Read lyrics from songbooks of the same decades.
2. Discuss the view of women in the different
   decades. Ask: What are the images of women in

the songs? Are the images of women limited and
limiting? How?
3. Listen to some songs of the women's movement.
   How is the image of women presented in these
   songs different from that in the popular songs?
4. Have the students write and perform a song ex-
   pressing a view of women that they would like to
   see prevail in today's society.

OTHER USES:

- Create a collage illustrating how women have been
  viewed in song during the three decades.
- Construct a bulletin board with song lyrics and
  pictures representing women in each decade.

COMMENTS:

1. This is project that can be presented in one class
   and continued as students add information from
   newly released songs.
2. This project can be easily adapted to a social
   studies class through a discussion of how music is
   representative of and often a political or social
   statement about the era in which it is written.

Adapted from: *Becoming Sex Fair: The Tredyffrin/Easttown Program. Stage Three Manual: Revising the Curriculum.* Developed by the
Tredyffrin/Easttown School District under a grant from the Women's Educational Equity Act Program. Newton, MA: Education Development Center, 1979. Pages 372–373.

4.0 Health and Physical Education

HEALTH*

Lesson Plans

4.1ᵃ Outline for Single Living. Rene Fishman. 1974. (Available from: Dumont High School, New Milford Avenue, Dumont, NJ 07628.)

A course outline for a unit in a family living or related course.[4] [10–12]

4.2ᵇ Values in Sexuality: A New Approach to Sex Education. Eleanor S. Morrison and Mila Underhill Price. New York: Hart Publishing Company, 1974. 319 p. $8.95.

Exercises and activities designed to make students examine and evaluate their values and feelings in the area of sexuality.[4] [10–12]

Supplementary Texts

4.3 Changing Learning, Changing Lives: A High School Women's Studies Curriculum from the Group School. Barbara Gates, Susan Klaw and Adra Reich. Old Westbury, NY: The Feminist Press, 1978. 256 p. $6.00.

This material was developed for young working class women at an alternative high school in Cambridge, Massachusetts. The curriculum is divided into nine areas including ''Messages from Society,'' ''Growing Up Female,'' ''Women and Work'' and ''Women Organizing Themselves.'' The units can be used as supplements to English, history, psychology, anthropology, career education or health courses. Throughout the packet recommendations are made on how to teach as well as what to teach.[14] [9–12]

4.4ᵇ Commonsense Sex. Ronald M. Mazur. Boston: Beacon Press, 1968. 110 p. $2.95 p.b.

Mazur's book is exactly what it purports to be: common sense about sex. Starting with the idea that sex should be a positive, rewarding,

---

*Subcategories of ''Health,'' indicated by superscript letters following entry numbers, are designated as follows: a=Health (Families); b=Health (Sex Education); c=Health (Rape); d=Health/PE.

collaboration between women and men, the author questions hypocritical attitudes and damaging feelings of shame and guilt. He explores such topics as petting, mutual masturbation, contraception, premarital intercourse, homosexuality and extramarital relationships matter-of-factly. He emphasizes responsibility for one's sexual activity again and again. Mazur says: ''Today, chastity means acting with integrity.'' In a gentle, reasonable and sensitive manner, this book gives young people a context in which to make their own decisions about sexual behavior. An excellent book to spark thoughtful discussion. [10–12]

4.5 Contraception, Abortion, Pregnancy. Alice L. Fleming. Nashville: Thomas Nelson, 1974. 92 p. $5.95.

Factual information about sexual intercourse, contraception, abortion, pregnancy and childbirth. A readable, informative source.

4.6ᵇ Dealing with Questions about Sex. Arlene Uslander and Caroline Weiss. Palo Alto, CA: Learning Handbooks, 1975. 94 p. $3.50.

Good classroom-tested program for teachers to use in sex education classes; glossary and resource list arranged by grade level.[4] [K–12]

4.7 Men's Bodies, Men's Selves. Sam Jultry. New York: Dell, 1979. 453 p. $9.95 p.b.

An outstanding resource book; comes close to providing everything a male needs to know to gain an understanding of his maleness and most importantly, his humanity. Written in a warm, supportive tone, the book explores such aspects as work, homosexuality, physical and emotional health, fathering, aging, sexuality, venereal disease and rape. Throughout the book, the author explodes masculine myths and stereotypes. Women are viewed as partners in life experiences rather than as sexual objects and/or second-class citizens. As such, women are encouraged to read this book. Each chapter contains an extensive list of other resource materials such as books, films, newsletters and organizations. The frankness of subject matter and sexually explicit language may make this book more appropriate for senior high students and above, but the book is an invaluable reference for every teacher. [9–12]

4.8ᵇ Sex & Birth Control. E. James Lieberman and Ellen Peck. New York: Schocken Books, 1975. 287 p. $3.45 p.b. (Originally published by Thomas Y. Crowell, 1973).

An excellent, straightforward, nonjudgmental book which deals with the various forms of birth control, abortion, sterilization and venereal disease. Perhaps more importantly, it discusses attitudes toward sex and sexual behavior, ''what's normal,'' ''what's moral,'' and overpopulation. Case histories and questions from young people of both sexes are helpful. Sources for obtaining more help and information are also included. This is a responsible book on sex for young people, and it encourages a responsibility for individual action which can only be attained with adequate knowledge. [9–12]

4.9   The Sexes: Male/Female Roles and Relationships. Betsy Ryan. New York: Scholastic Book Service, 1975. 186 p. Paperback.

A delightful book with more than 100 poems, photographs, songs, cartoons, articles and ads, which explore love, dating, marriage, and male and female sex roles today. This book is appropriate for free reading and would also provide an excellent resource for stimulating discussion about female and male roles and relationships in health, social studies or women's studies courses at the junior high or secondary level.

4.10   Single and Pregnant. Ruth I. Pierce. Boston: Beacon Press, 1970. 214 p. $5.95.

Without traditional moralizing, this book answers questions and provides information for the single, pregnant girl on abortion, adoption, marriage, and single parenthood. A wealth of information is offered, including facts on contraceptives, conception, the physical changes during pregnancy, relationships with family and friends, maternity homes, community resources, medical care, and counseling and therapy. The appendix includes abortion referrals, planned parenthood affiliates and maternity and infant care projects. However, some of the information is out-of-date, particularly regarding the legality of abortion and the treatment of minors. It is also geared toward white, middle-class girls, and some of the careers are stereotyped. With these cautions in mind, however, this book should provide an acceptable resource for young women.

4.11   Why Am I So Miserable If These Are the Best Years of My Life. Andrea Boroff Eagan. Philadelphia: J.B. Lippincott, 1976. 241 p. $7.95.

A positive, helpful guide for young women to learn how to have more control over their lives, to enjoy their school years and to make good choices for the future. The author frankly discusses sex and birth control in a clear, concise and objective way. Physiological, emotional and social aspects of sex are thoroughly discussed in regard to both girls and boys. The book emphasizes throughout the need to develop good decision-making skills that will affect future career plans, interpersonal relationships and one's overall happiness. The author has a good sense of humor and enormous respect for young women's potential for growth.

Photographs

4.12   Resource Photos for Mainstreaming. Women's Action Alliance. (Available from: Women's Action Alliance, 370 Lexington Avenue, New York, NY 10017. $5.00, Set One; $6.50, Set Two.)

Two sets of 11″ × 14″ black and white photographs. Set One has six photos of disabled men and women. Set Two has eight shots of school children in mainstreamed classrooms and a poster.[31]

Audiovisual Materials

4.13   A Day in the Life of Bonnie Consolo. Barr Films. 17 minutes, color. (Available from: Barr Films, P.O. Box 5667, Pasadena, CA 91107. $275.00; $27.50 rental.)

Shows a day in the life of a woman who functions fully as a mother and homemaker, though she was born without arms.[31]

4.14a   And They Lived Happily Ever After. National Film Board of Canada, 1974. 13 minutes, 16mm. (Available from: National Film Board of Canada, 150 Kent Street, Ottawa, Ontario, Canada.)

Discussion of some of the consequences of marriage, such as lack of privacy, children, possibilities of divorce and separation.[16] [7–12]

4.15   Della. Kenny Rehabilitation Institute. 12 minutes, b/w. (Available from: A/V Publication Department, Kenny Rehabilitation Institute, 1800 Chicago Avenue, Minneapolis, MN 55405.)

Focuses on the rehabilitation of a young paraplegic, also deaf, who now is an active member in her community.[31]

4.16a   Divorce/Separation: Marriages in Trouble. Guidance Associates, 1977. Two filmstrips with cassettes, teacher's guide. (Available from: Guidance Associates, A/V Subsidiary, 757 Third Avenue, New York, NY 10017.)

This two-part filmstrip is designed for use in high school classrooms and focuses on divorce as an emotional process. Taped interviews provide students with personal views from other young people of the divorce process.[16] [7–12]

4.17   The Family in a Changing Society. Encyclopedia Britannica Educational Corporation Films, 1978. Six filmstrips with cassette, guide. (Available from: Encyclopedia Britannica Educational Corporation Films, 425 North Michigan Avenue, Chicago, IL 60611.)

Divided into ''Marriage,'' ''Parenthood'' and ''Working Parents,'' general information, statistics and trends are presented and then illustrated by case studies of actual couples. Includes minorities.[28] [7–12]

4.18a   The Family in Transition: Program 3 of the Family Life Series. Butterick Publishing Co, 1976. Six, 10-minute filmstrips and cassettes. (Available from: Butterick Publishing Co., 161 Sixth Avenue, New York, NY 10013.)

Three segments with lessons and teacher's guide on divorce, aging, and new lifestyles. An excellent exploration of new lifestyles, the role of women and the problems of aging.[16] [8–12]

4.19a   The Future of the Family. Guidance Associates. Multimedia. Two filmstrips with discs or cassettes, discussion guide. (Available from: Guidance Associates, 757 Third Avenue, New York, NY 10017. $48.50.)

Examines past and present trends in family living and projects into the future—communes, nuclear family, women's liberation, urban versus suburban life.[1] [10–12]

4.20b   It Happens to Us. New Day Films. Multimedia. (Available from: New Day Films, P.O. Box 315, Franklin Lakes, NJ 07417. $30 rental.)

A documentary of women of different ages, classes, and races talking about their abortion experiences.[1] [10–12]

4.21[a]   Joyce at 34. New Day Films. (Available from: New Day Films, P.O. Box 315, Franklin Lakes, NJ 07417. $350.00; $35.00 rental plus $4.00 handling.)

This award-winning film explores the changes and adjustments made by a career woman and her husband as they start a family. It explores the conflict of work versus family and how it is handled by two generations of working women. Televised nationally on PBS, this film can be used with high school and adult groups.[2] [9–12]

4.22   Kelly. Women's Educational Equity Act Program. 27 minutes, color. (Available from: Education Development Center, 55 Chapel Street, Newton, MA 02160. $375.00; $25.00 rental.)

Story of a three-year-old black girl with cerebral palsy who enters a regular day care program at a public school.[31]

4.23[a]   Love and Marriage. Guidance Associates. Two filmstrips with two 12″ LPs or two cassettes, discussion guide (Available from: Guidance Associates, A/V Subsidiary, 757 Third Avenue, New York, NY 10017.)

A teenage couple, engaged couple, married couple, divorced couple and a couple living together discuss adjustments and concepts.[1] [10–12]

4.24   Make Out. Newsreel. Film. (Available from: Newsreel, 322 Seventh Avenue, New York, NY. $10.00 rental.)

Told from the women's point of view, a film of a girl and boy making out in the back seat of a car. Good for discussion openers with junior high and high school students.[1] [7–12]

4.25[a]   Male/Female: Changing Lifestyles. Educational AudioVisual. Four filmstrips, four discs or cassettes, teacher's notes. (Available from: Educational AudioVisual, 29 Marble Avenue, Pleasantville, NY 10670. $60.00 discs; $68.00 cassettes.)

This set begins by presenting facts about sexual development. There is a two-part history of sex roles, including the development of the women's movement from the 19th century to today. The final part offers comments by grade and high school students on issues such as the family, social pressures, work and relationships.[1] [10–12]

4.26   Mimi. Billy Budd Films. 12 minutes. (Available from: Billy Budd Films, 235 East 57th Street, New York, NY 10022. $150.00; $15.00 rental.)

An independent young woman, disabled since birth, combines marriage and artistic interests.[31]

4.27[a]   Parenthood: A Series, Preparing for Parenthood. Guidance Associates, 1971. 17 minutes, Two filmstrips with cassettes. (Available from: Guidance Associates, A/V Subsidiary, 757 Third Avenue, New York, NY 10017.)

This program discusses the changes children make in parents' lives and the responsibilities, as well as the joys, involved in parenthood.[16] [7–12]

4.28[c]   Rape: The Savage Crime. Audio Visual Narrative Arts, 1975. Two filmstrips and cassettes, teacher's guide.

(Available from: Audio Visual Narrative Arts, Box 9, Pleasantville, NY 10570.)

The first filmstrip is on the rapist and the reasons for rape, the laws on rape and the social views of rape. The second filmstrip looks at the victim and where the crime occurs, how fear of rape affects women, and how women are acting to change the situation.[16] [7–12]

4.29   Sexual Values: A Matter of Responsibility. Sunburst Communications. Two filmstrips with cassette, guide. (Available from: Sunburst Communications, 39 Washington Avenue, Pleasantville, NY 10570.)

Emphasizing the importance of honest communication between partners, couples discuss their sexual values. Contraception is presented as the responsibility of both partners, not just the female.[28] [7–12]

4.30[b]   A Woman's Place. Schloat Productions, 1974. Four filmstrips with cassettes. (Available from: Schloat Productions, 150 White Plains Road, Tarrytown, NY 10591.)

This set explores images and myths about women, along with a discussion of biological versus environmental theories of sex role development; it also describes the women's movement.[16] [9–12]

4.31[a]   You/Me/We: Making Marriage Work. Guidance Associates, 1975. Two filmstrips and cassettes. (Available from: Guidance Associates, A/V Subsidiary, 757 Third Avenue, New York, NY 10017.)

A discussion of the pioneering efforts in marriage relationships occurring today in which various couples discuss new roles and new marriage arrangements: childlessness, role exchange, divorce, interdependence.[16] [9–12]

Bibliographies/Resource Lists

4.32[d]   Bibliography of Research Involving Female Subjects. Waneen Wyrick Spirduso (ed.). 1974. 212 p. (Available from: American Alliance for Health, Physical Education and Recreation, 1201 16th Street, NW, Washington, DC 20036. $5.25.)

A compilation of theses and dissertations in physical education, health and recreation.[1]

PE/SPORTS*

Lesson Plans

4.33   A.C.T.I.V.E.: Sex Equity in Elementary Education (Teacher's Manual). Western Washington University, 149 p. (Available from: Education Development Center, 55 Chapel Street, Newton, MA 02160. $5.75.)

Using a movement education approach, the A.C.T.I.V.E. materials have been developed to help foster sex equality in elementary school

---

*Subcategories in "PE/Sports," indicated by superscript letters following entry numbers, are designated as follows: a=PE/Sports (Defense).

physical education. The Teacher's Manual provides curriculum material for use with students in grades K–6 in a wide range of areas—sports, dance, and gymnastics. It also describes how to identify stereotyped behavior of teachers and students and offers suggestions for change. Two teacher's manuals, one for a workshop component and the other for a competency-based teacher education program, are also available as part of the A.C.T.I.V.E. package. [K–6]

4.34 "Coed Sports in High School." Lee Johnson. (Available from: *Journal of Physical Education*, Vol. 48, No. 1, January 1977, pp. 23–25.)

Procedures for adapting the rules and strategies of five sports for coeducational play, including basketball, tag football, floor hockey, soccer, softball, volleyball and water polo. They are aimed at developing a fair sense of competition and eliciting equal participation from both sexes.

4.35 Curriculum Guide for Classroom Teachers, Grades K–3. Hanna Gillion. University of Alabama, Alabama General Assistance Center, 1976. (Available from: University of Alabama Press, Drawer 2877, University, AL 35486.)

Activities and classroom strategies for nonsexist physical education in the elementary school.[4] [K–3]

4.36 Equity in Physical Education. Cleveland State University. Women's Educational Equity Act Program, 1981. (Available from: Education Development Center, 55 Chapel Street, Newton, MA 02160. $4.25.)

An excellent book for designing programs based on students' ability and interest, regardless of sex. A detailed checklist is provided for teachers to observe and analyze students' motor performance and social interaction as a basis for planning equitable coeducational programs for grades K–12. Included is a review and explanation of Title IX regulations as they pertain to physical education. [K–12]

4.37 In Search of the Freedom to Grow: Report of the Physical Education Athletics Task Force. Karla Atkinson. Kalamazoo Public Schools, 1973. (Available from: EDRS MF-$.91—HC-$2.00 plus postage, ED 126 059.)

A report compiled by the United States Department of Health, Education, and Welfare on a study of sex discrimination in physical education and athletics. Discusses K–12 physical education programs offering specific strategies for change to achieve sex equity.[22] [K–12]

4.38 Strategies for Equality: Volume I, Guidance, Social Studies, Physical Education. Training Institute for Sex Desegregation. (Available from: Training Institute for Sex Desegregation, Rutgers University, Federation Hall-Douglass Campus, New Brunswick, NJ 08903. $3.50.)

A compendium of curricular projects devised and tested by educators in their own classrooms. For teachers, coaches, counselors and administrators.[16]

4.39 Teaching Guide for Out of the Bleachers. Barbara Bates. Old Westbury, NY: The Feminist Press, $3.50.

Creative ideas for teaching about women in sports.[13] [9–12]

4.40 Women in Athletics. Portland, ME: J. Weston Walch. $4.00.

Posters of famous women in sports, from Chris Evert to Wilma Rudolph.[1] [2–6]

4.41 Women in Sports Kit. SPRINT, Spring 1977. (Available from: SPRINT, WEAL Fund, 805 15th Street, NW, Suite 822, Washington, DC 20005. $4.00.)

Background materials, film and book lists, and some action ideas.

Course Outlines

4.42 Competitive Athletics: In Search of Equal Opportunity. Margaret C. Dunkle. 1976. (Available from: Resource Center on Sex Roles in Education, 400 North Capital Street, NW, Washington, DC 20001.)

Provides institutions with a guide for obtaining and evaluating information to assess equal opportunity in their athletic programs and for developing strategies to attain equal opportunity. Prepared primarily for athletic directors, administrators, coaches and others concerned with providing equal athletic opportunity in schools.[22]

4.43 Equity in School Athletics: A Guide. Training Institute for Sex Desegregation. (Available from: Training Institute for Sex Desegregation, Rutgers University, Federation Hall-Douglass Campus, New Brunswick, NJ 08903. $3.50.)

A guide to the development of an equitable 9–12 athletics program for teachers, administrators and coaches.[16] [9–12]

4.44 Philosophy and Standards in Girls' and Women's Sports. 1973. 66 p. (Available from: American Alliance for Health, Physical Education and Recreation, 1201 16th Street, NW, Washington, DC 20036. $2.50.)

A guide for those who administer, lead and participate in sports for women.[1]

4.45 Title IX Sex Integrated Programs that Work. Marjorie Blaufarb (ed.). 1978. 38 p. (Available from: American Alliance of Health, Physical Education and Recreation, 1201 16th Street, NW, Washington, DC 20036. $3.95.)

Provides in-depth descriptions of successful sex-integrated physical education programs at the junior and senior high school levels as well as 11 appendices which detail implementation and evaluation procedures used by schools across the country.[22] [7–12]

Supplementary Texts

4.46 American Women in Sports. Phyllis Hollander. New York: Grosset & Dunlap, 1972. 112 p.

A series of brief sketches of 52 American women athletes, from the early pioneers, who had to overcome society's disapproval of women athletes, to the athletes of today, who have entered and excelled in new areas of competition as well as fought for equal professional standing and remuneration.

4.47 Billie Jean. Billie Jean King with Kim Chapin. New York: Harper & Row, 1974. 208 p. $6.95.

This autobiography gives a very human account of the numerous struggles of a female athlete. Billie Jean King describes her career as a tennis player, her marriage, her family, and other significant people and events in her life. She reveals a feminist attitude when she discusses traditional inequality of the sexes in sports and her fight for women's equality in tennis. She points out her traditional family background and her expectations for marriage, and ideas on the women's liberation movement and its effects. This book provides an interesting account of the life of an ambitious, athletic and sensitive woman.

4.48   Contributions of Women: Sports. Joan Ryan. Minneapolis: Dillon Press, 1975. 136 p. $6.95.

Short biographies of six women who not only were champion athletes—setting world records and winning gold medals—but also contributed greatly to the acceptance of women in sports. Those featured are: Babe Didrikson Zaharias (outstanding golfer and track star); Kathy Kusner (Olympic equestrian and big-league jockey); Wilma Rudolph (Olympic runner); Billie Jean King (tennis champion); and Melissa Belote (Olympic swimmer).

4.49   Famous Modern American Women Athletes. Helen Hull Jacobs. New York: Dodd, Mead, 1975. 132 p. $4.95.

Short biographies of eight outstanding American women athletes who were Olympic stars, record setters and professional athletes, including Judy Cook Soutar, Janet Lynn, Micki King, Kathy Witworth, Cindy Nelson, Shirley Babashoff, Billie Jean King and Francie Larrieu.

4.50   Fundamentals of Athletic Training for Women. American Alliance for Health, Physical Education, and Recreation, 1975. 288 p. (Available from: American Alliance for Health, Physical Education, and Recreation, 1201 16th Street, NW, Washington, DC 20036. $7.95.)

A workbook and resource guide for athletic trainers of female athletes.[1] [9–12]

4.51   Girl Sports. Karen Folger Jacobs. New York: Bantam Books, 1978. 180 p. $1.50 p.b.

Fifteen girls aged 9 to 17, representing a variety of ethnic minority groups, tell what it is like to train, compete, win or lose in sports ranging from soccer to wrestling. Many of the girls compete in sports that until just recently were considered reserved for "boys only." Now girls are skateboarding, shooting pool and driving motorcycles. An inspiring book about young women who are successful competitors with rightfully earned self-respect. [6–12]

4.52   100 Greatest Women in Sports. Phyllis Hollander. New York: Grosset & Dunlap, 1976. 142 p. $4.95.

A comprehensive survey of women's accomplishments in a wide variety of sports, including basketball, bicycling, bowling, field hockey, figure and speed skating, golf, gymnastics, horseback riding, horse racing, skiing, softball, swimming, tennis, track and field, and volleyball. Emphasis is on record setting as well as the barriers women had to overcome in order to gain professional equality with men. Included are women from many countries who are young, old, married, single, professionals and amateurs.

4.53   Out of the Bleachers. Stephanie L. Twin. Old Westbury, NY: The Feminist Press. 272 p. $5.00.

A unique anthology of 20 historical and contemporary selections which explore the myths and realities of women's participation in sports. Includes essay, journal, biographical and autobiographical

selections. *Teaching Guide for Out of the Bleachers* also is available from The Feminist Press.[39] [9–12]

4.54ᵃ   Self-Defense and Assault Prevention for Girls and Women. Bruce Tegner and Alice McGrath. Ventura, CA: Thor Publishing, 1977. 123 p. Paperback.

A book of instruction in basic, practical self-defense for girls and women. The text is accompanied by photographs to illustrate various techniques. The book teaches women and girls not to view themselves as helpless victims, without being militant in tone. Self-defense is presented as an aspect of general competence and self-reliance. A teacher's guide to accompany the book is available from the publisher. [10–12]

4.55   Women in Sports: Swimming. Diana C. Gleasner. New York: Harvey House, 1975. 63 p.

These five stories about young women who are swimmers reveal the enormous amount of skill, self-discipline, stamina and fortitude involved in their sport. These young women are competitive and determined to excel. This book is highly recommended. [7–9]

Periodicals

4.56   In the Running. WEAL Education and Legal Defense Fund. Periodical, quarterly. (Available from: SPRINT Project, WEAL Education and Legal Defense Fund, 805 15th Street, NW, Washington, DC 20005. Free.)

Four-page, bold layout, newspaper style publication devoted to news regarding women and girls in sports and athletics; employment circumstances of coaches and physical education teachers; athletic scholarships; legal updates on athletic and sports issues, etc.[4] [9–12]

4.57   Women Sports. *Women Sports Magazine.* Periodical, monthly. (Available from: *Women Sports Magazine,* P.O. Box 50483, Palo Alto, CA 94303. $10.00/year.)

A monthly magazine written for the general public that focuses on women's achievements in sports. Includes a calendar of sporting events.[44] [9–12]

Photographs

4.58   Women and Girls in Sports Posters. Women Sports Foundation. (Available from: Women's Sports Foundation, P.O. Box 29384, San Francisco, CA 94122. $12.00.)

Six color posters measuring 17″ × 28″ depict girls and adults participating in active sports.[44] [7–12]

4.59   Women in Sports. Cathy Cade. (Available from Cathy Cade, 977 Bayview Avenue, Oakland, CA 946__. $3.35.)

Six 8″ × 10″ black and white photos of girls and women in gymnastics, track, softball, weightlifting, judo.[29] [K–12]

Multimedia Programs

4.60   Karate Girl: Tae Kwon Do. Educational Activities, 1975. Filmstrip with cassette and book. (Available from

Educational Activities, 1937 North Grand, Baldwin, NY 11510.)

A 14-year-old girl describes her enthusiasm for karate.[28] [K–6]

4.61   A Mirror of Our Society? Scholastic Book Service, 1975. Multimedia kit. (Available from: Scholastic Book Service, 906 Sylvan Avenue, Englewood Cliffs, NJ 07632. $99.50; includes anthology, $2.25; logbook, $1.25; posters, $5.25; records, $7.95; teacher's guide, $5.00.)

Readings to help students answer questions on why people compete, the problems of competition, sports as a reflection on society and the role of women in sports.[1]

4.62   "Sex Stereotyping in Math Doesn't Add Up"; "Girl, Boy or Person: Beyond Sex Differences"; "Equality in Science: Formula for Changing Sex Bias"; "Exercising Your Rights: Eliminating Sex Bias in Physical Education, Reading, Writing, and Stereotyping"; "Present but Not Accounted for: Women in Educational History"; "We the People: Sex Bias in American History." Patricia B. Campbell and Susan E. Katrin. Multimedia modules. (Available from: Education Development Center, 55 Chapel Street, Newton, MA 02160. $15.60 plus 20% postage, complete set; $2.50 each unit.)

This series of instructional modules on sex-role stereotyping in education includes cassette tapes, handouts, transparency masters and a bibliography for each topic area. The modules may be used alone or to complement an instructional unit.[14] [7–12]

Audiovisual Materials

4.63   The Flashettes. New Day Films. 20 minutes, color. Available from: New Day Films, P.O. Box 315, Franklin Lakes, NJ 07417. $335.00; $35.00 rental plus $3.00 postage.)

Documentary about an inner city girls' track club.[29]

4.64   Girls Sports: On the Right Track. Phoenix Films. 7 minutes, color, film, 16mm. (Available from: Phoenix Films, 470 Park Avenue South, New York, NY 10016.)

This film details the recent development in women's sports, focusing on three female high school athletes and illustrating the new opportunities for women in sports.[16] [9–12]

4.65   Making It Happen. Women's Educational Equity Act Program, 1981. 17 minutes, 16mm film or videotape. Available from: Education Development Center, 55 Chapel Street, Newton, MA 02160. Film $115.00, $8.00 rental; videotape $38.00, $5.00 rental.)

This 17-minute film explores the lives of three sports women involved in swimming, climbing, track, volleyball and basketball. A brief historical perspective is presented recounting women's participation in sports and highlighting some major contributions of women athletes.

4.66ª   Rape: Some Facts and Myths. Center for Cassette Studies, 1974. 41-minute cassette tape. (Available from: Center for Cassette Studies, 8110 Webb Avenue, North Hollywood, CA 91605.)

Two rape victims describe their personal experience with rapists and a defense expert recommends ways to counterattack.[16] [11–12]

4.67   Rookie of the Year. Time/Life Films, 1975. 47 minutes, color. (Available from: Time/Life Films, Eisenhower Drive, Paramus, NJ 07602. $550.00; $55.00 rental; $35.00 videotape.)

Story of a bat girl for a Little League baseball team who gets a chance to play in a game. She scores the winning run for her team.[29]

4.68   Serrina Becomes an Acrobat. Encyclopedia Britannica Educational Corporation Films. 11 minutes, 16mm. (Available from: Encyclopedia Britannica Educational Corporation Films, 425 North Michigan Avenue, Chicago, IL 60611.)

Ten-year-old Serrina narrates her story of a summer spent with the circus, training to fly on the trapeze. The viewer follows her as she gains control of her body, enjoys a warm camaraderie with her coaches (several of whom are women), up to the big moment when she conquers her fear and swings from the high bar.[21] [4–8]

4.69   Sugar Spikes. Insight Exchange. 30 minutes, videocassette. (Available from: Insight Exchange, P.O. Box 42584, San Francisco, CA 94101.)

Good overall description of the changes in women's sports, from recreational programs to college opportunities to the professional world of sports.[16] [7–12]

4.70   Women in Sports—An Informal History. Altana Films. 28 minutes, sound, color, 16mm. (Available from: Altana Films, 340 East 34th Street, New York, NY 10016.)

Excellent history of women's participation in sports; shows how they are entering more and more events which were formerly denied them.[28] [7–12]

4.71   Young Women in Sports. BFA Educational Media, 1974. 15 minutes, color. (Available from: BFA Educational Media, P.O. Box 1795, 2211 Michigan Avenue, Santa Monica, CA 90406. $240.00; $24.00 rental.)

Shows four high school athletes performing and discussing training and competing in track and field, gymnastics and swimming.[29]

Bibliographies/Resource Lists

4.72   Bibliographies on Educational Topics #2: Women's Athletics. 33 p. (Available from: ERIC Clearinghouse on Teacher Education, One Dupont Circle, NW, Suite 616, Washington, DC 20036. $1.00; or EDRS MF-$.91—HC $2.06 plus postage, ED 130 991.)

Annotated bibliography compiled from *Resources in Education* and *Current Index to Journals in Education*.[29]

4.73   Guinness Book of Women's Sports Records. New York: Sterling Publishing, 1979. $5.95.

An almanac-style publication devoted to the records and accomplishments of women in sports throughout modern history.[44] [7–12]

4.74   WEECN Resource Roundup: Girls and Women in Sports. Women's Educational Equity Communications Network, 1979. 6 p. (Available from: Women's Educational Equity Act Program, U.S. Department of Education, Donahoe Building, Room 1105, 400 Maryland Avenue, SW, Washington, DC 20202. Single copies are free by sending a self-addressed, stamped envelope.)

This bibliography was one of a series of Resource Roundups published by the Women's Educational Equity Communications Network. The resources listed deal with the participation of girls and women in sports and with sports issues in schools and colleges. Resources are listed under the following categories: general awareness, elementary and secondary school, higher education, research studies, nonprint resources, and national organizations and projects.

SAMPLE LESSON PLAN: HEALTH AND PHYSICAL EDUCATION
Coeducational Obstacle Course

AUDIENCE:

Middle school and junior high students

GOALS:

- To provide an opportunity for coeducational teams to use various group problem-solving techniques and to work together cooperatively.
- To use these situations as a skill-building and evaluation exercise.

OBJECTIVE:

To design a 12-step obstacle course requiring students to use the following skills: running, hopping, climbing, crawling, pushing, pulling, balancing, jumping, basic eye-hand coordination and basic body fitness.

MATERIALS:

The obstacle course should consist of the following equipment set up according to the project chart (see following page):
- uneven parallel bars
- side horse
- two sets of high jump standards
- jump ropes
- automobile inner tube
- 12 bowling pins
- high and low balance beams
- scooter, four hockey sticks and pucks
- five two-by-fours, four feet long
- high-jump bar
- mats, ladder
- one four-foot cage ball

HOW TO USE:

1. Form students into teams of eight to twelve students, with a fairly equal number of males and females on each team.
2. Have each student on the team complete each obstacle before the entire team moves on to the next one. (Up to four teams may be on the floor simultaneously.)
3. Access penalties of one or five seconds for errors made, such as touching the uprights of the uneven bars, crossing the boundary line with scooter, mounting the balance beam using the adjusting knob, and so on.

COMMENTS:

1. This activity is an excellent means of introducing important physical education concepts to students at the elementary and junior high level because it:
   - stresses development of the same individual skills for both males and females.
   - develops team effort.
   - gives teachers a chance to evaluate the strengths and weaknesses of the individual students.
2. The obstacle course is flexible enough to:
   - be used, with variations, for older and younger students and to sustain their interest at different age levels.
   - accommodate as many as 30 to 40 students at once.
3. It encourages female and male students to work together, regardless of sex differences.
4. It provides the basis for a valuable discussion with students about real and perceived differences between males and females in physical activity.
5. It can be included in a coed field day.

Reprinted by permission from: *Strategies for Equality: Guidance, Social Studies, Physical Education*. New Brunswick, NJ, Training Institute for Sex Desegregation, Rutgers, the State University, 1978.

GYM

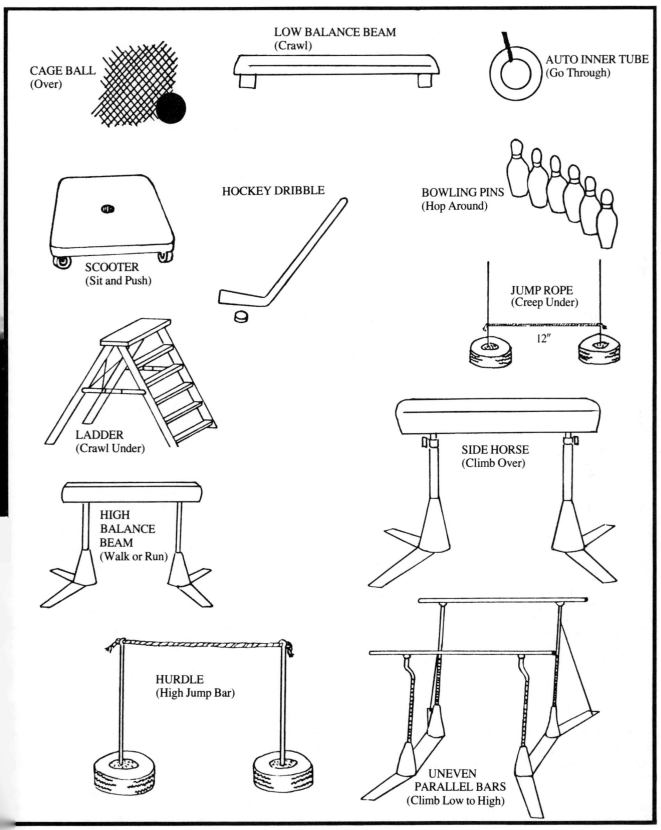

CAGE BALL
(Over)

LOW BALANCE BEAM
(Crawl)

AUTO INNER TUBE
(Go Through)

SCOOTER
(Sit and Push)

HOCKEY DRIBBLE

BOWLING PINS
(Hop Around)

JUMP ROPE
(Creep Under)

12"

LADDER
(Crawl Under)

SIDE HORSE
(Climb Over)

HIGH
BALANCE
BEAM
(Walk or Run)

HURDLE
(High Jump Bar)

UNEVEN
PARALLEL BARS
(Climb Low to High)

5.0 Language Arts

LITERATURE/CHILDREN'S BOOKS*

Lesson Plans

5.1 Again at the Looking Glass: Language Arts Curriculum Materials for Combatting Sex Stereotyping. Feminists Northwest. (Available from: Feminists Northwest, 5038 Nicklas Place, NE, Seattle, WA 98105 or EDRS MF-$.91 plus postage, ED 128 237.)

Ninety-two classroom activities designed to increase student awareness of sex role stereotyping in the area of language arts. The activities are grouped in four major sections: (1) sexist language; (2) autobiography, free lives; (3) nonsexist literature, sex stereotyping, women writers; and (4) sexism in the media. One sample activity has students collect and compare male and female grafitti, including how it reflects the roles of men and women in society. Another activity asks students to keep a tally of male and female personality traits portrayed on television. Although these activities are designed for secondary students, junior high teachers will find a number of activities appropriate for their classrooms. Criteria for analyzing curriculum materials and a bibliography of resource materials are included. [7–12]

5.2 Becoming Sex Fair: The Tredyffrin/Easttown Program (A Comprehensive Model for Public School Districts). Tredyffrin/Easttown (Pennsylvania) School District, 1979. (Available from: Education Development Center, 55 Chapel Street, Newton, MA 02160. $17.75.)

This program provides a model for assessing sex bias within a school district and specific materials and processes for moving toward the goal of sex fairness in all areas of school life. Designed to be carried out in three states under the leadership of a coordinator and a coordinating committee, the program systematically and gradually involves more and more people within the district for increased support and commitment. Of particular interest to the classroom teacher will be the *Stage Three Manual: Revising The Curriculum* (408p; $8.50). It outlines a process for revising curricula at the elementary and secondary level. Numerous sample materials and resources for use or adaptation within major subject matter areas are provided. [K–12]

5.3 Changing Learning, Changing Lives: A High School Women's Studies Curriculum from the Group School. Barbara Gates, Susan Klaw and Adra Reich. Old Westbury, NY: The Feminist Press, 1979. $6.00.

This material was developed for young working class women at an alternative high school in Cambridge, Massachusetts. The curriculum is divided into nine areas including "Messages from Society," "Growing Up Female," "Women and Work," and "Women Organizing Themselves." The units can be used as supplements to English, history, psychology, anthropology, career education or health courses. Throughout the packet recommendations are made on how to teach as well as what to teach.[14] [9–12]

5.4 Classroom Practices in Teaching English, 1976-77 Responses to Sexism. Ouida H. Clapp (ed.). National Council of Teachers of English. (Available from: National Council of Teachers of English, 1111 Kenyon Road, Urbana, IL 61801. $4.95.)

Includes classroom activities to develop students' awareness of sexism; lesson plans on language, sexism, and women in literature and feminist literary criticism.[22] [9–12]

5.5 The Emerging Woman: Quest for Equality. Anita Wilkes Dore. New York: Globe Books.

Activities and exercises for use in the classroom, using excerpts from literature to show women's roles in society; a good consciousness-raiser.[4] [10–12]

5.6 In Praise of Diversity: Multicultural Classroom Applications. Gloria Grant (ed.). Teacher Corps, 1977. 318 p. (Available from: Teacher Corps, Center for Urban Education, The University of Nebraska at Omaha, 3805 North 16 Street, Omaha, NE 68110 or EDRS MF-$.91—HC-$16.7 plus postage, ED 144 854.)

---

*Subcategories of "Literature/Children's Books," indicated by superscript letters following entry numbers, are designated as follows: a=Literature/Children's Books (Poetry); b=Literature/Children's Books (Drama); c=Literature/Children's Books (Women Writers).

Fifty-one activity units written for the classroom teacher who is interested in implementing multicultural and nonsexist education in the areas of social studies, language arts, science, math, and art. Each activity unit offers a rationale, desired learning experiences, suggestions for implementation, supplementary activities and instructional and background resources for teachers. The wealth of activities may be modified and adapted by teachers so that they are relevant to a particular grade level and to the needs of students. One sample activity has parents and students forming a book club to encourage at-home reading and to allow students to become acquainted with nonsexist books. Many of the activities are designed to incorporate ideas and materials from the companion document: *In Praise of Diversity: A Resource Book for Multicultural Education.* [K–8]

5.7 Sexism, Racism and Other Isms: Hidden Messages in Children's Stories ("The Princess and the Pea"). Council on Interracial Books for Children (CIBC). (Available from: CIBC Resource Center, Room 300, 1841 Broadway, New York, NY 10023. $1.50.)

A "fun" lesson plan for 5th grade through college. "The Princess and the Pea" opens a discussion of subtle ways in which sexism, racism, materialism and elitism permeate the simplest of stories. The level of discussion will vary with age, but participants learn how to spot hidden messages while enjoying a lively discussion.[10] [5–12]

5.8 Teaching Guide for Women Working. Florence Howe and Alexandra Weinbaum. Old Westbury, NY: The Feminist Press. $3.50.

A teaching guide developed with the help of college and high school teachers who have tested *Women Working: An Anthology of Stories and Poems* in their classrooms. The guide, conceived as a kind of inservice course for teachers, includes creative teaching suggestions, student projects and annotated bibliographies of books, articles and films. [9–12]

Course Outlines

5.9 Women's Studies for Teachers and Administrators. Merle Froschl, Florence Howe and Sharon Kaylen. Old Westbury, NY: The Feminist Press. $10.00.

Materials to help schools start inservice courses on women in history, literature, social studies and sexism in education. Includes syllabi, sample curriculum materials and a list of resource organizations.[11]

Supplementary Texts

5.10 Ariel: Poems by Sylvia Plath. Sylvia Plath. New York: Harper & Row, 1961. 85 p. $2.25 p.b.

A collection of Sylvia Plath's final poems before her suicide. The power of her poetry is a result of her honest portrayal of other people, other things and herself. There are many demeaning terms used to describe both minorities and women, as well as much explicitness of language. However, *Ariel* is valuable as a brilliant articulation of madness and self-destructiveness. [9–12]

5.11 The Bell Jar. Sylvia Plath. New York: Bantam Books, 1972. 216 p. $2.50 p.b. (Originally published by Harper & Row, 1971).

A scarcely disguised autobiography covering six months in the life of 20-year-old Sylvia Plath, who provides a self-portrait of a very fragile young woman. Through vivid images the reader sees Plath's descent into madness, her mental breakdown and her attempted suicide. Subject matter may make this book more appropriate for older readers. [9–12]

5.12 By and about Women: An Anthology of Short Fiction. Beth Kline Schneiderman (ed.). New York: Harcourt, Brace & Jovanovich, 1973. 325 p.

A collection of short stories by well-known American and British women writers. The stories represent a variety of experiences encountered by women, with an emphasis on the necessity of coping with life. It should be noted that none of the stories focus on women in even slightly nontraditional careers; "coping" often means learning to live with defeat. A few of the stories contain rather explicit sexual references, and the subject matter may make this anthology more appropriate for senior high readers. However, the selective teacher will find examples of fine literature which will serve as valuable catalysts for thought and provocative class discussion. [9–12]

5.13 Crazy Salad: Some Things about Women. Nora Ephron. New York: Alfred A. Knopf, 1975. 201 p. $7.95.

Twenty-five articles written by Nora Ephron for several different magazines. Some articles are political in nature and all are somewhat satirical. Topics include women's liberation, politics, the women of Israel, consciousness-raising groups and several individual women, including Dorothy Parker. Ephron takes a piercing look at these topics but also produces articles that are fun to read. Secondary students should enjoy this book. [7–12]

5.14 Feminine Plural: Stories by Women about Growing Up. Stephanie Spinner. New York: Macmillan, 1972. 240 p. $5.95.

This excellent collection of ten short stories by women includes: Carson McCullers's "Wunderkind"; Doris Lessing's "Notes for a Case History"; Colette's "Green Sealing Wax"; Shirley Ann Grau's "Miss Yellow Eyes"; Katherine Ann Porter's "Virgin Violetta"; R. Prawer Jhabvala's "My First Marriage"; Edna O'Brien's "Irish Revel"; Kay Boyles's "Your Body is a Jewel Box"; Tillie Olsen's "O Yes"; and Flannery O'Connor's "A Temple of the Holy Ghost." The stories are about growing up and new beginnings, which in some cases mean the end of romantic illusion and learning the rules of adult behavior. An excellent anthology for use in a high school literature class or for free reading. [9–12]

5.15 George Sand. Ruth Jordan. London: Constable, 1976. 367 p.

A biography of Aurore Dupin de Francueil Dudevant, who under the name of George Sand, became one of the best-known literary figures in 19th century France. Although the biography is somewhat dry and would provide heavy reading for a high school student, the author provides a well-researched look at the life, works and personal relationships of this complex and controversial woman. The numerous excerpts from the writings of George Sand, as well as from the writings of her peers and contemporaries, are particularly intriguing. [9–12]

5.16 The Heart Is a Lonely Hunter. Carson McCullers. New York: Bantam Books, 1978. 307 p. $1.95 p.b. (Originally published by Houghton Mifflin, 1940).

This moving yet unsentimental novel was written by Carson Mc-Cullers at the age of 23. It provides a vividly realistic portrait of the isolation and despair of the poor and disenfranchised—black and white—in a small southern town. The story focuses on Singer, a deaf-mute, and the four characters who bring to him their problems and despair: Mick, a 15-year-old girl seeking beauty in an ugly world; Blount, a bitter, drunken radical; Dr. Copeland, a bitterly disillusioned black doctor; and Biff, a lonely, hardboiled cafe owner. The subject matter may be more appropriate for junior high readers. [9–12]

5.17   The Member of the Wedding. Carson McCullers. New York: Bantam Books, 1975. 153 p. $1.75 p.b. (Originally published by Houghton Mifflin, 1946).

A realistic and moving novel of the growing pains of a young girl's adolescence. Twelve-year-old Frankie, who is determined to become F. Jasmine, finds herself searching for the "we of me," after her best friend moves away and her father says she's too old to share his bed any longer. To combat an overwhelming sense of loneliness and to find someone to belong to, Frankie decides to go with her brother and his new bride after the wedding. This book provides a moving portrait of human beings isolated from one another—man from woman, child from adult and black from white. [9–12]

5.18   Persuasion. Jane Austen. New York: New American Library, 1964. 256 p. $1.75 p.b. (Originally published by John Murray, London, 1818).

A 19th century novel about the world of country gentry in Regency England. The hero, Anne Elliot, is a woman of perfect breeding, profound depth of emotion and unswerving integrity. While the hero exhibits remarkable strength and understanding, her aspirations do not go beyond the traditional role of wife. The characters are highly stereotyped and in many instances reveal the shallowness and hypocrisy of that society. [9–12]

5.19   Plays by and about Women. Victoria Sullivan and James Hatch (eds.). New York: Random House, 1974. 421 p. $3.95 p.b.

This collection of plays includes Alice Gerstenberg's *Overtones*; Lillian Hellman's *The Children's Hour*; Clare Boothe's *The Women*; Doris Lessing's *Play With a Tiger*; Megan Terry's *Calm Down Mother*; Natalia Ginzburg's *The Advertisement*; Maureen Duffy's *Rites*; and Alice Childress's *Wine in the Wilderness*. All of the plays are written from a female, but not necessarily feminist, point of view and deal with a wide range of themes. Some of the plays are experimental in form. Due to subject matter, language, violence, and/or sophisticated form, all except *Overtones* are recommended for mature readers. [9–12]

5.20   The Prime of Miss Jean Brodie. Muriel Sparks. New York: Dell, 1978. 156 p. $1.25 p.b. (Originally published by J. B. Lippincott, 1961).

The Prime of Miss Jean Brodie probes with skill the halcyon years of a fiercely independent and unorthodox schoolteacher and her relationship with six favorite pupils. How Miss Brodie enjoys, exploits and ultimately becomes a victim of her vaunted "prime" forms the basis of this novel. [9–12]

5.21   Tell Me a Riddle. Tillie Olsen. New York: Dell, 1979. 125 p. $1.25 p.b.

In four timeless short stories, Tillie Olsen explores the struggles and pain of contemporary existence, with verbal richness and beauty that no reader will forget. Included are: "I Stand Here Ironing"; "Hey Sailor, What Ship?"; "O Yes"; and "Tell Me a Riddle." This collection would be an excellent resource for a high school literature class. [9–12]

5.22   Women and Fiction: Short Stories by and about Women. Susan Cahill (ed.). New York: New American Library, 1975. 379 p. $2.95 p.b.

Women and Fiction provides the reader with a very rich portrait of the lives of women from all walks of life. This selection of short stories by some of our most creative modern women writers will especially appeal to readers from high school age on up. The ironies, tragedies, joys and day-to-day experiences of women from all socio-economic strata of society are portrayed. The introduction and brief biographical sketch of each of the 26 authors also add to the reader's understanding of the struggle which many of these writers experienced to become career fiction writers. [7–12]

5.23   Women of Wonder: Science Fiction Stories by Women about Women. Pamela Sargent (ed). New York: Vintage, 1974. 285 p. $1.95 p.b.

An excellent anthology of 12 intriguing and well-written science fiction stories by women, in which women characters play major roles. In addition to biographical sketches and brief introductions to the authors and stories, the editor provides a thoughtful, well-researched discussion on the role of women in the time-honored, male preserve of science fiction. The introduction provides an excellent resource for a class on women and science fiction or other literature units focusing on the science fiction genre. Several stories explore changing sex roles and sexual mores and are perhaps most appropriate for mature readers; one of the stories portrays a particularly violent rape. [9–12]

5.24   Women Working: An Anthology of Stories and Poems. Nancy Hoffman and Florence Howe. Old Westbury, NY: The Feminist Press. 304 p. $5.50.

Thirty-four selections chosen to capture the intensity of women's experience of work, paid and unpaid, both in and outside the home. Includes: "Oppressive Work: Anzia Yezierska, Willa Cather, Nikki Giovanni"; "Satisfying Work: Sarah Orne Jewett, Zora Neal Hurston, Barbara Smith"; "Family Work: Carmen Taffola, Tillie Olsen, Sheila Ballantyne"; "Transforming Work: Margaret Walker, Dorothy Canfield Fisher, Meridel Le Suer." (Partial listing.) *Teaching Guide for Women Working* also is available from The Feminist Press.[39] [9–12]

Multimedia Programs

5.25   Black Literature: The Journey, The Scene, The Search, The Black Hero, Major Black Writers, Black Perspectives. Scholastic Book Service, 1975. Multimedia (Available from: Scholastic Book Service, 906 Sylvan Avenue, Englewood Cliffs, NJ 07632. Each set includes paperback, $1.35; teaching guide, $3.10; posters $7.50; record $5.95.)

A series of six sets which contain works by Gloria Davis, Mari Evans, Nikki Giovanni, Maya Angelou, Gwendolyn Brooks, Margaret Walker, Alice Childress and others.[1] [7–12]

Audiovisual Materials

5.26[a]   Black Poetry Kit. Scholastic Book Service. Two filmstrips, with records or cassettes. (Available from

Scholastic Book Service, 906 Sylvan Avenue, Englewood Cliffs, NJ 07632. $36.00.)

Poetry from young black poets of the 70s, including Julia Fields and Nikki Giovanni.[1] [7–9]

5.27[b] Breaking Out of the Doll's House. 30 minutes, color, sound, 16mm. (Available from: Learning Corporation of America, 1350 Avenue of the Americas, New York, NY 10019.)

An edited version of a television production of Henrik Ibsen's "The Doll's House." Excellent both as literature and history and as a vehicle to discuss sex roles.[16] [8–12]

5.28[b] A Doll's House. Caedmon Records. Three discs or cassettes. (Available from: Caedmon Records, Inc., 505 Eighth Avenue, New York, NY 10018. $21.94 discs; $23.85 cassettes.)

Claire Bloom and Donald Madden star in this version of *A Doll's House*, a 19th century play with an ironically modern note.[1] [10–12]

5.29[b] Man and Woman: Myths and Stereotypes. Center for Humanities, Inc., 1975. 30 minutes, slide carousels, cassettes and records. (Available from: Center for Humanities, Inc., 2 Holland Avenue, White Plains, NY 10603.)

Using paintings, photography, theater and movie scripts and popular music, these sets describe how our views of men and women developed in western culture and how these stereotypes are changing today.[16] [9–12]

5.30[a] Poetry Is Alive and Well and Living in America. Media Plus. Six filmstrips, discs or cassettes, teacher's guide. (Available from: Media Plus, Inc., 60 Riverside Drive, New York, NY 10024. $90.00.)

Visual interpretations of May Swenson's poems "Still Turning" and "The Pregnant Dream" and G. C. Oden's "The Way It Is" and "Speculation."[1] [7–12]

5.31 The Practical Princess. Sterling Educational Films. 10 minutes, 16mm. (Available from: Sterling Educational Films, Division of Walter Reade Organization, 241 East 34th Avenue, New York, NY 10016.)

A full-dress fairy tale about a princess who devises ways to thwart the advances of evil Lord Garp. Imprisoned in a tower, she briefly languishes, then gives herself a shake and reminds herself that no prince is coming to rescue her so she had better start making her own plans.[21] [4–6]

5.32 The Seven Ravens. Learning Corporation of America. 22 minutes, 16mm. (Available from: Learning Corporation of America, 1350 Avenue of the Americas, New York, NY 10019.)

A fairy tale from the Brothers Grimm in which the main character is truly a hero. A little girls sets out to free her brothers who have been changed into ravens by a disgruntled witch. She carries her quest to the kingdom under the sea, to the sun and moon, and finally to the crystal mountain which she must climb. Successful, she is given a hero's welcome by her family.[21] [2–6]

5.33 Tatterhood Tales on Tape. The Feminist Press. Three cassette tapes. (Available from: The Feminist Press, Box 334, Old Westbury, NY 11568. $6.95 each.)

Series of three cassettes: (1) "Humour T
and Enchantment"; and (3) "Tales o
stories are taken from *Tatterhood and*
fairy and folk tales chosen for their portraya...
and courageous females.[39] [K–12]

5.34[c] Women in Literature. Educational Audio-Visual, 1976. Four filmstrips with four cassettes, guide. (Available from: Educational Audio-Visual, 29 Marble Avenue, Pleasantville, NY 10670.)

Deals with women both as characters in literary works and as writers, beginning with classical literature and continuing to the present day.[16] [9–12]

Bibliographies/Resource Lists

5.35 Advisory List of Instructional Media for Reduction of Sex Bias. North Carolina State Department of Public Instruction. (Available from: North Carolina State Department of Public Instruction, Division of Educational Media, Raleigh, NC or EDRS MF-$.91—HC-$2.06 plus postage, ED 149 755.)

Instructional media appropriate to schools' efforts to reduce sex bias are described in this advisory list. Entries were favorably reviewed by educators. Most materials were evaluated by members of the Raleigh, North Carolina, Chapter of the National Organization for Women. Materials range from primary to senior high school grade levels and are arranged in these categories: biographies; history, sociology, and biology of sex roles; and curriculum materials illustrating balanced sex roles. Books, films, posters, slide sets and filmstrips are included. Entries include citation, price if available, grade level and annotation.[3] [K–12]

5.36 Articles on Non-Sexist, Non-Racist Children's Literature. Maureen Pastine, 1975. 27p. (Available from: EDRS MF-$.91—HC-$2.06 plus postage, ED 117 654.)

An unannotated bibliography of articles, ERIC documents, alternative publishers, book review sources, and books and pamphlets to aid users in finding appropriate nonsexist, nonracist books for children. [K–8]

5.37 Bibliography of Materials on Sexism and Sex-Role Stereotyping in Children's Books. Kathleen Gallagher and Alice Peery. Chapel Hill, NC: Lollipop Power, Inc., 1976. 9 p.

An unannotated bibliography of journal articles, newsletters, monographs, reports and resources focusing on sexism and sex role stereotyping in children's books. Although many of the references cited focus on primary and intermediate grade education, the bibliography should prove useful to the junior high school teacher. [K–8]

5.38 Books for Today's Children: An Annotated Bibliography of Non-Stereotyped Picture Books. Jeanne Bracken and Sharon Wigutoff. Old Westbury, NY: The Feminist Press. 42 p. $2.00.

A critically annotated list of 200 recent picture books in such categories as working mothers, handicaps, multiracial and adoption. [1–8]

5.39 A Guide to Non-Sexist Children's Books. Judith Adell and Hilary Dole Klein. Chicago: Academy Press, 1976. 149 p. $3.95.

An annotated bibliography of nonsexist children's books. Titles are divided into the broad categories of fiction and nonfiction within the three major categories of preschool through third grade, third grade through seventh grade and seventh grade through twelfth grade. The bibliography provides a wealth of titles and includes the publisher, copyright date, recommended grade level and price; however, no criteria for determining reading level or nonsexist content has been provided. [K–12]

5.40   A Selected Bibliography of Bias-Free Materials: Grades K–12. Nancy R. Motomatsu (ed.). Washington Office of the State Superintendent of Public Instruction, 1976. 23 p. (Available from: Washington Office of the State Superintendent of Public Instruction, Olympia, WA, or EDRS MF-$.91—HC-$1.67 plus postage, ED 127 408.)

Bibliography of nonsexist books and films appropriate for K–12 students. Annotations are provided for the film citations. [K–12]

5.41   Strong Women: An Annotated Bibliography of Literature for the High School Classroom. Deborah Silverton Rosenfelt. Old Westbury, NY: The Feminist Press, 1976. 56 p. $1.95.

A selective, annotated bibliography for high school teachers and students who want inexpensive supplementary readings by women, which emphasize the strengths and accomplishments of women. The bibliography is organized according to anthologies, autobiography and biography, drama, novels, short stories and poetry. A cross topical index with the following categories also is provided: adolescence, female sexuality, women in the arts and professions, women and political commitment, third-world women and working class women. [9–12]

5.42c   200 Plus: A Framework for Non-Stereotyped Human Roles in Elementary Media Center Materials. Kalamazoo Public Schools, September 1977. 25 p. (Available from: Media Services, Kalamazoo Public Schools, 1220 Harvard Street, Kalamazoo, MI 49008. $.79.)

200 Plus lists elementary materials, indicating grade use and reading level for each item. Over 80 percent of the 206 books are in the first three categories—picture books, fiction, and social studies; other categories are language arts, miscellaneous and audiovisuals. The Kalamazoo bibliographies are updated every year. Orders are filled with the latest editions, which include all items that were listed in previous editions. [12] [K–8]

5.43c   Women and Literature: An Annotated Bibliography of Women Writers. Cambridge, MA: Women and Literature Collective, 1976. 212 p. $3.80.

Extensive bibliography of women's fictional writings and essays; useful subject and name indices.[4]

WOMEN WRITERS

Supplementary Texts

5.44   Breakthrough: Women in Writing. Diana Gleasner. New York: Walker and Company, 1980. 143 p. $9.95.

An interesting book in which the author presents the personal insights of and the problems encountered by five women writers: Judy Blume, Erica Jong, Erma Bombeck, Jessamyn West, and Phyllis Whitney. This is a delightful book which will no doubt inspire aspiring writers, female and male. [9–12]

5.45   In Her Own Image: Women Working in the Arts. Elaine Hedges and Ingrid Wendt. Old Westbury, NY: The Feminist Press, 1980. 301 p. Paperback.

Excellent anthology of works of Western women in the arts, represented by selections from their poetry, fiction, autobiographies, essays, journals and letters, and photographs; their sculpture, painting, graphics, photography, ceramics, needlework, music and dance. In all these forms, the women are making statements about their view of themselves as women. The book is organized in a way that shows the relationship between women's art and the condition of women's lives. Each section is introduced with an essay which explores and connects the book's themes; each artist is introduced with a brief biography. [8–12]

Multimedia Programs

5.46   Black Literature: The Journey, The Scene, The Search, The Black Hero, Major Black Writers, Black Perspectives. Scholastic Book Service, 1975. Multimedia. (Available from: Scholastic Book Service, 906 Sylvan Avenue, Englewood Cliffs, NJ 07632. Each set includes paperback, $1.35; teaching guide, $3.10; posters, $7.50; record, $5.95.)

A series of six sets which contain works by Gloria Davis, Mari Evans, Nikki Giovanni, Maya Angelou, Gwendolyn Brooks, Margaret Walker, Alice Childress and others.[1] [7–12]

Audiovisual Materials

5.47   The Brontes: Fantasy and Reality. Guidance Associates, 1975. Two filmstrips with cassettes. (Available from: Guidance Associates, A/V Subsidiary, 757 Third Avenue, New York, NY 10017.)

Part I describes the Bronte family and emphasizes the limitations and restrictions placed on women in this era. Part II describes the Brontes' life and work.[16] [9–12]

5.48   Edith Sitwell Reading Her Poems. Caedmon Records. Disc or cassette. (Available from: Caedmon Records Inc., 505 Eighth Avenue, New York, NY 10018. $6.90 disc; $7.95, cassette.)

Sitwell reads from a wide variety of her poetry.[1] [10–12]

5.49   Edna St. Vincent Millay Reading Her Poetry. Caedmon Records. Disc or cassette. (Available from Caedmon Records, Inc., 505 Eighth Avenue, New York, NY 10018. $6.98, disc; $7.95, cassette.)

This reading—which includes some of Millay's political poetry, i.e., "Where Can the Heart Be Hidden in the Ground" (dedicated Sacco and Vanzetti)—was recorded in 1941 when she was 49. [10–12]

5.50   Gertrude Stein Reads from Her Works. Caedmon Records. Disc or cassette. (Available from: Caedmon

Records, Inc., 505 Eighth Avenue, New York, NY 10018. $6.98, disc; $7.95, cassette.)

Stein reads "The Making of Americans, parts 1 and 2," "A Valentine to Sherwood Anderson," "If I Told Him: A Complete Portrait of Picasso," "Matisse," and "Madame Recamier."[1] [10–12]

5.51 Pearl S. Buck., Films Incorporated. 28 minutes. (Available from: Films Incorporated, 1144 Wilmette Avenue, Wilmette, IL 60091.)

A conversation with one of her adopted Asian children discloses the influence of Asia on her life and work, as well as an interpretation of contemporary events in China.[21] [10–12]

5.52 The Private World of Emily Dickinson. Guidance Associates, 1971. 25 minutes, two filmstrips with cassettes. (Available from: Guidance Associates, A/V Subsidiary, 757 Third Avenue, New York, NY 10017.)

Part I presents a biography of Dickinson and the conditions which helped to create the poet; Part II examines her personality and self-created world. Both are filled with excerpts from her poetry and letters.[16] [7–12]

5.53 Profiles of Black Achievement: Margaret Walker Alexander/James Van Der Zee. Guidance Associates. Two filmstrips with two 12" LP's or two cassettes, discussion guide. (Available from: Guidance Associates, A/V Subsidiary, 757 Third Avenue, New York, NY 10017. $48.50.)

Part I: Alexander recalls her southern childhood, northern college years, her teaching novel *Jubilee;* reads from her poem. Part II: Van Der Zee's life as photographer of black experience.[1] [10–12]

5.54 To Be a Woman and a Writer. Guidance Associates, 1976. Two filmstrips with cassettes, guide. (Available from: Guidance Associates, A/V Subsidiary, 757 Third Avenue, New York, NY 10017. $48.50.)

Portraits of 19th- and 20th-century women writers: their desires, writings, problems, and images. Some of the writers whose works are discussed are George Eliot, Tillie Olsen, Jane Austen, Louisa May Alcott, Emily Bronte, Virginia Woolf, Adrienne Rich, Doris Lessing and Lorraine Hansbury.[16] [9–12]

5.55 Women in Literature Reading Their Own Works. Caedmon Records. Six cassettes. (Available from: Caedmon Records, Inc., 505 Eighth Avenue, New York, NY 10018. $45.00.)

Gwendolyn Brooks, Marianne Moore, Katherine Anne Porter, Edith Sitwell, Gertrude Stein and Eudora Welty read from their works.[1] [10–12]

WRITING/LANGUAGE

Lesson Plans

5.56 ABC Workbook. Jean Mangi. Old Westbury, NY: The Feminist Press, 1975. 32 p. $1.95.

Coloring book with nonsexist text and humorous illustrations of all kinds of people and activities.

Supplementary Texts

5.57 Changing Words in a Changing World. Arizona State University. Women's Educational Equity Act Program, 1981. (Available from: Education Development Center, 55 Chapel Street, Newton, MA 02160. $2.00.)

A study of language communication and how it defines and shapes culture. The book is organized around four linguistic principles: a language reflects the culture and values of its speakers; language forms reflect the viewpoint of the majority of the powerful groups in a society; exaggeration is an integral part of communication; and language changes continuously but in different ways with different speakers. Additional activities, discussion topics and instructions for incorporating this material into linguistics courses are included in an accompanying 32-page *Instructor's Guide* ($1.75). [10–12]

5.58 The Handbook of Nonsexist Writing for Writers, Editors and Speakers. Casey Miller and Kate Swift. New York: Lippincott & Crowell, 1980. 134 p.

This handbook provides practical suggestions for those committed to equality in style. Hundreds of examples, mostly from published sources, illustrate the subtle messages conveyed by biased language. Word substitution and rewriting are offered as the most frequent solutions to biased writing. [9–12]

5.59 A Teacher's Guide to Sexist Words. Mary W. Matthews. *Social Education,* Vol. 41, No. 6 (May 1977), pp. 389–397.

Teaching guide for increasing students' awareness of sexism in language. Extensive word lists and suggested teaching activities are provided for the following groups of words: (1) no-parallel job titles; (2) comparisons; (3) words of approval and words of disapproval; and (4) words and phrases derived from names. [K–3]

Multimedia Programs

5.60 "Sex Stereotyping in Math Doesn't Add Up"; "Girl, Boy or Person: Beyond Sex Differences"; "Equality in Science: Formula for Changing Sex Bias"; "Exercising Your Rights: Eliminating Sex Bias in Physical Education, Reading, Writing, and Stereotyping"; "Present but Not Accounted for: Women in Educational History"; "We the People: Sex Bias in American History." Patricia B. Campbell and Susan E. Katrin. Multimedia modules. (Available from: Education Development Center, 55 Chapel Street, Newton, MA 02160. $15.60 plus 20% postage, complete set; $2.50 each unit.)

This series of instructional modules on sex role stereotyping in education includes cassette tapes, handouts, transparency masters and a bibliography for each topic area. The modules may be used alone or to complement an instructional unit.[14]

Audiovisual Materials

5.61 Inequality of Language: An Analysis of Sexist Language and Terminology in Textbooks. Center for Cassette Studies, 1974. 59 minutes, two cassette tapes. (Available from: Center for Cassette Studies, 8110 Webb Avenue, North Hollywood, CA 91605.)

Discusses textbook writers whose biased language has distorted the impact and image of women in history and culture.[16] [10–12]

SAMPLE COURSE OUTLINE: LANGUAGE ARTS
20th Century Women Writers

AUDIENCE:

12th grade English students (quarter elective course)

GOAL:

To explore concepts and ideas expressed by some of the best women writers of the 20th century concerning women's experiences and the realities of being female as opposed to what society says women experience or should experience in their lives; to try to bring a new awareness of a woman's condition and the possibilities open to her for growth, equality and self-actualization.

OBJECTIVES:

- *To recognize* the inequality between male and female as it now exists in the culture and to gain an insight into the term "androgyny."
- *To explore* the historical reasons for this condition.
- *To analyze* the economic consequences to both women and the society as a whole.
- *To debate* the possibilities for eliminating war by opening up the upper decision making levels which govern all our lives and which is directly connected to economics.
- *To awaken* to the realities of black women in this culture.
- *To discuss* how the body itself has been an object to be owned and controlled by an outside authority (organized religion and marriage), and to explore the tragic consequences of this usurped ownership.
- *To discuss* and rejoice in the contributions which women bring to the new era of consciousness whose evolution characterizes our time.

MATERIALS:

1. *Orlando* by Virginia Woolf
2. *A Room of One's Own* by Virginia Woolf
3. *Three Guineas* by Virginia Woolf
4. *Under a Glass Bell* (short story collection); "Birth" by Anais Nin
5. *I Know Why the Caged Bird Sings* by Maya Angelou or *The Autobiography of Miss Jane Pittman* by Ernest Gaines
6. *The Awakening* by Kate Chopin
7. *The Way of All Women* by Dr. M. Esther Harding
8. Two sound filmstrips which explain the contribution to literature made by Mary Wollstonecraft, Mary Shelley, Jane Austen, Elizabeth Browning, the Brontes, Harriet Beecher Stowe, Emily Dickinson, Virginia Woolf, Gertrude Stein, Anais Nin, Flannery O'Connor, Lillian Hellman, Sylvia Plath, Doris Lessing, Nikki Giovanni and others: Part I, "Fanny Burney to Kate Chopin"; Part II, "The Twentieth Century"

LEARNING ACTIVITIES:

1. Course will concentrate upon reading, writing, speaking and listening.
2. Small and large group discussion techniques will focus on the various ideas and concepts to be found in the literature.
3. Students will be asked to write papers and exams exploring the various objectives and questions previously stated.

Note:

Teachers may wish to include literature written by other ethnic minority group women, such as Native American, Asian or Hispanic. This particular lesson plan focuses on the contributions of white and black women.

Adapted from a Sex Equity Action Plan developed by Lucille W. Evans (Lakeridge High School, Lake Oswego (Oregon) School District), in BIAS (Building Instruction Around Sex Equity) inservice training workshop, January 1980.

6.0 Math and Science

MATH*

Lesson Plans

6.1 Beating the Numbers: A Math Careers Program Handbook. Boston Community School Board and Boston University. Women's Educational Equity Act Program, 1981. (Available from: Education Development Center, 55 Chapel Street, Newton, MA: 02160. $8.00.)

An increasing number of jobs require strong math skills. This handbook describes a successful Boston-based program that combines math instruction and counseling to help undereducated and underemployed women develop basic math skills, broaden their career aspirations and overcome barriers to job advancement. Designed as a short-term continuing education or tutorial program for women with high school or general equivalency diplomas, the handbook can also be used in high schools. It includes a bibliography of mathematics, counseling and career information; a 16-week lesson plan model; eight counseling workshops; and occupational math modules for traditional and nontraditional careers. [9–12]

6.2ª Becoming Sex Fair: The Tredyffrin/Easttown Program (A Comprehensive Model for Public School Districts). Tredyffrin/Easttown (Pennsylvania) School District, 1979. (Available from: Education Development Center, 55 Chapel Street, Newton, MA 02160. $17.75.)

This program provides a model for assessing sex bias within a school district and specific materials and processes for moving toward the goal of sex fairness in all areas of school life. Designed to be carried out in three stages under the leadership of a coordinator and a coordinating committee, the program systematically and gradually involves more and more people within the district for increased support and commitment. Of particular interest to the classroom teacher will be the *Stage Three Manual: Revising The Curriculum*

Subcategories of ''Math,'' indicated by superscript letters following entry numbers, are designated as follows: a=Math/Science; b=Math (Careers); c=Math/Science (Careers).

(408p., $8.50). It outlines a process for revising curricula at the elementary and secondary level. Numerous sample materials and resources for use or adaptation within major subject matter areas are provided. [K–12]

6.3ª Expanding Your Horizons in Science and Mathematics: Conferences for Young Women Interested in New Career Options: A Handbook for Conference Planners. Joanne Koltnow. Mills College, 1979. 50 p. (Available from: Education Development Center, 55 Chapel Street, Newton, MA 02160. $3.00.)

A handbook that uses quotes, examples and questions to aid the reader in creating a conference that aims to stimulate female involvement in math and science classes. A very helpful appendix includes six hands-on workshop activities plus useful forms, samples, quizzes, etc.[44] [7–12]

6.4ª In Praise of Diversity: Multicultural Classroom Applications. Gloria Grant. 1977. 318 p. (Available from: Teacher Corps, Center for Urban Education, The University of Nebraska at Omaha, 3805 North 16th Street, Omaha, NE 68110 or EDRS MF-$.91—HC $16.73 plus postage, ED 144 854.)

Fifty-one activity units written for the classroom teacher who is interested in implementing multicultural and nonsexist education in the areas of social studies, language arts, science, math and art. Each activity unit offers a rationale, desired learning experiences, suggestions for implementation, supplementary activities and instructional and background resources for teachers. The wealth of activities may be modified and adapted by teachers so that they are relevant to a particular grade level and to the needs of students. Many of the activities were designed to incorporate ideas and materials from the companion document: *In Praise of Diversity: A Resource Book for Multicultural Education*. [K–8]

6.5 Mind over Math. Stanley Kogelman. New York: Dial Press, 1978.

Discusses the use of informal workshops to alleviate the fear and anxiety often associated with learning math. Offers tips for reading math texts and performing math problems under pressure. Reviews basics of algebra and calculus.[34] [9–12]

6.6   Overcoming Math Anxiety. Sheila Tobias. New York: W. W. Norton, 1978. 278 p. $10.95.

A discussion of how intimidation, misunderstanding and missed opportunities have made people fear learning math. Appendices include a composite math anxiety scale and programs for math anxious people.[44] [9–12]

6.7ª   Strategies for Equality: Volume IV, Mathematics/ Science. Training Institute for Sex Desegregation of the Public Schools, 1980. 118p. (Available from: Training Institute for Sex Desegregation of the Public Schools, Rutgers University, Federation Hall-Douglass Campus, New Brunswick, NJ 08903. $4.00.)

A compendium of curricular projects, focusing on math and science, devised and tested by educators in their own classrooms. [K–12]

Supplementary Texts

6.8   Math Equals: Biographies of Women Mathematicians and Related Activities. Teri Perl. Menlo Park, CA: Addison-Wesley, 1978. 250 p. Paperback.

Biographies of nine women mathematicians, with related math activities. The women range from Hypatia of Greece (370-415 A.D.) to Emmy Noether (1882–1935). The relatively brief biographies are fascinating. Each one notes the particular problems which the female mathematician faced by virtue of her sex. The mathematical activities are related to the work of the mathematicians covered in the book and are presented in original and thought-provoking ways. Appendices and solutions to the problems are included, and the book is well-illustrated. [9–12]

6.9ᵇ   Women Engineers. Engineering Council for Professional Development. (Available from: Engineering Council for Professional Development, 345 East 47th Street, New York, NY 10017. $.25.)

Career pamphlet.

Periodicals

6.10   AWIM Newsletter. Wellesley College. (Available from: Association of Women in Mathematics, c/o Department of Mathematics, Wellesley College, Wellesley, MA 02181. $10.00.)

This quarterly newsletter contains information on women in mathematics as well as resources and employment news.[42]

Multimedia Programs

6.11ᶜ   How High the Sky? How Far the Moon? Sharon L. Menard (ed.). 1979. Multimedia. (Available from: Education Development Center, 55 Chapel Street, Newton, MA 02160. $10.00.)

This program is designed to help educators encourage female students to pursue careers in mathematics and the sciences. Varied curriculum materials for use with students, grades K–12, provide activities intended to increase interest and skill in scientific and technical fields. Extensive information about careers in science and annotated listings of print and audiovisual materials appropriate for each grade level are provided. One section of materials, ''The Role Models,'' explores outstanding accomplishments of women in science and includes short biographies of seven women currently active in a variety of scientific fields. Four audiotape cassettes containing interviews with these seven women supplement the program. [K–12]

6.12   Multiplying Options and Subtracting Bias. National Council of Teachers of Mathematics, 1981. Four, 30-minute color, sound videotapes (¾" videocassette, ½" open reel, VHS or Beta 1); facilitator's guide. (Available from: National Council of Teachers of Mathematics, 1906 Association Drive, Reston, VA 22091. $125.00 each; $375.00 set of four.)

A videotape and workshop intervention program designed to eliminate sexism from mathematics education. Each of the four videotapes, narrated by Marlo Thomas, is directed to a specific junior and senior high school audience: students, parents, teachers and guidance counselors. Each tape uses a variety of formats—candid interviews, dramatic vignettes, and expert testimony—to address the problem of mathematics avoidance and some possible solutions. A facilitator's guide, which provides special workshop materials to develop an awareness of sexual bias and math anxiety, is an integral part of the program. The guide contains an overview of the workshops, detailed instructions on how facilitators can prepare for conducting the workshops, and four separate step-by-step sets of workshop instructions for each of the target audiences. Overhead transparencies and handout masters are included. [7–12]

6.13ª   ''Sex Stereotyping in Math Doesn't Add Up''; ''Girl, Boy or Person: Beyond Sex Differences''; ''Equality in Science: Formula for Changing Sex Bias''; ''Exercising Your Rights: Eliminating Sex Bias in Physical Education, Reading, Writing, and Stereotyping''; ''Present but Not Accounted for: Women in Educational History''; ''We the People: Sex Bias in American History.'' Patricia B. Campbell and Susan E. Katrin. Multimedia modules. (Available from: Education Development Center, 55 Chapel Street, Newton, MA 02160. $15.60 plus 20% postage, complete set; $2.50 each unit.)

This series of instructional modules on sex role stereotyping in education includes cassette tapes, handouts, transparency masters and a bibliography for each topic area. The modules may be used alone or to complement an instructional unit.[14]

Audiovisual Materials

6.14ᶜ   Count Me In: Educating Women for Science and Math. Mills College Department of Mathematics. Video tape cassettes. (Available from: Education Development Center, 55 Chapel Street, Newton, MA 02160. $34.00 $5.00 rental.)

Documents successful curricular-career program to interest women in entering scientific and technical fields. For high school students math and science faculty, guidance people, administrators and others.[14] [9–12]

6.15ᶜ   The Math/Science Connection: Educating Young Women for Today. Mills College, 1979. 18 minutes sound, color, 16mm or videotape cassette ¾". (Available from: Education Development Center, 55 Chapel Street, Newton, MA 02160. 16mm $115.00, $8.00 rental; videotape cassette $32.00, $5.00 rental.)

Excellent film depicts strategies in mathematics and science to encourage girls and women to learn and enjoy these subjects.[47] [7–12]

6.16[c]   Sandra, Zella, Dee and Claire: Four Women in Science. 19 minutes, color, 16mm or videotape cassette ¾". (Available from: Education Development Center, 55 Chapel Street, Newton, MA 02160. 16mm $120.00, $8.00 rental; videotape cassette $32.00, $5.00 rental.)

Film for junior and senior high school students who have an interest in science; explores the work and lives of four women: an astronomer, an engineer, a veterinarian, and a laser physicist. [7–12]

6.17[b]   Women's Work: Engineering. 26 minutes, sound, color, 16mm. (Available from: Education Development Center, 55 Chapel Street, Newton, MA 02160.)

Interviews with women engineers (civil, materials and chemical) who discuss education and training necessary to become engineers. This film shows women at work and at home, providing excellent role models.[47] [7–12]

Bibliographies/Resource Lists

6.18[a]   Science and Engineering Careers: A Bibliography. Eleanor Babco. Scientific Manpower Commission, 1974. (Available from: Scientific Manpower Commission, 1776 Massachusetts Avenue, NW, Washington, DC 20036. $2.00.)

A bibliography of guidance literature published by various organizations interested in science and engineering education.[44]

6.19[a]   Women in Science and Mathematics Bibliography. Phyllis Chinn. American Association for the Advancement of Science, 1979. 38 p. (Available from: American Association for the Advancement of Science, 1515 Massachusetts Avenue, NW, Washington, DC 20036. $1.00.)

This bibliography begins with a list of other bibliographies on related subjects and is followed by a ''journals and periodicals'' section. The main section consists of monographs and periodical articles. A rather lengthy addenda includes entries up to 1979.[44] [9–12]

SCIENCE*

Supplementary Texts

6.20[a]   The Cancer Lady: Maud Slye and Here Heredity Studies. J. J. McCoy. New York: Thomas Nelson, 1977. 84 p. $6.95.

This is a story of cancer research more than a biography of geneticist Maud Slye. Other than glimpses of her poetry and the fact that she

cried over each death of a laboratory mouse, the author tells almost nothing about her personal life and nothing at all about her childhood. The reader does find out a lot about her work: cancer research. Maud Slye's mouse studies proved that heredity was a factor in cancer, a theory that was not accepted by the majority of cancer researchers in her day. Working with little money, assistance or support of any kind, Slye devoted her life to something that is a common diagnostic tool today. Because of its technical style, this book may be most appropriate for serious secondary science students. [8–12]

6.21[a]   Chemistry Careers. L.B. Taylor. New York: Franklin Watts, 1978. 62 p.

Excellent introduction for junior and senior high school students to careers available in the field of chemistry, from chemists and chemical engineers to technical writers and patent agents. Included are salary information and required educational preparation. Book is exemplary in its use of nonsexist language, and women and ethnic minorities are represented in the photographs. [11–12]

6.22   Contemporary Women Scientists in America. Iris Noble. New York: Julian Messner, 1979. 158 p.

Brief history of women in science precedes biographies of famous women of science, such as Estelle Ramey, physiologist, and Dixie Lee Ray, marine biologist.[47] [K–6]

6.23   Contributions of Women: Aviation. Ann Genett. Minneapolis: Dillon Press, 1975. 115 p.

Biographies of six remarkable aviators: Earhart, Lindbergh, Cochran, Mock, Cobb and Howell.[47] [K–6]

6.24   Contributions of Women: Science. Diane Emberlin. Minneapolis: Dillon Press, 1977. 159 p.

Brief biographies of six American scientists: Cannon, Gilbreath, Mead, Carson, Patrick and Clark.[47] [K–6]

6.25[a]   Dentistry: The Career of Choice for Women. Council on Dental Education. (Available from: Council on Dental Education, American Dental Association, 211 East Chicago Avenue, Chicago, IL 60611. Free.)

Career pamphlet.

6.26[a]   Doctors for the People. Elizabeth Levy and Mara Miller. New York: Dell, 1979. 111 p. $1.25 p.b.

Profiles of two female and three male doctors. All not only care for, but care about their patients since they have placed commitment to patient care above anything else. One of the women is a black surgeon and legislator; the other is a feminist gynecologist. The men include a geneticist, a family practitioner and a general practitioner who works with migrant farm workers. In addition to the individual profiles, the book describes a unique clinic for teenagers which provides a wide range of medical, psychological and vocational services. [7–9]

6.27[a]   Looking Forward to a Career: Veterinary Medicine. Helen L. Gillum. Minneapolis: Dillon Press, 1976. 107 p.

This book explains what a veterinarian does and what preparation is needed for the career of veterinary medicine as well as related careers. Print size and use of photographs make this book appropriate for junior high readers.

Subcategories of ''Science,'' indicated by superscript letters following entry numbers, are designated as follows: a=Science Careers).

6.28ᵃ   Medicine—A Woman's Career. American Midical Women's Association. (Available from: American Medical Women's Association, 1740 Broadway, New York, NY 10019.)

Career pamphlet.

6.29ᵃ   New Women in Medicine. Kathleen Bowman. Mankato, MN: Creative Educational Society, 1976. 47 p.

Brief biographies of seven notable women in the medical field: Mary Calderon, sex education expert; Kathryn Nichol, pediatrician; Anna Ellington, neurologist; Mary Louise Robbins, medical researcher; Estell Rainey, endocrinologist; Margaret Hewitt, nurse-midwife; and Elisabeth Kubler-Ross, international consultant on death and dying. Unlike most of the exemplary books in the ''New Women'' series, only one of the characters in this book, Anna Ellington, is an ethnic minority (black). Book provides portraits of excellent role models. [7–9]

6.30ᵃ   Science Career Exploration for Women. Walter Smith and Kala Stroup. National Science Teachers Association. (Available from: National Science Teachers Association, 1742 Connecticut Avenue, NW, Washington, DC 20009. Stock No. 471-14748. $2.50.)

Junior high and high school level materials for teachers and others influential in science education. Includes curriculum suggestions, resource lists and background material on females at adolescence regarding careers, etc.[14] [K–12]

6.31ᵃ   Science Experiments You Can Eat. Vicki Cobb. New York: J. B. Lippincott, 1972. 127 p. $4.95 p.b.

Thirty-nine edible experiments which can be performed in the home kitchen and will make learning about science fun! Ways to investigate the properties of solutions, suspensions, colloids and emulsions; the cooking action of microbes and enzymes; and phenomena concerning carbohydrates, fats and proteins are presented in an understandable and entertaining manner. The author takes for granted that both girls and boys can be cooks and experimenters, and that the adult cook in the house is not necessarily the mother. These are excellent enrichment activities as well as a source of classroom and ''science fair'' demonstrations. [6–9]

6.32ᵃ   Science, Sex and Society. Ann E. Kammer, Cherlyn S. Granrose and Jan B. Sloan (eds.). Kansas State University, 1979. 569 p. (Available from: Education Development Center, 55 Chapel Street, Newton, MA 02160. $10.50.)

A collection of readings examining a multitude of issues relevant to the interrelationships among science and society and to the effects on the lives of women as scientists. The readings in one unit compare the experiences of women in the past with contemporary women providing a perspective on the education of women in science. Another section explores the nature of science as a field of study and career choice. This particular section also examines some ways science influences society and, conversely, how biased beliefs of a society can shape individuals' lives. Other units focus on combining family and professional responsibilities and the process by which women choose careers. An extensive bibliography accompanies each unit. An appendix provides additional references, career counseling information and extensive resources for developing an introductory course designed to encourage women to explore opportunities in science. [7–12]

6.33ᵃ   Space for Women. American Astronomical Society. (Available from: American Astronomical Society, 211 Fitz Randolph Road, Princeton, NJ 08540. Free.)

Career pamphlet.

6.34ᵃ   Watching the Wild Apes: The Primate Studies of Goodall, Fossey, and Galdikas. Bettyann Kevles. New York: E.P. Dutton, 1976. 164 p. $8.95.

This fascinating book is appropriate for free reading or as a resource or text supplement for classrooms studying the natural or behavioral sciences. The book focuses on the primate studies of Jane Goodall, Dian Fossey and Birute-Galdikas, and their observations of chimpanzees, mountain gorillas and orangutans in the primates' natural habitats. Their work opened up the field of primate ethology with startling new information that also has impact on the study of human behavior. The descriptions of the three women and their pioneering efforts, as well as the great apes themselves, provide informative and entertaining reading.

6.35ᵃ   Witches, Midwives and Nurses: A History of Women Healers. Barbara Ehrenreich and Deirdre English. Old Westbury, NY: The Feminist Press, 1973. 48 p. $1.95 p.b.

This brief, fascinating and well-researched history of women healers chronicles the participation of women in the healing arts. It also details their suppression by an elitist medical establishment composed of upper-class, white males from the middle ages to the present century. The first section of the book, 'Witchcraft and Medicine in the Middle Ages,'' discusses the witchhunt craze (14th-17th centuries) during which time thousands of women were burned at the stake, accused not only of murdering and poisoning, sex crimes and conspiracy but of helping and healing. The second section of the book, ''Women and the Rise of the American Medical Profession,'' discusses the Popular Health Movement and the political confrontation between the ''regular'' doctor (in a time when there was little medical ''science'') and the lay-practitioners, many of whom were women, blacks and poor white males.

6.36ᵃ   Women in Physics. American Physics Society. (Available from: American Physics Society, Committee on the Status of Women in Physics, 335 East 45th Street, New York, NY 10017. $.50.)

Career pamphlet.

6.37ᵃ   Women in Science and Technology: Careers for Today and Tomorrow. ACT Publications. (Available from ACT Publications, Box 168, Iowa City, IA 52240. $1.50.)

Career pamphlet.

Periodicals

6.38   AWIS Newsletter. (Available from: Association for Women in Science, 1346 Connecticut Avenue, NW, Suite 1122, Washington, DC 20036. $10.00.)

This bimonthly newsletter includes some short biographies, interviews with women working in science, as well as current events and employment information.[47]

Posters

6.39 Women in Science. Barbara Stanford. Portland, ME: J. Weston Walch, 1975.

Photographs of successful women of science, in all fields, are accompanied by a short text describing their achievements and activities.[47] [K–6]

Audiovisual Materials

6.40 Alice Evans: Bacteriologist. Center for Cassette Studies, 1972. 22-minute tape. (Available from: Center for Cassette Studies, 8110 Webb Avenue, North Hollywood, CA 91605.)

Story of the first and highly gifted female bacteriologist in the U.S.; how she persisted with her research and was eventually elected President of the Society of American Bacteriologists.[16] [7–12]

6.41 Careers in Energy. Pathescope Educational Media, Inc., 1977. Two filmstrips with cassette (13 and 12 minutes), guide. (Available from: Pathescope Educational Media, Inc., 71 Weyman Avenue, New Rochelle, NY 10802.)

Shows the great diversity of careers in the energy field and discusses the requirements for a variety of jobs, from professional engineer to coal miner and offshore rig operator.[28] [7–12]

6.42ª Careers Related to Science. Denoyer-Geppert Audio-Visuals, 1977. Three filmstrips with cassette, guide. (Available from: Denoyer-Geppert Audio-Visuals, 5235 Ravensword Avenue, Chicago, IL 60640.)

Based on interviews with women and men working in science, this program shows how they started, what they think about their work and how they work. Part I includes: meteorology, tool and die machining, chemical technology. Part II includes: drafting, nursing, gardening and National Park Service. Part III includes: pharmaceutical industry, dentistry, chemical engineering and medical illustration.[28] [7–12]

6.43ª I'm Going to Be. . . . University of California. Sound, color, 16mm. (Available from: University of California, Extension Media Center, 2223 Shattuck Avenue, Berkeley, CA 94720.)

With a little bit of magic, a girl and boy find out all about the different types of engineers. Useful for career education and elementary classes and staff development.[47] [K–6]

6.44ª Intern: A Long Year. Encyclopedia Britannica Educational Corporation Films, 1972. 20 minutes, sound, color, 16mm. (Available from: Encyclopedia Britannica Educational Corporation Films, 425 North Michigan Avenue, Chicago, IL 60611.)

Shows a woman intern rotating through different departments and experiencing day-to-day occurrences in an inner city hospital; includes her home and social life. (Note: some scenes are not for the faint-hearted.)[47] [7–12]

6.45ª People Who Help: Careers in Aviation. Bailey Film Associates. 16 minutes. (Available from: Bailey Film Associates, 2211 Michigan Avenue, P.O. Box 1795, Santa Monica, CA 90406.)

Reviews careers available in three major areas of aviation: commercial, general and aerospace. Among specific jobs touched on are commercial pilot, flight attendant, crop duster, weather forecaster, airplane repairer and aeronautical engineer. Excellent onsite footage of aviation careers in action and interviews with men and women on the job vitalize message. Good color, well-paced and a nice general summary of aviation careers, which gives special emphasis to women working in the field.[21] [10–12]

6.46ª Women in Science: Illustrated Interviews. American Association of Physics Teachers, 1975. Slides and three cassettes. (Available from: American Association of Physics Teachers, Graduate Physics Building, State University of New York, Stony Brook, NY 11794.)

This package presents interviews with six successful women scientists. Each woman talks about her background, how she became interested in science, her training and career specialty and what it is like to be a woman in a traditionally male field. [9–12]

Bibliographies/Resource Lists

6.47ª Keys to Careers in Science and Technology. National Science Teachers Association, 1973. 74 p. (Available from: National Science Teachers Association, 1742 Connecticut Avenue, NW, Washington, DC 20009.)

Lists resources for information on different careers in science and technology; includes lists of societies and associations. [7–9]

6.48ª Women in Medicine. Sandra L. Chaff, Ruth Haimbach, Carol Fenichel and Nina Woodside. Metuchen, NJ: Scarecrow Press, 1977. 1136 p. $37.50.

This annotated bibliography comprehensively covers the published literature about women physicans. International in scope, it provides over 4,000 citations to material which documents the lives of specific women physicians and groups of women physicians, as well as the history of women physicians and healers and the institutions and issues related to that history. Complete bibliographic citations are provided, along with carefully written annotations which convey the flavor as well as the content of the items. The bibliography provides citations to literature which documents the increasing involvement of women in medicine and examines the causes and future course of this trend. It includes materials that help provide insight into how the careers of most women physicians have differed from their male colleagues. The work should prove useful to persons representing a wide range of interests and information needs: researchers, guidance counselors and people and agencies in general wishing to know woman's heritage.[45]

SAMPLE LESSON PLAN: MATH AND SCIENCE
Math Stories

AUDIENCE:
Middle elementary and junior high students

OBJECTIVE:

The student recognizes sexism in a math book and rewrites one problem to make it sex-fair.

MATERIALS:

Copies of an elementary or junior high math book.

TIMING:
40 minutes

HOW TO USE:

1. Pass out math books, asking students to find a page with word problems.

2. Analyze a number of problems together:
   - What do the boys do?
   - What do the girls do?
   - Who seems to be smarter, who solves more problems?
   - Who does the most interesting activities?
   - Could the opposite sex do the same things as well?
3. List conclusions on the board.
4. Have each student choose and copy one problem as it is in the book. Then ask each student to rewrite it to eliminate any stereotyping.
5. Ask students to read aloud each original and revised problem.

COMMENT:

This work combines math, reading and writing skills.

Adapted from: *Becoming Sex Fair: The Tredyffrin/Easttown Program. Stage Three Manual: Revising the Curriculum*. Developed by the Tredyffrin/Easttown School District under a grant from the Women's Educational Equity Act Program. Newton, MA: Education Development Center, 1979. Pages 154–155.

7.0 Social Studies

HISTORY

Lesson Plans

7.1 Aba Women's Rebellion and **Hoda Sha'Arawi: Nationalist and Feminist.** African-American Institute. (Available from: African-American Institute, 833 United Nations Plaza, New York, NY 10017 or EDRS MF-$.91 plus postage, ED 132 088.)

Two papers with accompanying lesson plans designed to show the characteristics of colonialism and imperialism and their links to feminism and the women's movement. Hoda Sha'arawi was an Egyptian nationalist who carried her convictions to the feminist struggle in 1919. The paper on the Aba Women's Rebellion provides background discussion of the women's movement and colonialism in Nigeria. The lesson plans provide discussion questions, some enrichment activities and a bibliography. [7–12]

7.2 Harriet Tubman: The Moses of Her People. Ida S. Meltzer. Brooklyn, NY: Book-Lab, 1971. 30 p.

Exercise book on Harriet Tubman, to encourage reading and comprehension.[4] [4–6]

7.3 Ideas for Men and Women of the World. Kenneth Burke and Julie Kranhold. Belmont, CA: Fearon Publishers, 1974. 24 p. $1.75.

Suggestions for bulletin board displays; list of selected biographical dates.[4] [4–6]

7.4 Teaching Guide for Black Foremothers. Barbara Christian. Old Westbury, NY: The Feminist Press, 1980.

A teaching guide, developed with the help of college and high school teachers who have tested *Black Foremothers: Three Lives* in their classrooms. The guide, conceived as a kind of inservice course for teachers, includes creative teaching suggestions, student projects and annotated bibliographies of books, articles and films. [9–12]

7.5 Teaching Our Story in the Elementary Classroom: Fourteen Specific Suggestions for Teachers. Margaret Carter. *Social Education,* Vol. 39, No. 3 (March 1975), pp. 37–39.

Fourteen suggestions for lesson plans which teachers may expand upon to present women's contributions to society. Activities vary from having students gather data on how women are portrayed on television to compiling a newspaper from 1867, 1917 or 1970, noting what women as well as men were accomplishing. [K–8]

Course Outlines

7.6 "Women's Studies: Women in American History" and **"HIStory or HERstory: Changing Roles of American Women."** Beth Millstein, et al. Bureau of Social Studies, New York City Board of Education. (Available from: EDRS MF-$.91—HC-$3.29 plus postage, ED 071 954.)

Two experimental courses which can stand alone or from which teachers can select specific activities and lesson plans to incorporate into their social studies curriculum. The first course, "Women In American History," provides suggested activities to promote inquiry, discovery, independent study, research and debate around two major themes: (1) women's role in America and (2) women's struggle for equality. Sample activities include topics for debate and discussion; analysis of cartoons and advertisements for the depiction of women and the liberation movement; review of statistics on the economic and occupational status of women; and citations from literary works showing how women have been portrayed throughout history. The second course, "HIStory or HERstory: Changing Roles of American Women," provides an outline for discussion and study on the following themes: (1) the problem, (2) school case study in different roles, (3) how did we get where we are, (4) the socialization of women, (5) the role of women in the 1970s, (6) black women, and (7) toward the future. A sample activity has students examine female and male representation in their school personnel, the curriculum and student activities and then create hypotheses regarding sex role expectations. A bibliography of supplementary books, audiovisual materials and women's organizations is included. [9–12]

Supplementary Texts

7.7 An American in History (second edition). Rebecca Brooks Gruver. Reading, MA: Addison-Wesley, 1976.

Includes study guide and workbook, test items book and instructor's manual. Some good materials on women in U.S. history.[4] [10–12]

7.8   The American Women's Gazetter. Lynn Sherr and Jarate Kazickas. New York: Bantam Books. $7.95.

A geographical dictionary that lists over 1,500 places in the U.S., state by state, where women contributed to the history of our country. The alphabetical arrangement by state and city makes this gazetteer easy to use. A bibliography is available for further study, and the work is completely indexed.[22] [7–12]

7.9   Beautiful Also Are the Souls of My Black Sisters. Jeanne Noble. Englewood Cliffs, NJ: Prentice-Hall, 1978. 346 p.

A powerful history of the black woman in America, written by a black female historian. This is not a dry history book; rather, it is a history ranging from African queens who were engineers and city planners to black women in the current women's movement. Again and again their strength, capacity to endure, and to do much more than endure is emphasized. The preslave history is particularly fascinating, but the entire book will grip the reader. [10–12]

7.10   Black Foremothers: Three Lives. Dorothy Sterling. Old Westbury, NY: The Feminist Press. 192 p. $4.25.

Biographies of Ellen Craft, runaway slave and abolitionist; Ida B. Wells, crusading journalist; and Mary Terrell, suffragist and labor organizer. *Teaching Guide for Black Foremothers* also is available from The Feminist Press.[39] [9–12]

7.11   Contributions of Black Women to America: 1776-1977. Benedict College, 1979. (Available from: Benedict College, Community Development Institute, Harding and Blanding Street, Columbia, SC 29204.)

A series of booklets depicting the contributions of black women in the areas of commerce and business, the arts, education, law, medicine and health care, science, civil rights, sports and media.[44] [9–12]

7.12   Enterprising Women. Caroline Bird. New York: W. W. Norton, 1976. 256 p. $12.95.

A fascinating chronicle of the economic achievements made by women during the last 200 years of American history. The short essays about little known women not mentioned in traditional history books keep the reader's interest and show women who have influenced the status of their sex for both the better and the worse. The careers portrayed cover a variety of fields, ranging from farming and canning to banking and publishing. This book provides a clear view of what women have accomplished and will continue to contribute to the economic makeup of America. [9–12]

7.13   Famous American Women. Hope Stoddard. New York: Thomas Y. Crowell, 1970. 440 p.

Forty-one biographies of famous American women of the 19th and 20th centuries, from Jane Addams to Babe Didrikson Zaharias. The women included in this book represent a wide range of backgrounds and talents, but all have made a major contribution to the cultural and social progress of America. Each woman is viewed in terms of events and attitudes of her time, so that the reader gains an understanding of history as well as a knowledge of the historical figure herself. [9–12]

7.14   Feminism: The Essential Historical Writings. Miriam Schneir (ed.). New York: Random House, 1972. 355 p. $2.95 p.b.

This anthology of "essential historical writings" on feminist issues includes excerpts from works dating from 1776 (Abigail Adams) to 1929 (Virginia Woolf). A wide variety of selections (more than 40), accompanied by context-setting introductions by the editor, focus on feminist issues of relevance today. Contrary to popular belief, the "old" feminism concentrated on more than the suffrage issue. One section entitled, "Men as Feminists" contains excerpts from ideological and literary works written by men who were sympathetic to the condition of womankind. An informative and thought-provoking introduction to the history of feminism, this book is appropriate for high school women's studies and history courses. [10–12]

7.15   From Parlor to Prison. Sherna Gluck (ed.). New York: Random House, 1976. 285 p. $3.95 p.b.

Five American suffragists talk about their lives in this collection of oral histories. All five were involved in the early 20th century suffrage movement. Neither prominent leaders nor "unsung heros" of the movement, their stories lend another dimension to the history of the struggle for women's rights. [7–9]

7.16   In Search of Our Past. Berkeley Unified School District. Women's Educational Equity Act Program, 1981. (Available from: Education Development Center, 55 Chapel Street, Newton, MA 02160. $9.00 U.S. History Teacher Guide; $5.25 U.S. History Student Book; $11.75 World History Teacher Guide; $6.00 World History Student Book.)

These multiethnic curriculum materials for junior high school students present women's involvement during three periods in American history and three eras of world history. Through short stories, essays and a variety of activities, students learn to connect events that happened in the past with their lives today and gain insight into perceptions of themselves as females and males. The U.S. History unit is divided into "Native American Women in Pre-Columbian America," "Southern Women, 1820–1860," and "Women in Struggle, Immigration and Labor, 1820–1940." Historical information about African Americans, Chicanos, Asian Americans, Native Americans and white Americans is included. The sections in the world history unit are "Women under Feudalism in Western Europe and China," "The Industrial Revolution," and Women in Change, Twentieth Century Women in Transition." The unit includes the study of non-Western as well as Western people. [7–9]

7.17   Making Our Way. William Loren Katz and Jacqueline Hunt Katz. New York: Dial Press, 1978. 170 p. $7.95. (Originally published by Ethrac Publications, Inc. 1975).

Making Our Way is a profoundly moving collection of personal histories of men and women struggling to survive the squalor surrounding them in turn-of-the-century America. Many of the stories describe the dreams and ultimate nightmares of American immigrants. Each person who contributed to the colorful tapestry of this collection was, in one sense, a minority member wrestling with oppression. The authenticity of their portraits provides us with intimate insight, historically and personally. Ethnic minorities are well represented. Book is appropriate for junior and secondary high school students. [7–12]

7.18   Stereotypes, Distortions and Omissions in U.S. History Textbooks. Council on Interracial Books for Children.

dren (CIBC), 1977. 143 p. (Available from: CIBC Resource Center, 1841 Broadway, Room 300, New York, NY 10023. $7.95.)

A very readable and helpful book covering Asian American, black, Chicano, Native American, Puerto Rican and women's history, with bibliographies.[5]

7.19   Women and Womanhood in America. Ronald W. Hogeland (ed.). Lexington, MA: D. C. Heath, 1973. 183 p. Paperback.

A collection of essays, from Cotton Mather in colonial times to Alice S. Rossi, a contemporary sociologist, which illustrate a historical view of woman's role in America. The book does not dwell on the accomplishments or contributions of women. Rather, women as a group are seen in American history through the eyes of their male and female contemporaries. Not all of the selections are easy to read, and the flow of selections is somewhat disjointed. The teacher should note that the last essay was written in 1964. However, the book is a good supplement to the study of periods of American history. [10–12]

7.20   Women in American History: A Series. Beverly Sanders (ed.). American Federation of Teachers, 1979. (Available from: Education Development Center, 55 Chapel Street, Newton, MA 02160. $6.50.)

This series of books sketches the lives of Native American, black and white women whose lives and work influenced the development of the United States. Included are "Women in the Colonial Era and the Early American Republic 1607–1820" (56 pp.); "Women in the Ages of Expansion and Reform 1820–1860" (80 pp.); "Women during and after the Civil War 1860–1890" (72 pp.); and "Women in the Progressive Era 1890–1920" (92 pp.). Questions for inquiry and discussion are provided for each chapter, as are suggestions for projects, independent study and group activities. A general bibliography for each of the four major periods is also included. [9–12]

.21   Women of the West. Dorothy Levenson. New York: Franklin Watts, 1973. 88 p. $3.90.

Unromanticized stories of the hardships of American women— black, white and Indian—accompanied by photographs and prints.[1] [4–6]

.22   Women's Rights. Janet Stevenson. New York: Franklin Watts, 1972. 90 p. Paperback.

An introductory history of the battle to obtain votes for women in America. Short biographies of suffragists, fictionalized chapters and brief excerpts from primary source materials help make this a very readable, supplementary text for junior high students. [7–9]

ames

23   Cooperative Game about Women and Minorities American History. Dr. Nancy Schniedewinde, 1979. (Available from: Dr. Nancy Schniedewinde, 155 Plains Road, New Paltz, NY 12561.)

Board game designed to represent the roles of women and minorities in American history.[44] [9–12]

Photographs

7.24   American Women's Role: Yesterday and Today. Elgin, IL: David C. Cook Publishing, 1975.

This set of large pictures with resource guide demonstrates women's contributions to society.[4] [K–3]

Posters

7.25   Emerging Woman. Perfection Form Co., 1976. (Available from: Perfection Form Co., 1000 N. 2nd Avenue, Logan, IA 51546. $8.95.)

Two posters illustrating the history of women in the 19th and 20th centuries: Part 1: Toward Equality, and Part 2: Change and Achievement.[22] [6–12]

Multimedia Programs

7.26   America in Crisis: The Women's Movement. Audio Visual Narrative Arts. Two filmstrips, discs or cassettes, guide. (Available from: Audio Visual Narrative Arts, Box 9, Pleasantville, NY 10570. $37.50 discs; $41.50 cassettes.)

Part I: The Suffragettes describes the long struggle of women to get the vote. *Part II: The Women's Libbers* (an unfortunate title) describes the birth of NOW and the need for the women's movement.[1] [K–6]

Audiovisual Materials

7.27   Abigail Adams. Susan and John Lee, 1977. Four books and cassettes. (Available from: Children's Press, 1224 West Van Buren Street, Chicago, IL 60607.)

A biography of the extraordinary woman who actively supported the Revolution.[28] [8–12]

7.28   And Ain't I a Woman? Schloat Productions, 1975. Six, 13-minute filmstrips with cassettes. (Available from: Schloat Productions, 150 White Plains Road, Tarrytown, NY 10591.)

The struggle for women's equality is depicted through the writings and speeches of women from colonial to modern times. Outstanding artists and activists from each time period with samples of their work are identified. Topics include "Early Signs," "Feminist Fifties," "Hearthside," "Outside," "Society and Attitudes," "Toward a New Consciousness."[16] [7–12]

7.29   Angelina and Sara Grimke. Pacifica Tape Library. 30 minutes, cassette tape. (Available from: Pacifica Tape Library, Department W 3761, 5316 Venice Boulevard, Los Angeles, CA 90019.)

Portrait of two sisters, born around 1800, who became public speakers and writers on abolition and women's rights.[16] [7–12]

7.30   Aunt Molly Jackson. Rounder Records. Record. (Available from: Rounder Records, 727 Somerville Avenue, Somerville, MA 02143. $4.00.)

Songs from the 1930s in Kentucky are sung by a union organizer and a storyteller.[1] [7–12]

7.31   But the Women Rose . . . Voices of Women in American History. Folkways Records, 1971. Two cassette tapes/records. (Available from: Folkways Records, 701 7th Avenue, New York, NY 10036. $5.95.)

Excerpts from letters, diaries and speeches of well-known American women from Abigail Adams to Shirley Chisholm, discussing their status and rights.[16] [9–12]

7.32   Cavalcade of America: Frontier Widow. Perfection Form. 20 minutes, cassette. (Available from: Perfection Form Company, 1000 N. 2nd Avenue, Logan, IA 51546.)

Story of Ann Robertson, a pioneer teacher.[16] [7–12]

7.33   Dorothea Dix. Pacifica Tape Library. Cassette. (Available from: Pacifica Tape Library Department W 3761, 5316 Venice Blvd., Los Angeles, CA 90019. $11.00.)

Starting as a volunteer in the Cambridge jail, Ms. Dix became the prime mover in reforming laws affecting the insane in prison. She also organized, much to the displeasure of the male doctors, nurses for the Civil War.[1] [10–12]

7.34   Elizabeth Cady Stanton and Susan B. Anthony. Gerda Lerner. 28 minutes, cassettes. (Available from: Pacifica Tape Library, Department W 3761, 5316 Venice Blvd., Los Angeles, CA 90019.)

These two women who struggled for women's rights, especially for the right to vote, are presented as individuals with their own way of problem solving.[16] [10–12]

7.35   The Emerging Woman. Film Images, 1974. 45 minutes, sound, 16mm. (Available from: Film Images/Radim Films, 17 West 60th Street, New York, NY 10023.)

The best available film about the history of women in America from 1800 to the present; made up of original photos and films and produced and filmed by women.[16] [8–12]

7.36   Famous Women. Valiant IMC. (Available from: Valiant IMC., 195 Bonhomme Street, Hackensack, NJ 07602. $117.50.)

Series of tapes of lives and contributions of 24 women, including Carrie Nation; Harriet Beecher Stowe; Mary, mother of Christ; Queen Victoria; Eva Peron; Cleopatra. [4–12]

7.37   Florence Luscomb, Suffragist. Public Television Libraries. 29 minutes, color, videocassette. (Available from: Public Television Libraries, 475 L'Enfant Plaza, SW, Washington, DC 20024.)

Interview with a woman who was an active participant in the suffragist movement 50 years ago.[16] [7–12]

7.38   Frances Willard. Pacifica Tape Library. Cassette. (Available from: Pacifica Tape Library, Department W 3761, 5316 Venice Blvd., Los Angeles, CA 90019. $11.00.)

Willard's temperance crusade and her Political School for Women were significant because they were the first mass political movements for women in this country (mid-19th century) and provided women with organizational training.[1] [10–12]

7.39   Harriet Tubman and the Underground Railway. McGraw-Hill. 27 minutes. (Available from: McGraw-Hill, Department 410, 1221 Avenue of the Americas, New York, NY 10020.)

An all-star cast of Ruby Dee, Brock Peters, Ossie Davis and Ethel Waters recreate Tubman's first rescue mission.[21] [7–12]

7.40   Hatshepsut: The First Woman of History. Multimedia Productions, 1975. Two filmstrips with cassette, guide. (Available from: Multimedia Productions, P.O. Box 5097, Stanford, CA 94305.)

Hatshepsut ruled Egypt during the New Kingdom period and gave her country a period of peace and prosperity.[28] [7–12]

7.41   Las Chicanas: Historical and Contemporary View of Mexican-American Women. Center for Cassette Studies, 1974. 17 minutes, cassette tape. (Available from: Center for Cassette Studies, 8110 Webb Avenue, North Hollywood, CA 91605.)

Both accurate and inaccurate images of the Chicana in history are discussed, and a Chicana attorney interviews Chicanas active in La Causa.[16] [7–12]

7.42   Letters from a Woman Homesteader. Pacifica Tape Library. Three cassettes. (Available from: Pacifica Tape Library, Department W 3761, 5316 Venice Blvd., Los Angeles, CA 90019. $28.00.)

A dramatic production from the diary of Elinore Pruitt Stuart, a young widow who left her job in 1909 in Denver to go to Wyoming; farmed on 320 acres; hired herself out as a housekeeper; and married her employer with the provision that she work her own land and pay for it herself.[1] [10–12]

7.43   Life in 1900. Clearwater Publishing, 1971. Cassette tape. (Available from: Clearwater Publishing, 1995 Broadway, New York, NY 10023.)

An 84-year-old Cheyenne Sioux is interviewed about her childhood at the turn of the century.[16] [7–12]

7.44   Ms.—A Struggle for Women's Rights. Counselor Films. 14 minutes. (Available from: Counselor Films, 2100 Locust Street, Philadelphia, PA 19103.)

Rare film footage and historic sound statements portray the pioneering suffragettes who led the crusade for women's right to vote. The significance of World War II in the movement of women into the labor force and the subsequent struggle for ratification of the Equal Rights Amendment are also examined.[21] [4–12]

7.45   Ms. America. Scholastic Book Service, 1974. Filmstrip with cassette. (Available from: Scholastic Book Service, 906 Sylvan Avenue, Englewood Cliffs, NJ 07632.)

An examination of the roles women have played from colonial times to the present and how these roles are changing.[16] [7–12]

7.46   The Negro Woman. Folkways Records, 1966. Record and guide. (Available from: Folkways Records, 701 7th Avenue, New York, NY 10036.)

Excerpts (read by Dorothy Washington) from books and speeches of famous black women, such as Sojourner Truth, Ida Wells Barnett and Mary McLeod Bethune. Guide includes illustrations and bibliography.[16] [7–12]

7.47 Oh, Freedom. Sterling Educational Films. 28 minutes. (Available from: Sterling Educational Films, Division of Walter Reade Organization, 241 E. 34th Street, New York, NY 10016.)

Depicts the triumphs and tragedies of the civil rights movement that shaped the struggle for black equality in America today.[21] [11–12]

7.48 Rebecca Lukens: Woman of Steel. Center for Cassette Studies, 1972. 22 minutes, cassette. (Available from: Center for Cassette Studies, 8110 Webb Avenue, North Hollywood, CA 91605.)

Story of a determined business woman, an executive in the iron industry in 1825.[16] [7–12]

7.49 Recovering Our Past. Feminist History Research Project, 1974. 22 minutes, slides in carousel with tape. (Available from: Feminist History Research Project, P.O. Box 1156, Topanga, CA 92090.)

Using the recollections of suffragists still living, the story of the suffrage movement is vividly recounted.[16] [9–12]

7.50 Side by Side: Re-Enactments of Scenes from Women's History, 1848 to 1920. Galaxia Women Enterprises. 90 minutes, two records. (Available from: Galaxia Women Enterprises, P.O. Box 212, Department A, Woburn, MA 01801. $9.83.)

This double record album uses a narrative "You are there" technique to tell the story of how American women got the vote.[30]

7.51 Tapestry: History of Chinese and Japanese Women. Organization of American Women , 1979. 45 minutes, slide show. (Available from: Organization of American Women, P.O. Box M-71, Hoboken, NJ 07030. $25.00 rental.)

No annotation available.

7.52 The Trial of Susan B. Anthony. Bailey Film Associates. 22 minutes. (Available from: Bailey Film Associates, 2211 Michigan Avenue, P.O. Box 1795, Santa Monica, CA 90406.)

Shows the enormous inequities of the legal system and effectively spotlights a key event in women's history.[21] [7–12]

7.53 Union Maids. Julia Reichert, James Klein and Miles Mogulescu. 48 minutes, b/w. (Available from: New Day Films, P.O. Box 315, Franklin Lakes, NJ 07417. $55.00 rental, plus $5.00 handling cost.)

Three women in their 60s—Sylvia, Kate and Stella—tell the way things really were back in the days when people risked their jobs and lives to organize trade unions. They are the stars of *Union Maids,* a vivid slice of almost forgotten American history. What is especially moving is the way the film provides a quietly hopeful sense of continuity between the past and future. (San Francisco Chronicle, quoted in New Day Films publicity brochure.)[5]

7.54 Women: An American History. Encyclopedia Britannica, 1976. Six filmstrips with cassettes, 15–17 minutes each. (Available from: Encyclopedia Britannica, Educational Corporation Films, 425 North Michigan Avenue, Chicago, IL 60611.)

Excellent history of women in America from colonies to present including Indian, black and Spanish women, with each filmstrip covering a different historical period: colonial era, early 19th century, late 19th century, 20th century and current women's movement.[16] [8–12]

7.55 Women at Work: Choice. Guidance Associates, 1975. 18 minutes, color, sound filmstrips. (Available from: Guidance Associates, A/V Subsidiary, 757 Third Avenue, New York, NY 10017. $48.50.)

This unit contains two-color, sound filmstrips designed for high school students and adults which explores the changing role of women in the labor force and alternate lifestyles available to women. Part I summarizes the development of women's work roles throughout important periods in United States history. Part 2 provides interpersonal insights into the effects of work on women. A 40-page discussion guide accompanies the units.[9] [9–12]

7.56 Women in American History. Educational Activities, 1974. Six filmstrips with three records or cassettes, teacher's guide. (Available from: Educational Activities, Baldwin, NY. $61.95 record; $64.95 cassette.)

Woman's role in our history, from the colonies through the revolution, slavery, suffrage, to the present. Many well-known and lesser-known women are mentioned.[42] [4–6]

7.57 Women in the Civil War. Multimedia Productions, 1979. One filmstrip with cassette, guide. (Available from: Multimedia Productions, Box 5097, Stanford, CA 94305.)

This program shows the contributions made by women during the war, not only on the homefront but also on the frontline. Demonstrates that women's involvement in war work also affects gains in civil rights.[28] [7–12]

7.58 Women in World War II. Multimedia Productions, 1979. One filmstrip with cassette, guide. (Available from: Multimedia Productions, Box 5097, Stanford, CA 94305. $19.95.)

This illustrates the many changes which occurred during the war in women's lives in many areas—work, family responsibilities and social expectations.[28] [7–12]

7.59 Women of the American Revolution: Six Biographies. Eye Gate House, 1977. Six filmstrips with three cassettes, guide. (Available from: Eye Gate House, Inc., 146-01 Archer Avenue, Jamaica, NY 11435.)

Stories of Molly Pitcher, Deborah Sampson, Catherine Schuyler, Frederika von Riedesel, Mercy Warren and Phillis Wheatley are told within the context of their times.[28] [K–6]

7.60 Women on the March: The Struggle for Equal Rights. National Film Board of Canada. Two 30-minute films. (Available from: National Film Board of Canada, 1251 Avenue of the Americas, New York, NY 10020.)

A film record of the tempestuous struggle for equal rights that characterized the suffrage movement. Spearheaded by resolute women like Emmeline Pankhurst, the movement thrived on imprisonment, martyrdom and exile and soon caught the attention of the world. The film is divided into two parts: the first dealing with the fight for the franchise, the second with the status of women today.[21] [10–12]

7.61   Women without History/History without Women. Training Institute for Sex Desegregation of the Public Schools, 1977. Slides in Kodak carousel and script. (Available from: Training Institute for Sex Desegregation, Rutgers University, Federation Hall-Douglass Campus, Brunswick, NJ 08903.)

This slide show describes the multiple roles women played in American society between 1860 and 1920.[16] [7–12]

7.62   Women's Rights in the U.S.—An Informal History. Altana Films. 27 minutes, color, 16mm. (Available from: Altana Films, 340 East 34th Street, New York, NY 10016. $375.00; $40.00 rental.)

An award winning film about the social history of women in America.[1] [10–12]

7.63   Women's Work America: 1620-1920. Schloat Productions, 1974. Four filmstrips with cassette tapes. (Available from: Schloat Productions, 150 White Plains Road, Tarrytown, NY 10591.)

These filmstrips survey the diverse roles filled by women since the colonization of America and its subsequent history. Part I covers the life of women in colonial America; Part II, women in the world of work in industrialized society; Part III, the growth of the women's rights movement; and Part IV, the fight against prejudice and legal and social barriers which deny women equal participation in society.[16] [9–12]

7.64   The Work of Women—A History in Song. Educational Activities Inc. (Available from: Educational Activities, Inc., 1937 Grand Avenue, Baldwin, NY 11510. $6.95, LP; $7.95, cassette.)

Songs of women's concerns and needs from the Revolution till today.[1] [10–12]

7.65   Working Women's Music: The Songs and Struggles in the Cotton Mills, Textile Plants, and Needle Trades. Evelyn Alloy. Sommerville, MA: New England Free Press, 1976. 44 p. $2.50.

History of the words and music of working women of the 19th century.[4] [10–12]

Bibliographies/Resource Lists

7.66   The American Woman in Colonial and Revolutionary Times, 1565–1800: A Syllabus with Bibliography. Eugene Andruss Leonary. Westport, CT: Greenwood Press, 1962.

An organized bibliography to give students sources for obtaining a picture of the colonial woman in all aspects of her life and work. Consists of three parts: (1) a syllabus with references grouped under specific headings and subheadings, (2) a list of 104 outstanding women, with references grouped under the name of each woman, and (3) a bibliography consisting of books, magazine articles and pictorial publications about colonial women.[29] [9–12]

7.67   Women in American Labor History, 1825-1935: An Annotated Bibliography. Martha Jane Soltow and others. East Lansing, MI: Michigan State University, 1972. 150 p.

Annotated bibliography covering specific industrial trade unions, working conditions, protective legislation, etc.[4]

7.68   Women in Antiquity: An Annotated Bibliography. Leanna Goodwater. Metuchen, NJ: Scarecrow Press, 1975. $8.00.

Even a brief look at women in antiquity reveals a rich and fascinating history worthy of serious, scholarly study. *Women in Antiquity* offers an extensive, annotated bibliography of materials about the historical women of antiquity, from the earliest records to 476 A.D., covering ancient Greece, the Minoans, Etruscans, Hellenistic kingdoms, Rome and the provinces of the Roman Empire. Biographies of individual women constitute a considerable portion of the works listed.[45]

7.69   Women in U.S. History: An Annotated Bibliography. Common Women Collective. (Available from: Common Women Collective, 5 Upland Road, Cambridge, MA 02140. $2.00.)

In an excellent introduction, the authors explain their purposes and criteria used for evaluating the materials included in their bibliography. The annotations, like the introduction, show a high degree of consciousness. Arranged by subject, with no author or title index, but nonetheless a very useful book.[5]

SOCIAL STUDIES

Lesson Plans

7.70   Becoming Sex Fair: The Tredyffrin/Easttown Program (A Comprehensive Model For Public School Districts). Tredyffrin/Easttown (Pennsylvania) School District 1979. (Available from: Education Development Center, 55 Chapel Street, Newton, MA 02160. $17.75.)

This program provides a model for assessing sex bias within a school district and specific materials and processes for moving toward the goal of sex fairness in all areas of school life. Designed to be carried out in three stages under the leadership of a coordinator and coordinating committee, the program systematically and gradually involves more and more people within the district for increased support and commitment. Of particular interest to the classroom teacher will be the *Stage Three Manual: Revising the Curriculum* (408p., $8.50). It outlines a process for revising curricula at the elementary and secondary level. Numerous sample materials and resources for use or adaptation within major subject matter areas are provided. [K–12]

7.71   Checklist to Rate Your School for Racism and Sexism. Council on Interracial Books for Children (CIBC) (Available from: CIBC Resource Center, Room 300, 184 Broadway, New York, NY 10023. $2.50.)

Questions for use by students or teachers in discussing how the school and most schools are and how schools ought to be. Contain discussion pointers, group activities and readings.[10]

7.72   A Comparative View of the Roles of Women (Experimental Learning Unit, revised edition). Barbara Miller and Jacquelyn Johnson. 1976. 110p. (Available from EDRS MF-$.91—HC-$6.01 plus postage, ED 128 263.)

Twenty-two activities arranged so that students may consider two questions: (1) What are the appropriate roles of women today? and (2) What changes could equality bring to students' personal lives, the community, the nation and the global society? Each activity provides an introduction, objective, time required, materials needed, step-by-step procedures, suggested follow-up and evaluation procedures. Sample activities include asking students to examine how toys and books note sex stereotyping for children; to compare attitudes toward childbearing in various cultures; and to examine a reversal of male and female marital roles.

7.73   Crossing Cultures: Third World Women: A Book of Materials, Activities, and Ideas for the Classroom Teacher. Sharon Valiant. Training Institute for Sex Desegregation of the Public Schools. 32 p. (Available from: Training Institute for Sex Desegregation of the Public Schools, Rutgers University, Federation Hall-Douglass Campus, New Brunswick, NJ 08903. $2.50.)

These materials give a sampling of lives in other worlds; materials are on countries, lifestyles, architecture, food and costume.[44] [K–12]

7.74   The ERA Comes to New Columbia: A Simulation. Jack Rubin and Donald B. Dodd. Auburn University, 1973. 14 p. (Available from: EDRS MF-$.91—HC-$.50 plus postage, ED 099 301.)

A simulation designed to introduce students to the legislative process and the ERA. Seven students are asked to roleplay members of the Senate Judiciary Committee of the State of New Columbia, whose vote for or against the ERA will determine its passage. The committee members, each of whom represents a different point of view regarding the ERA (1) review their task, (2) break for a strategy negotiating session to discuss the issue and create a coalition, and (3) attend a session where a debate and the final vote take place. Background information, roleplay instructions and schedule outline are included. [7–12]

7.75   Images of People: Sociological Resources for the Social Studies. Boston: Allyn and Bacon, 1967.

Workbook on stereotypes and images for high school students.[4] [–12]

7.76   In Praise of Diversity: Multicultural Classroom Applications. Gloria Grant (ed.). Teacher Corps. (Available from: Teacher Corps, Center for Urban Education, The University of Nebraska at Omaha, 3805 N. 16th Street, Omaha, NE 68110 or EDRS MF-$.91—HC-$16.73 plus postage, ED 184 854.)

Fifty-one activity units written for the classroom teacher who is interested in implementing multicultural and nonsexist education in the areas of social studies, language arts, science, math and art. Each activity unit offers a rationale, desired learning experiences, suggestions for implementation, supplementary activities and instructional and background resources for teachers. The wealth of activities may be modified and adapted by teachers so that they are relevant to a particular grade level and to the needs of students. One sample activity has students developing supplementary history texts, which take into account the interests and diversity of the contributions of the many varieties of cultural groups and of both men and women. Many of the activities were designed to incorporate ideas and materials from the companion document *In Praise of Diversity: A Resource Book for Multicultural Education.* [K–8]

7.77   Sexism, Racism and Other Isms: Hidden Messages in Children's Stories ("The Princess and the Pea"). Council on Interracial Books for Children (CIBC). (Available from: CIBC Resource Center, Room 300, 1841 Broadway, New York, NY 10023. $1.50.)

A "fun" lesson plan for 5th grade through college. "The Princess and the Pea" opens a discussion of subtle ways in which sexism, racism, materialism and elitism permeate the simplest of stories. The level of discussion will vary with age, but participants learn how to spot hidden messages while enjoying a lively discussion.[10] [5–12]

7.78   Strategies for Equality: Volume I, Guidance, Social Studies, Physical Education. Training Institute for Sex Desegregation. (Available from: Training Institute for Sex Desegregation, Rutgers University, Federation Hall-Douglass Campus, New Brunswick, NJ 08903. $3.50.)

Compendium of curricular projects devised and tested by educators in their own classrooms. For teachers, coaches, counselors and administrators.[16]

7.79   Toward Equality. Betsy Wesner (ed.). Dallas Independent School District. (Available from: Dr. Joe M. Pitts, Dallas Independent School District, Box 12, Dallas, TX 75204. Limited copies.)

This collection of already existing materials and strategies may be used by classroom teachers and staff development planners interested in implementing educational change relating to sexism and racism. The materials included are geared for upper elementary and secondary levels as well as adults. A nine-page annotated reading list is also included.[14] [7–12]

Course Outlines

7.80   Changing Roles of Women: Social Studies. Betti Pate. Dade County (Florida) Public Schools. (Available from: Textbook Services, 2210 SW Third Street, Miami, FL 33135 or EDRS MF-$.91—HC-$3.29 plus postage, ED 079 227.)

A course which analyzes changes occurring in the role of American women by having students examine (1) the history of women, (2) the psychology of being a woman, (3) the various physical and emotional changes which women undergo, and (4) women's choices for a full life. The course, which outlines six major goals, provides teachers with suggested objectives and specific activities which will enable students to have a better understanding of women's roles from colonial times to the present. The guide offers discussion questions; recommended books, films and magazine articles; self-assessment quizzes; a brief history of the women's movement; and a variety of other activities designed to help students reflect on male and female images and sex role stereotypes in our society. Also included is a game, "When I Grow Up I'm Going to Be Married," which gives girls a greater awareness of the realities of women's lives, e.g., most will have a family *and* a career, whether they plan for it or not. Teachers may choose specific activities to incorporate into the curriculum or may teach the courses as a complete unit. [10–12]

7.81   Sources of Strength: Women and Culture. Far West Laboratory for Educational Research and Development, 1979. Multimedia package; teacher's guide, annotated bibliography, two audiocassettes. 701 p. (Available from:

Education Development Center, 55 Chapel Street, Newton, MA 02160. $40.00.)

Sources of Strength: Women and Culture is a high school course designed to help students relate information about how women live in other cultures—traditionally and in modern times—to their own lives and choices. Through readings, films, activities and interviews, students trace the exercise of political, economic and social power among Nigerian, Chinese, African American and Asian American women. Three units presented in the teacher's guide may be taught consecutively or separately. In "Cultural Comparisons," students use autobiographical essays to study the degree and kinds of power traditionally held by women in Nigeria and China and how that power has changed over time; in "Oral History Interviewing," students conduct indepth interviews of women they know; in "Personal Lives," students concentrate on decision making in their own lives. The annotated bibliography contains listings pertinent to the four cultures studied, cross-cultural bibliographies, teacher background resources and student readings for each unit. [9–12]

Supplementary Texts

7.82   Child of the Dark: The Diary of Carolina Maria de Jesus. Carolina Maria de Jesus. New York: New American Library, 1962. 159 p. $1.50 p.b. (Originally published by E. P. Dutton, 1962).

A diary providing a starkly realistic look at the plight of slum dwellers in a squalid Brazilian favela. Originally written on scraps of paper picked from gutters, this is the raw, primitive journal of a young black woman who struggled for survival for herself and her three children. Despite a daily battle against hunger, disease and people grown callous and brutal from deprivation, Carolina Maria de Jesus managed to write a deeply disturbing, compassionate and moving chronicle. Print size, formatting and subject matter make this book appropriate for junior high and secondary students. [7–12]

7.83   Daughters of the Earth (The Lives and Legends of American Indian Women). Carolyn Niethammer. New York: Collier Books, 1977. 281 p. $7.95 p.b. (Originally published by Macmillan, 1977).

This absorbing book presents a chronology of multiethnic Native American women's lives. Herbal remedies, childbirth and marriage rituals, sexuality, menstrual taboos, puberty rites, spiritual experiences and many other fundamental aspects of daily life are discussed in great detail. [9–12]

7.84   Fighting Shirley Chisholm. James Haskins. New York: Dial Press, 1975. 211 p. $7.95.

This is an easy-to-read biography of Shirley Chisholm, a "fighter" known for not giving up in the face of adversity and one of the most influential black politicians in recent years. The author follows Shirley's life from Brooklyn ward politics to a closely fought election in which she becomes the first black woman elected to serve in the House of Representatives. This book places special emphasis on Shirley's close family tie with her father and her parents' almost obsessive goal to educate their children.

7.85   Man's World, Woman's Place: A Study in Social Mythology. Elizabeth Janeway. New York: William Morrow, 1971. 307 p. $8.95.

A comprehensive discussion of women and their relationship to the world. The author looks at women from several perspectives: histor-

ical, biological, psychological, sexual, sociological and economical. She carefully examines social myths and roles from where and how she supposes they developed and makes comparisons between American values and norms and those of other cultures. A particularly interesting and thorough discussion on proposed differences between the sexes runs throughout the book, looking at biological, intellectual and social differences and possible explanations for their existence. This work is stimulating and probing—a useful and complete introduction to women's issues.

7.86   Masculine/Feminine. Readings in Sexual Mythology and the Liberation of Women. Betty Roszak and Theodore Roszak (eds.). New York: Harper & Row, 1969. 316 p. $4.50 p.b.

An anthology of readings viewing the subjugation of women from a variety of perspectives—sociological, psychological and anthropological. The contents are organized into four major sections: (1) a brief survey of sex stereotypes as promulgated by playwrights, philosophers, sociologists and psychologists which have been integrated in the pedagogy, psychotherapy and mass media imagery of today; (2) excerpts from the writings of male allies of feminism over the last half-century; (3) feminist writings from the thirties up to the present, including readings from the "new militancy"; and (4) a collection of women's liberation manifestos. Provides a variety of materials which teachers may use to supplement texts, build units around, provide background information, or use as take-off points for discussion.

7.87   Mirror Mirror: Images of Women Reflected in Popular Culture. Kathryn Weibel. Garden City, NY: Anchor Press, 1977. 256 p. $3.95.

A well-researched, historical survey of the images of women reflected in popular culture. The author discusses how the myths and cultural norms for women have been defined and distorted by the popular images of women in fiction, television, movies, magazines and advertising, and fashion. Although this book would be fairly heavy free reading for a high school student, it would provide a valuable resource for use in classes studying fiction, media, and the culture and sociology of women and American society. The images of minority women are only briefly discussed.

7.88   Popcorn Venus. Margorie Rosen. New York: Avon, 1974. 447 p. $1.95 p.b. (Originally published by Coward, McCann & Geoghegan, 1973).

In this fascinating and somewhat "gossipy" retrospective on women in films—on camera and off—the author asks the question whether "art" (pop culture) reflects life or life reflects "art." Although that judgment is left to the reader, the author suggests it is time to reinterpret the American Dream and the fantasy roles movies define for women as part of that dream. This book provides an excellent resource for a student or class studying the sociology of women and American pop culture by contrasting the lives of women as they were and are in reality versus the lives of women portrayed on the silver screen. Especially commendable is the emphasis placed on labor statistics and the variety of careers and jobs performed by women in "real life" since the turn of the century.

7.89   The Social Roles of Women and Men: A Sociological Approach. Helen Mayer Hacker. New York: Harper & Row, 1975. 51 p.

A guide placing women in a sociological perspective; good stimulating student discussion.[4] [10–12]

7.90   A Student Guide to Title IX. Myra Sadker. 1977. 45 p. (Available from: The Resource Center on Sex Roles in Education, The National Foundation for the Improvement of Education, 1201 Sixteen Street, NW, Room 701, Washington, DC 20036.)

Guide to rights and responsibilities of students, emphasizing right to nonsexist education.[4] [10–12]

Periodicals

7.91   Bulletin. Council on Interracial Books for Children (CIBC). Periodical, eight issues per year. (Available from: CIBC, 1841 Broadway, New York, NY 10023. $15.00 for institutions; $10.00 for individuals.)

Contains resources on sexism and racism for educators. Each issue contains editorials, articles, book and media reviews which are free from sexism and racism. Professional literature and parenting materials are also included.[44] [K–8]

Photographs

7.92   The Changing Family. Sammy Ruetenik. Set of four color pictures. (Available from: MSSAM, 6505 Alden Drive, West Bloomfield, MI 48033. $16.00.)

Four, full-color pictures printed on 13″ × 18″ sturdy board with varnished finish. Complete teaching unit is printed on reverse side, covering women in families at their work, at play, old and young, black and white, as a single head of a household and married, as they face family changes, such as moving, role reversals, death, birth of siblings, etc. Also included are suggested questions, vocabulary words, activities for art and games, and a bibliography. [K–6]

Multimedia Programs

.93   Competence Is for Everyone. University of Vermont, Department of Psychology, 1979. Multimedia. Available from: Education Development Center, 55 Chapel Street, Newton, MA 02160.)

This classroom program involves students in examining the process making judgments or appraisals of people and discovering how praisals based on sex, race or minority status can limit learning d career opportunities. Through activities, readings and video-pes, students analyze their appraisals of others and themselves; stomary actions of social institutions relating to employment, ucation and the mass media; and current changes in legal prac-es. The materials may be used as a complete course of study or as upplement to existing programs. Both the upper and intermediate el programs include teacher's guides and student texts for each of r units, two videotape cassettes, discussion guides and back-und readings. The two levels contain similar information but y in level of difficulty. [4–12]

94   Multimedia Curriculum Aids for Teaching about inority Women. Urban Affairs Department, 1979. vailable from: Indiana School District #625, Urban Af-rs Department, 360 Colhorne Street, St. Paul, MN 102.)

riculum packets, including a slidetape/filmstrip and a teacher's ual, on each of the following: minority group women, American ans, Asian and Pacific Americans, blacks and Hispanics. [K–12]

7.95   Winning Justice for All. Council for the Women's Educational Equity Act Program. Three filmstrips, student workbook and teacher's edition. (Available from: Council on Interracial Books for Children (CIBC) Resource Center, Room 300, 1841 Broadway, New York, NY 10023. $70.00.)

This curriculum unit was developed and tested in 13 classrooms across the nation. Tests revealed that the curriculum achieves a reduction in students' stereotypes about "proper" sex roles and an increase in students' knowledge of why and how to combat sexism and racism. The content includes U.S. history, focused on women of all colors and on minority people; current social practices; language arts; and some math. The 35 lesson plans can easily fit into regular reading or social studies period. The many exciting activities provide opportunities for successful integration into the entire school curriculum. Included in this package are three filmstrips: "An Equal Chance," "The Secret of Goodasme," and "Fighting Discrimination."[10] [5–6]

Audiovisual Materials

7.96   American Woman's Search for Equality. Current Affairs Films. Filmstrip with disc or cassette, discussion sheet. (Available from: Current Affairs Films, Division of Key Productions, 24 Danbury Road, Wilton, CT 06897. $20.00 disc; $22.00 cassette.)

The major issues in the women's movement are discussed, including opposition to and various levels of interest in the movement. The need for an end to job inequality is stressed.[1] [9–12]

7.97   An Equal Chance. Council for the Women's Educational Equity Act Program. Sound, color filmstrip. (Available from: Council on Interracial Books for Children (CIBC) Resouce Center, Room 300, 1841 Broadway, New York, NY 10023. $27.50.)

This sound-color filmstrip on historic and current barriers to sex and race equality uses a cartoon style. This filmstrip shows that white male babies born in the United States grow up to earn more money and have more social power than babies born female or dark-skinned. As babies race through an obstacle course, the reasons for such unequal results become clear. Some solutions are also indicated. Accompanied by supportive lesson plans.[10] [5–8]

7.98   Anything You Want to Be. New Day Films, 1971. Eight minutes, b/w, sound, 16mm. (Available from: New Day Films, P.O. Box 315, Franklin Lakes, NJ 07417. $115.00; $17.00 rental.)

This is a short, fast-paced film showing how society subtly socializes women into accepted and stereotyped roles. The main character is a bright high school girl who is told she can be anything she wants to be but receives signals that in reality she can't. This film would be useful with junior high students through adults for discussion about sex stereotypes.[9] [7–12]

7.99   Beyond Black and White. Motivational Media. 28 minutes, color, 16mm. (Available from: Motivational Media, 8271 Melrose Avenue, Los Angeles, CA 90046.)

Deals with the perpetuation of cliches about minorities which have no factual validity; parallels sex stereotyping.[16] [10–12]

7.100   The Bill of Rights in Action. Bailey Film Associates. 22 minutes. (Available from: Bailey Film Associates, 2211 Michigan Avenue, P.O. Box 1795, Santa Monica, CA 90406.)

Rosalind Wallace wants to swim on the high school boys' team but there are state by-laws which prohibit this. In an exciting medley race, we see her almost win against one of the boys' top swimmers, proving that she is capable of competing on the boys' varsity team. A lawyer takes her case to prominent members of the athletic conference but, after repeatedly being rebuffed, decides to challenge the by-laws in court.[21] [6–12]

7.101   Breaking Out of the Doll's House. Learning Corporation of America, 1975. 30 minutes, color, sound, 16mm. (Available from: Learning Corporation of America, 1350 Avenue of the Americas, New York, NY 10019.)

An authentic portrayal of 19th century society and values—which remain vestigially rooted in our social codes. The story of Nora closing the door behind her yesterday opens windows on issues of feminine identity that affect us all today.[21] [8–12]

7.102   Campaign. Churchill Films. 20 minutes. (Available from: Churchill Films, 662 N. Robertson Boulevard, Los Angeles, CA 90069.)

This film follows the state senate campaign of Kathy O'Neill, an articulate and dynamic young woman. Her superb organizational team—with women in the key positions—and her strong answers to a male interviewer's questions about her husband and children are depicted. A fine documentary with multiple uses.[21] [7–12]

7.103   The Eve of Change. Westinghouse Learning Corporation, 1973. Six filmstrips with tape cassettes. (Available from: Westinghouse Learning Corporation, 100 Park Avenue, New York, NY 10017.)

This filmstrip series covers many facets of sex discrimination. Some of the topics are discrimination in education; problems of discrimination in employment; homemaking as a career for both men and women; flight attendants and discrimination, changing attitudes toward marriage; the problems and benefits of the working wife; and discrimination in the banking and financial world.[16] [7–12]

7.104   Felipa: North of the Border. Learning Corporation of America. 15 minutes, 16mm. (Available from: Learning Corporation of America, 1350 Avenue of the Americas, New York, NY 10019.)

The intent of this film is to interest children in the ethnic diversity in the United States by acquainting them with the life of one Mexican American family.[21] [4–8]

7.105   Fighting Discrimination. Council for the Women's Educational Equity Act Program. Sound, color filmstrip. (Available from: Council on Interracial Books for Children (CIBC) Resource Center, Room 300, 1841 Broadway, New York, NY 10023. $27.50.)

A sound-color filmstrip based on a boy's dream of Sojourner Truth visiting his older sister's high school. Tactics useful in winning justice through the years are presented, such as marches, strikes, lobbies, boycotts, etc. Sojourner Truth helps the students make plans to achieve sex equity in their school.[10] [5–9]

7.106   Immigrant from America. Sterling Educational Films. 20 minutes. (Availavle from: Sterling Educational Films, Division of Walter Reade Organization, 241 E. 34th Street, New York, NY 10016.)

A remarkable film that confronts with unprecedented candor the injustice of racism in a nation of immigrants.[21] [10–12]

7.107   Indian Students. Clearwater Publishing, 1971. Cassette. (Available from: Clearwater Publishing, 1995 Broadway, New York, NY 10023.)

An Oglala Sioux senior student reviews her college experiences and contrasts them to other Native American students.[16] [7–12]

7.108   Joyce at 34. New Day Films, 1973. 28 minutes, color, sound, 16mm. (Available from: New Day Films, P.O. Box 315, Franklin Lakes, NJ 07417. $350.00; $35.00 rental.)

This award-winning film explores the changes and adjustments made by a career woman and her husband as they start a family. It explores the conflict of work versus family and how it is handled by two generations of working women. Televised nationally on PBS, this film can be used with high school and adult groups.[2] [9–12]

7.109   Male/Female: Changing Lifestyles. Educational Audio-Visual, 1974. Four filmstrips with four cassettes, guide, duplicating masters. (Available from: Educational Audio Visual, 29 Marble Avenue, Pleasantville, NY 10670.)

Surveys scientific and cultural differences between the sexes which are the basis of sex roles, traces history of sex roles and how they are changing, and shows the development of the women's movement.[16] [10–12]

7.110   Man and Woman: Myths and Stereotypes. Center for Humanities, Inc., 1975. 30 minutes, two slide carousels, cassettes and records. (Available from: Center for Humanities, Inc., 2 Holland Avenue, White Plains, NY 10603.)

Using paintings, photography, theater and movie scripts, and popular music, these sets describe how our views of men and women developed in Western culture and how these stereotypes are changing today.[16] [9–12]

7.111   Mother of Many Children. National Film Board of Canada, 1980. (Available from: National Film Board of Canada, 1251 Avenue of the Americas, 16th Floor, New York, NY 10020.)

This 1980 winner of the American Indian Film Festival award as best "semi-documentary" is a beautiful and memorable film written, produced and directed by Alanis Obomsaivire. It is much more than a story about women as told by Native American women of Canada; it becomes a story of all people and their relationships, family and community.[36]

7.112   National Organization for Women. Center for Cassette Studies, 1974. 24 minutes, cassette. (Available from: Center for Cassette Studies, 8110 Webb Avenue, North Hollywood, CA 91605.)

Founding members discuss the history, goals and accomplishments of the National Organization for Women (NOW).[16] [9–12]

7.113   The Secret of Goodasme. Council for the Women's Educational Equity Act Program. Sound-color filmstrip. (Available from: Council on Interracial Books for Children (CIBC) Resource Center, Room 300, 1841 Broadway, New York, NY 10023. $27.50.)

In this filmstrip, space creatures discuss stereotypes with a white girl, black boy and Cherokee boy, convincing the children that stereotypes: (1) are not true; (2) cause harm; and (3) are used to justify unfair treatment of women and minorities. Accompanied by supportive lesson plans. [4–7]

7.114   The Shopping Bag Lady. Learning Corporation of America. 21 minutes. (Available from: Learning Corporation of America, 1350 Avenue of the Americas, New York, NY 10019.)

The Shopping Bag Lady focuses on the humanistic values of compassion, tolerance and empathy. Raises the viewer's awareness that one day he or she will be middle-aged and old.[21] [4–12]

7.115   String Bean. McGraw-Hill. 17 minutes. (Available from: McGraw-Hill, Department 410, 1221 Avenue of the Americas, New York, NY 10020.)

A beautiful film about a very old Parisian woman who lives alone and lovingly nurtures her string bean plant. Recognizing that it needs more space and sun, she plants it in a park. Children respond to this film—one of the very few to portray old age.[21] [K–12]

7.116   We Are Women. Motivational Media. 16 minutes. (Available from: Motivational Media, 8271 Melrose Avenue, Suite 204, Los Angeles, CA 90046.)

We Are Women makes a strong case for individual rights for women and an equally strong case for what this means for men. Designed to depolarize men and women regarding women's nontraditional concept of themselves.[21] [6–12]

7.117   Woman Candidate—Running for Office Is a Victory. Blue Ridge Films. 13 minutes, color, 16mm. (Available from: Blue Ridge Films, 9003 Glenbrook Road, Fairfax, VA 22030. $200.00; $22.00 rental.)

A film about the campaign of Flora Crater—the first woman to run for statewide office in Virginia.[1] [9–12]

7.118   A Woman's Place. Schloat Productions, 1974. Four filmstrips with cassettes. (Available from: Schloat Productions, 150 White Plains Road, Tarrytown, NY 10591.)

This set explores images and myths about women, along with a discussion of biological versus environmental theories of sex role development; it also describes the women's movement.[16] [9–12]

7.119   A Woman's Place—Parts One and Two. Xerox. ? minutes. (Available from: Xerox, 245 Long Hill Road, Middletown, CT 06457.)

The traditional role of women and how it is changing in American society today is examined in this film. Details how women are now rethinking their roles in society, acting in concert to air their feelings, seeking solutions to their problems and reaching out to men to participate and help with their quest.[21] [7–12]

7.120   Women! Prentice-Hall, 1977. Ten filmstrips with cassettes, packaged in four units. (Available from: Prentice-Hall, Englewood Cliffs, NJ 07632.)

Unit I: Health and Reproduction; Unit II: Business and Women; Unit III: Lifestyles of Women; Unit IV: Women and Men Talk about Change. Each filmstrip involves a variety of women and men and viewpoints and deals with the various problems, areas and viewpoints of the women's movement of today.[16] [9–12]

7.121   Women and the Law. WTL Distribution. (Available from: WTL Distribution, Box 351, Primos, PA 19018.)

A color video course put together at the Seton Hall University Law Center. It contains 15 programs, 30 minutes each, on selected aspects of the law as it affects women. Each is an independent unit and may be used that way.[36]

7.122   Women in Politics—Why Not? Pacifica. One cassette. (Available from: Pacifica Tape Library, Department W 3761, 5316 Venice Blvd., Los Angeles, CA 90019. $14.00.)

Shirley Chisholm, New York congresswoman, speaks about the key role of women in forming a coalition of the powerless to gain power.[1] [10–12]

7.123   Women vs. the System, or the Games Men Play. Anti-Defamation League of B'nai B'rith. Two records and guide. (Available from: Anti-Defamation League of B'nai B'rith, 315 Lexington Avenue, New York, NY 10016.)

Series of recorded, dramatic incidents, illustrating some aspects of discrimination against women in the business and social world.[16] [9–12]

7.124   Worldview: Unit I. Scholastic Book Service, 1976. Five filmstrips with cassettes. (Available from: Scholastic Book Service, 906 Sylvan Avenue, Englewood Cliffs, NJ 07632.)

Using the concepts of food, clothing, homes and families, water, and arts and crafts, children are shown various cultural styles, giving them a cross-cultural perspective of society and basic social studies concepts. Differences in sex roles in various cultures are also shown.[28] [K–6]

Bibliographies/Resource Lists

7.125   American Black Women in the Arts and Social Sciences: A Bibliographic Survey. Ora Williams. Metuchen, NJ: Scarecrow Press. $6.00.

A book containing over 1200 entries of works by American black women including movies, tapes and recordings, as well as printed materials.[1]

7.126   American Women and the Labor Movement, 1825-1974: An Annotated Bibliography. Martha Jane Soltow and Mary K. Wery. Metuchen, NJ: Scarecrow Press, 1976. $9.00.

This annotated bibliography on women in the American labor movement updates an earlier edition published in 1972 under the title *Women in American Labor History, 1825-1935: An Annotated Bibliography*. The new edition contains 269 additional items, an increase of more than 50 percent over the 1972 work, and additional sections which take into account post-1935 developments. Books, monographs, journal articles, pamphlets and U.S. government publications are included. Clear annotations add to the usefulness of this bibliography and help make it a valuable source for research scholars interested in the field of women in American labor history. Thoroughly indexed.[45]

7.127   The Psychology of Women: A Partially Annotated Bibliography. Joyce Jennings Walstedt. Pittsburgh, PA: KNOW, Inc. $2.30.

Distinctly feminist, this bibliography reports objectively about what has been researched with the author's reactions as a woman in the comments. Classic and especially important entries are highlighted. The timely bibliography contains listings for infancy and childhood, young adulthood, middle and old age in Part I. Part II lists cross-cultural, general source material, primate studies, minority group status (discrimination), psychoanalytic theories (mental health) and sexuality, and physiology.[20]

7.128   Strong Women: An Annotated Bibliography of Literature for the High School Classroom. Deborah Silverton Rosenfelt. Old Westbury, NY: The Feminist Press, 1976. 56 p.

A selective, annotated bibliography for high school teachers and students who want inexpensive supplementary readings by women, which emphasize the strengths and accomplishments of women. The bibliography has organized the materials to include anthologies, autobiography and biography, drama, novels, short stories and poetry. A cross-topical index with the following categories also is provided: adolescence, female sexuality, women in the arts and professions, women and political commitment, third-world women and working class women. [9–12]

7.129   Teaching Women about Women in the Social Studies. Jean Desden Grambs. National Council for the Social Studies, 1976. (Available from: National Council for the Social Studies, 2030 M Street, NW, Suite 406, Washington, DC 20036.)

Resource book for social studies teachers who want to avoid sexism in their teaching and who want to make the contributions of women part of the study of history. Presents basic concepts to help teachers and school systems analyze their current social studies offerings, units and courses. Includes references.[34]

7.130   Women and World Development: An Annotated Bibliography. Mayra Buvinic. 1976. 162 p. (Available from: Overseas Development Council, 1717 Massachusetts Avenue, NW, Washington, DC 20036. $2.50.)

Annotated bibliography of published and unpublished works. Over 400 entries, grouped geographically within nine subject categories: (1) general studies; (2) impact of society on women's roles and status; (3) women's behavior patterns and customs; (4) socio-economic participation of rural women; (5) women's education; (6) women's work and economic development; (7) women and health, nutrition, and fertility; (8) women's formal and informal associations; and (9) women, law and policies. Critical review of research.[5]

7.131   Women: Sexuality, Psychology and Psychotherapy: A Bibliography. Emily A. Cary. Boston, MA: Womanspace.

Includes bibliographies on Counseling Women (1975) and Issues in the Psychology and Counseling of Women (1976).[4]

WOMEN'S STUDIES

Lesson Plans

7.132   Appalachian Women: A Learning/Teaching Guide. Model Sex-Fair Training Program in Educational Psychology and Guidance, University of Tennessee, 1979. 184 p. (Available from: Education Development Center, 55 Chapel Street, Newton, MA 02160.)

These materials were developed to be used for a graduate level course in guidance and counseling. However, all or some of the units could be used in the high school classroom. The four units included are "Appalachian Women: An Introduction through Poetry, Music and Prose"; "Sex Roles in Appalachia"; "Female Role Models: Historical and Contemporary"; and "Psycho-Social Aspects of the Female Experience in Appalachia." Each unit includes an introduction, objectives, facilitator's directions, learning activities, bibliography and appendix of readings and worksheets. [9–12]

7.133   The Black Female Experience in America: A Learning Teaching Guide. Model Sex-Fair Training Program in Educational Psychology and Guidance, University of Tennessee, 1979. 138 p. (Available from: Education Development Center, 55 Chapel Street, Newton, MA 02160.)

These materials were developed to be used in a graduate level course in guidance and counseling. However, all or some of the units could be used for teacher resource materials or in a high school classroom. The four units included are "Black Woman History"; "Black Women: Maintaining Personal Power"; "Relationships, Roles and the Family Life of Black Women"; and "Being Black and Female Toward Healthy Development." Each unit includes an introduction, objectives, facilitator's directions, learning activities, bibliography and appendix of readings and worksheets. [9–12]

7.134   Breaking the Mould: Lesson Aid Plans to Explore Sex Roles, K–8. Margot Smith and Carol Pasternak (editors). 122 p. (Available from: The Ontario Institute for Studies in Education, 252 Bloor Street West, Toronto, Ontario, Canada. M5S 1V6.)

Thirty-seven class projects and resources for use with K–8 students. The projects, which focus on beginning and advanced consciousness-raising, work roles, Canadian history, media and texts, are designed to offer teachers help in combatting sex stereotyping elementary schools. In addition to the curricular materials, suggestions for identifying and altering sexist attitudes and behaviors at the informal level—the "hidden curriculum"—are also included. [K–8]

7.135   Changing Learning, Changing Lives: A High School Women's Studies Curriculum from the Group School. Barbara Gates, Susan Klaw and Adra Reich. Old Westbury, NY: The Feminist Press, 1978. 256 p. $6.00.

This material was developed for young working class women at alternative high school in Cambridge, Massachusetts. The curriculum is divided into nine areas including "Messages from Society," "Growing Up Female," "Women and Work," and "Women Organizing Themselves." The units can be used as supplements English, history, psychology, anthropology, career education health courses. Throughout the packet recommendations are made on how to teach as well as what to teach.[14] [9–12]

7.136   Contributions of Contemporary Indian Women/ Curriculum Units for Intermediate Grades. Minnesota Chippewa Tribe, 1979. (Available from: Minnesota Chippewa Tribe, P.O. Box 217, Cass Lake, MN 56633.)

Eight curriculum units.[44] [4–6]

7.137   Distinguished Women. Social Studies School Service. 12 posters with teacher's guide. (Available from: Social Studies School Service, 10000 Culver Blvd., Culver City, CA 90230. $19.95.)

A series of 12 17″ × 23″ posters portraying prominent women, reproduced from photographs or paintings. Each poster includes brief captions including quotations and basic biographical information. Also includes a teacher's guide with biographical information on the women, suggested readings on each, a bibliography, and lesson plans on women's history and sex roles.[22] [7–12]

7.138   Non-Sexist Curricular Materials for Elementary Schools. Laurie Olson Johnson. Old Westbury, NY: The Feminist Press, 1974. 97 p. $6.95.

A collection of nonsexist lesson plans and projects for elementary school classrooms. Included are exercises in consciousness-raising, quizzes, checklists, a student workbook, background resources, classroom activities focusing on career awareness, history and math; and a student bibliography. Looseleaf pages may be easily reproduced for the classroom. [K–8]

7.139   Strategies for Equality: Volume III, Multi-Cultural Women's Studies. Training Institute for Sex Desegregation. (Available from: Training Institute for Sex Desegregation, Rutgers University, Federation Hall-Douglass Campus, New Brunswick, NJ 08903. $3.50.)

Compendium of curricular projects devised and tested by educators in their own classrooms. For teachers, coaches, counselors and administrators.[16] [K–12]

7.140   A Teacher's Guide to Women's Studies. Andrea B. Karls. New York: Dell, 1978. 63 p. $1.00.

Consists of short biographies, student activities, discussion (or essay) questions, resource materials and related readings to aid students in understanding the roles and options for women.[44]

7.141   Teaching Guide for Rights and Wrongs. Neale McGoldrick. Old Westbury, NY: The Feminist Press. $3.00.

A teaching guide, developed with the help of college and high school teachers who have tested *Rights and Wrongs: Women's Struggles* in their classrooms. The guide, conceived as a kind of inservice course for teachers, includes creative teaching suggestions, student projects and annotated bibliographies of books, articles and films. [7–12]

Course Outlines

7.142   Breaking the Silence: Seven Courses in Women's Studies. Feminist Studies, Goddard College, 1979. 167 p. (Available from: Education Development Center, 55 Chapel Street, Newton, MA 02160. $4.75.)

A course guide for adolescent and adult women whose access to education and employment has been limited because of race, sex or class discrimination. Written from a feminist viewpoint, the materials explore the effects of sex role stereotyping on the lives of third world, poor, working class and institutionalized women. The manual includes seven course descriptions titled: "Black Women Writers," "Introduction to Women's History in the United States," "Reading and Writing about Women's Lives," "Sex Roles and Socialization," "Women in Cross-Cultural Perspective," "Women in Prison," and "Women and Their Working Lives." A user's guide, bibliographies, suggestions for audiovisual and supplementary reading materials are also included. Each of the courses contains material for six one- to two-hour sessions. All the courses use consciousness-raising, skill building and resource sharing as methods for supporting women's efforts at change. Certain topics, such as mentors and role models, relationships, sexuality and violence against women are examined in all the courses.

7.143   Chicana Studies Curriculum Guide, Grades 9– 12. Odalmira L. Garcia. National Educational Laboratory Publishers, 1978. (Available from: National Educational Laboratory Publishers, 813 Airport Blvd., Austin, TX 78702. $7.00.)

Curriculum materials in history, education, literature, society, art and music. Includes bibliographies in topic areas.[44] [9–12]

7.144   The Choice Is Yours: A Women's Studies Curriculum for Non-College Bound High School Girls. Cynthia P. Green. (Available from: HEW, Educational Resources Information Center, Washington, DC. $5.00.)

Career awareness for non-college bound high school girls.[4] [9–12]

7.145   Female Studies VIII: Do-It-Yourself Women's Studies. Sara S. Schramm. Pittsburgh, PA: KNOW, Inc., 1975. 221 p.

A curriculum source book for teachers of women's studies courses and units.[1]

7.146   Liberating Our Children, Ourselves. Suzanne Howard. 1975. (Available from: American Association of University Women, 2041 Virginia Avenue, Washington, DC 20037.)

This is a description of women's studies courses. It includes course objectives, syllabi and readings.[8]

7.147   Women's Art and Culture. Nancy Fire Conklin and Vivian M. Patraka; **New Women, New World: The American Experience.** Carlene Bagnall, et al.; **A Cross-Cultural Study of Women.** Margot Morrow, et al.; **Women and Identity.** Ann Coleman, et al. 1977. (Available from: Women's Studies Curriculum Series, Women's Studies Program, 1058 LS&A Building, University of Michigan, Ann Arbor, MI 48109. $10.00 total set, plus $2.00 handling; $2.50 each.)

These four interdisciplinary course outlines offer conceptual frameworks and resource materials. The books include themes to be developed, lecture outlines, bibliographies and discussion questions. They may be used as the basis of a women's studies course or may be used as supplementary materials for other courses. Although designed for junior college and university level, they would be suitable for older high school students also.[14] [10–12]

7.148   Women's Studies. Gail Thomas McLure and John W. McLure. 1977. (Available from: National Education

Association, 1201 16th Street, NW, Washington, DC 20036.)

This book offers assistance to educators in structuring women's studies programs in school systems.[8]

7.149   Women's Studies for Teachers and Administrators. Merle Froschl, Florence Howe and Sharon Kaylen. Old Westbury, NY: The Feminist Press.

Materials to help schools start inservice courses on women in history, literature, social studies and sexism in education. Includes syllabi, sample curriculum materials and a list of resource organizations.[11]

7.150   "Women's Studies: Women in American History" and "HIStory or HERstory: Changing Roles of American Women." Beth Millstein, et al. Bureau of Social Studies, New York City Board of Education. (Available from: EDRS MF-$.91—HC-$3.29 plus postage, ED 071 954.)

Two experimental courses which can stand alone or from which teachers can select specific activities and lesson plans to incorporate into their social studies curriculum. The first course, "Women in American History," provides suggested activities to promote inquiry, discovery, independent study, research and debate around two major themes: (1) women's role in America and (2) women's struggle for equality. Sample activities include topics for debate and discussion; analysis of actions and advertisements for the depiction of women and the liberation movement; review of statistics on the economic and occupational status of women; and citations from literary works showing how women have been portrayed throughout history. The second course, "HIStory or HERstory: Changing Roles of American Women," provides an outline for discussion and study on the following themes: (1) the problem, (2) school: a case study in different roles, (3) how did we get where we are, (4) the socialization of women, (5) the role of women in the 1970s, (6) black women, and (7) toward the future. A sample activity has students examine female and male representation in their school personnel, the curriculum and student activities and then create a hypothesis regarding sex role expectations. A bibliography of supplementary books, audiovisual materials and women's organizations is included. [9–12]

Supplementary Texts

7.151   Crazy Salad: Some Things about Women. Nora Ephron. New York: Alfred A. Knopf, 1975. 201 p. $7.95.

Twenty-five articles written by Nora Ephron for several different magazines. Some articles are political in nature and all are somewhat satirical. Topics include women's liberation, politics, the women of Israel, consciousness-raising groups and several individual women, including Dorothy Parker. Ephron takes a piercing look at these topics but also produces articles that are fun to read. Secondary students should enjoy this book, also. [7–12]

7.152   Daughter of Earth. Agnes Smedley. Old Westbury, NY: The Feminist Press, 1976. 412 p. $4.50 p.b.

An autobiographical novel about a woman born to an impoverished midwest farm family in the 1890s. The reader sees her struggle to overcome the scars of her childhood and her vow to never love or have children which she believes are the downfall of all women. Although living in poverty in order to maintain total self-suffi-

ciency, she also manages to become educated, help other members of her family, and work for political and social causes. The author paints a vivid and often painful picture of a lonely woman in a changing world. This book examines many nontraditional roles, careers and families with an emphasis on the feminist viewpoint. The subject matter is particularly appropriate for high school students. [9–12]

7.153   Famous American Women. Hope Stoddard. New York: Thomas Y. Crowell, 1970. 440 p.

Forty-one biographies of famous American women of the 19th and 20th centuries, from Jane Addams to Babe Didrikson Zaharias. The women included in this book represent a wide range of backgrounds and talents, but all have made a major contribution to the cultural and social progress of America. Each woman is viewed in terms of events and attitudes of her time, so that the reader gains an understanding of history as well as a knowledge of the historical figure herself. [9–12]

7.154   The Feminine Mystique. Betty Friedan. New York: Dell, 1979. 420 p. $2.25 p.b. (Originally published by W. W. Norton, 1963.)

The Feminine Mystique is a sophisticated, comprehensive study articulating the essence of the women's movement in America. It is, therefore, rather intense reading, recommended for highly motivated young women and men. Selected excerpts may provide excellent impetus for class discussion and debate. [9–12]

7.155   Feminism: The Essential Historical Writings. Miriam Schneir (ed.). New York: Random House, 1972. 355 p. $2.95 p.b.

This anthology of "essential historical writings" on feminist issues includes excerpts from works dating from 1776 (Abigail Adams) to 1929 (Virginia Woolf). A wide variety of selections (more than 40), accompanied by context-setting introductions by the editor, focus on feminist issues of relevance today. Contrary to popular belief, the 'old" feminism concentrated on more than the suffrage issue. One section entitled, "Men as Feminists" contains excerpts from ideological and literary works written by men who were sympathetic to the condition of womankind. An informative and thought-provoking introduction to the history of feminism, this book is appropriate for high school women's studies and history courses. [10–12]

7.156   From Parlor to Prison. Sherna Gluk (ed.). New York: Random House, 1976. 285 p. $3.95 p.b.

Five American suffragists talk about their lives in this collection of oral histories. All five were involved in the early 20th century suffrage movement. Neither prominent leaders nor "unsung heroines" of the movement, their stories lend another dimension to the history of the struggle for women's rights. [7–9]

7.157   I'm Running Away from Home but I'm Not Allowed to Cross the Street. Gabrielle Burton. Pittsburgh: KNOW, Inc., 1972. 206 p. $4.50.

This very readable book has been subtitled "A Primer of Women's Liberation." It will provide young women of all ages a gentle, humorous and thoughtful introduction to feminist issues as well as a guide for "learning to cross the street." Highly recommended!

7.158   A Pictorial History of Women in America. Ruth Warren. New York: Crown, 1975. 228 p. $7.95.

A very readable history that pays tribute to American women—from Jamestown and Plymouth colony settlers to 20th century women active in sports, politics, the sciences and the performing arts. Although women are shown in a wide variety of careers and roles, the contributions of American ethnic minority women are fragmented primarily into two chapters: "Indian Women—the First American Women" and "The Black Revolution." The contributions of other ethnic minorities have been ignored.

7.159 Rights and Wrongs: Women's Struggles. Susan Cary Nicholas, Alice M. Price and Rachel Rubin. Old Westbury, NY: The Feminist Press, $3.25.

A concise overview of the law as it affects women in such areas as employment, domestic relations, constitutional rights and reproductive control. *Teaching Guide for Rights and Wrongs* also is available from The Feminist Press.[39]

7.160 We, the American Women. U.S. Department of Commerce, Bureau of the Census, 1973. 13 p. (Available from: Superintendent of Documents, U.S. Government Printing Office, Washington, DC 20402. $.45.)

Colorful graphics and photographs effectively highlight this brief but salient presentation of statistics on women in America. Much of the material could be used to make transparencies or otherwise be used in a workshop or classroom setting.[44] [9–12]

7.161 Woman's Almanac: 12 How-To-Handbooks in One. Kathryn Paulsen and Ryan A. Kuhn (eds.). Philadelphia: Lippincott, 1976. 624 p.

Practical information on health, education, money, politics, legal problems, etc., for women; presented in an easy-to-use and fascinating way.[4] [10–12]

7.162 Women of Crisis: Lives of Struggle and Hope. Robert Coles and Jane Hallowell Coles. New York: Dell, 1978. 291 p. $4.95 p.b.

Five poor, working class American women—two whites, one black, one Eskimo and one Chicana—describe in their own words their hopes, dreams, fears, conflicts and struggles. Despite the fact that none of these women sees herself as a feminist or as politically aware or educated, each shares a common sense of what it is like to grow up as a woman in America. The authors supply additional information and observations, providing a book in which complex issues of race, class and sex vividly come to life. [9–12]

7.163 Women Working: An Anthology of Stories and Poems. Nancy Hoffman and Florence Howe (eds.). Old Westbury, NY: The Feminist Press, 1979. 264 p. Paperback.

An excellent collection of 34 short stories and poems about women working: in the office, in the factory and at home, as artists, political activists, servants and professionals. More than half the selections focus on women doing unpaid work, which commonly goes unrecognized as "work." Many unknown women writers are represented, as well as better known authors, such as Willa Cather and Sholem Asch. Interesting biographical information on the authors and poets and a thought-provoking introduction to each section. [9–12]

7.164 Women's Liberation and Revolution. Sheila Rowbotham. Old Westbury, NY: The Feminist Press, 80 p. $3.95.

An exciting reading list which focuses on the relationship between feminism and revolutionary politics.[39] [9–12]

7.165 Young and Female. Pat Ross (ed.). New York: Vintage Sundial, 1972. 107 p. $2.95 p.b. (Originally published by Random House, 1972).

An anthology of easy-to-read, first-person accounts of turning points in the lives of eight American women: Shirley MacLaine, Shirley Chisholm, Dorothy Day, Emily Hahn, Margaret Sanger, Althea Gibson, Edna Ferber and Margaret Bourke-White. The selections have been taken from the women's autobiographies, where they describe with spirit, self-confidence and humor how they overcame the limited roles traditionally assigned to girls. Appropriate for free reading or as supplemental classroom text.

7.166 The Young Woman's Guide to Liberation. Karen DeCrow. Indianapolis: Bobbs-Merrill, 1971. 200 p. Paperback.

This introduction to feminist issues and the liberation movement, written by the former director of National Organization for Women (NOW), provides a cogent analysis of the various sources in our culture that have continued to make women feel, think and act like second-class citizens. Although it is rather "militant," this book is an invaluable aid for encouraging high school aged young women and men to examine the influences deeply rooted in our culture for the past 6,000 years which have tended to keep women from participating in society as fully-equipped, competent and self-loving individuals.

Periodicals

7.167 Heresies: A Feminist Publication on Art and Politics. (Available from: *Heresies*, P.O. Box 766 Canal Street Station, New York, NY 10013. $11.00 one year/4 issues for individuals; $18.00 for institutions.)

Heresies is an idea-oriented journal devoted to examining art and politics from a feminist perspective. Each issue has both a different theme and a different editorial staff made up of women from the community who want to work on the issue. An open meeting is held both to form the issue collective and to evaluate the issue after it is published. *Heresies* seeks the participation and involvement of all feminists, in this country and abroad. ISSUES: #6 On Women & Violence; #7 Women Working Together; #8 Third World Women in the U.S., The Politics of Being Other; #9 Women Organized/ Women Divided: Power, Propaganda & Backlash; #10 Women & Music; #11 Women & Architecture; #12 Sexuality; and #13 Feminism & Ecology.[7]

7.168 Women's Studies Newsletters. (Available from: The Feminist Press, Old Westbury, NY 11568. $7.00 per year/4 issues for individuals; $12.00 for institutions.)

A quarterly published by The Feminist Press and the National Women's Studies Association. Contains articles on women's studies at all levels of education: new programs, innovative courses, teaching techniques, curricular materials, book reviews, conference reports, bibliographies and job information.

Photographs

7.169 Asian Women in the U.S. Visual Communications. (Available from: Visual Communications, 313 South San Pedro Street, Los Angeles, CA 90013. $20.00 rental.)

Includes 43 photos with text.[35]

7.170   Distinguished Women. Social Studies School Service, 1976. (Available from: Social Studies School Service, 10000 Culver Blvd., Culver City, CA 90230. $19.95.)

A series of 12 17½" × 23" posters portraying prominent women. Each poster includes a brief caption; the set includes a teacher's guide.[44]

Multimedia Programs

7.171   Edupak on Sex Role Stereotyping. Multimedia package (Available from: NEA Order Department, Academic Building, Sawmill Road, West Haven, CT 06516. $79.50.)

This package contains the two filmstrip units "Cinderella Is Dead!" and "The Labels and Reinforcement of Sex Role Stereotyping"; three books on nonsexist education, sex stereotyping in schools and women's studies; four cassette tapes including discussions on sexism, racism and classism in schools; a four-part tape on women's rights and multicultural equity; and two research reports and pamphlets. Each item can also be ordered separately. A publication list is available.[2]

Audiovisual Materials

7.172   Accomplished Women. Films Incorporated. 25 minutes, color, 16mm. (Available from: Films Incorporated, 440 Park Avenue, South, New York, NY 10046. $360.00; $26.00 rental.)

If they were men, this movie would not have been made—interviews with Katherine Graham, Dr. Virginia Apgar, LaDonna Harris, Shirley Chisholm, Nikki Giovanni and Helen Reddy.[1] [7–12]

7.173   American Woman: New Opportunities. Chrome Yellow Films. Two filmstrips with two cassettes, 9–11 minutes, teacher's guide. (Available from: Butterick Publishing, 161 Sixth Avenue, New York, NY 10013. $45.00.)

Successful women discuss their lives; high school students discuss their ideas. Teacher's manual includes classroom activities and suggested reading. Preview available.[5] [7–12]

7.174   American Women: Portraits of Courage. McGraw-Hill. 53 minutes. (Available from: McGraw-Hill, Department 410, 1221 Avenue of the Americas, New York, NY 10020.)

A survey of outstanding American women and their contributions to the American experience.[21] [7–12]

7.175   Asian American Women vs. The Women's Movement. Pacifica, 1979. 33 minutes, cassette tape. (Available from: Pacifica Tape Library, Department W801, 5316 Venice Boulevard, Los Angeles, CA 90019. Order #AZ0297. $11.00.)

A panel of Asian American women talk about their experiences with the women's movement.[35]

7.176   Chinatown Celebration of International Women's Day. Chinese for Affirmative Action, 1973. 30-minute tapes, videoreels or videocassettes. (Available from:

Chinese for Affirmative Action, 950 Stockton, San Francisco, CA 94111. $30.00 deposit, $10.00 returned for 1" videoreels; $40.00 deposit, $20.00 returned, for ¾" videocassettes.)

A tribute to the contributions women have made at home, at work, in our society and in our culture.[5]

7.177   Growing Up Female. New Day Films, 1971. 50 minutes, b/w, sound, 16mm. (Available from: New Day Films, P. O. Box 315, Franklin Lakes, NJ 07417. $400.00; $60.00 rental.)

This film shows the socialization of women through a personal look at six females, ages 4 to 35. Their backgrounds vary from poor black to upper middle-class white. The influences of parents, teachers, counselors, media and advertising, pop music and marriage are examined. This film was presented nationally as a PBS television special in 1974.[2] [10–12]

7.178   Helen Keller and Her Teacher. McGraw-Hill. 27 minutes, 16mm. (Available from: McGraw-Hill, Department 410, 1221 Avenue of the Americas, New York, NY 10020.)

Obviously done on a small budget, this film shows the strain in settings that are less than authentic, an over-reliance on music and amateurish performances. What does emerge, though, is the depth of love between the two women and their incredible strength.[21] [4–12]

7.179   Hey, Big Spender! Women in Advertising. Perfection Form Company, 1977. Filmstrips with cassette. (Available from: Perfection Form Company, 1000 N. 2nd Avenue, Logan, IA 51546.)

Shows how advertising reinforced the woman's role as nurturer and servant to her husband and children and how women were encouraged to develop new roles in careers now considered stereotyped and traditional.[16] [7–12]

7.180   Images of Country Women: A Patchwork Quilt. Blue Ridge Films, 1975. 29 minutes, 16mm. (Available from: Blue Ridge Films, 9003 Glenbrook Road, Fairfax, VA 22030.)

Four country women shown in their everyday lives discuss their experiences and roles as women. The women are a black secretary, dairy farmer, a housewife and an artist. An excellent portrait of rural life in America.[16] [8–12]

7.181   Lucy Covington: Native American Indian. Encyclopedia Britannica Educational Corporation Films, 1978. 16 minutes, sound, color, 16mm. (Available from: Encyclopedia Britannica Educational Corporation Films, 425 North Michigan Avenue, Chicago, IL 60611.)

Granddaughter of a chief, this Native American woman ranches the Colville Reservation and serves as a spokesperson for her people, protecting their heritage.[28] [7–12]

7.182   Pearls. Educational Film Center, 1979. Five minute videotapes, color. (Available from: Educational Film Center, 5401 Port Royal Road, Box 1444, Springfield, VA 22151. Free rental.)

A five-part series. The video entitled "Ourselves" features women of diverse ages and backgrounds discussing their views on the Asian female experience in America.[35]

7.183 Portraits of Three Chinese-American Women. Chinese for Affirmative Action, 1973. 30 minutes, b/w, videoreel or videocassette. (Available from: Chinese for Affirmative Action, 950 Stockton, San Francisco, CA 94111. $15.00 deposit, $5.00 returned, for 1″ videoreel purchase; $20.00 deposit, $10.00 returned, for ¾″ videocassette rental.)

Made for young adults to demonstrate the use of oral history material and to document Asian American history. Three Chinese American actresses portray three Chinese American women of widely varying ages and experiences, each talking about her own life. The dialogue moves fast and sometimes overlaps, so it is not always readily understandable. Since the presentation takes up only the first half of the tape, it could be played several times for greater clarity. This tape can also be used to demonstrate one way students can elaborate on the oral histories they will gather.[5] [10–12]

7.184 The Silenced Majority. Media Plus, Inc. Multimedia. Five filmstrips with discs or cassettes, multimedia guide, posters, stickers. (Available from: Media Plus, Inc., 60 Riverside Drive, Suite 11D, New York, NY 10024. $85.00.)

A five-part media kit produced by feminists covering jobs, education, advertising and other women's issues. A recommended first purchase. Includes: "Liberation Now"; "Women, Jobs and the Law"; "Women and Education"; "This Ad Insults Women"; and "Rapping with the Feminists."[1] [8–12]

7.185 Sometimes It's Awful Hard. Women and Work Video and Discussion Project. 30 minutes, videocassette. Available from: Women and Work Video and Discussion Project, University of Michigan, Ann Arbor, Michigan 48109.)

Interviews with a number of women in different life situations: homemaker, lawyer, retired household worker, ambulance attendant and grocery store clerk.[16]

7.186 Watch Out Girlie: Women's Liberation Is Gonna Get Your Momma. University Christian Movement. Available from: University Christian Movement, 11 Garden Street, Cambridge, MA 02138.)

An effective slide show about the issues of the women's movement. The pop background music makes a humorous and moving introduction to feminist issues.[1] [9–12]

7.187 Women of Russia. International Films Foundation, Inc. 11 minutes, color. (Available from: International Films Foundation, Inc., Suite 916, 475 Fifth Avenue, New York, NY 10017. $150.00.)

The role of women in Russia—from ballerinas to bricklayers, students to peasants—all working for family and country.[1] [4–9]

7.188 Women: The Forgotten Majority. Denoyer Geppert Audio-Visuals, 1971. Two filmstrips with cassettes. Available from: Denoyer Geppert Audio-Visuals, 5235 Ravenswood Avenue, Chicago, IL 60640.)

A provocative and thought-provoking discussion of the recent women's movement, based on a speech by Gloria Steinem.[16] [9–12]

7.189 Women Today. Guidance Associates. Two filmstrips with discs or cassettes, discussion guide. (Available from: Guidance Associates, A/V Subsidiary, 757 Third Avenue, New York, NY. $48.50.)

Explores key feminist issues and challenges students to discuss the movement's effect on their lives, with commentary by activists.[1] [7–12]

7.190 Young and Female; Selected Biographies from the Book by Pat Ross. Caedmon Records, 1975. Record/cassette. (Available from: Caedmon Records, Inc., 505 Eighth Avenue, New York, NY 10018.)

Excerpts read from the works of well-known American women—Margaret Sanger, Shirley Chisholm, Margaret Bourke-White, etc.[16] [9–12]

Bibliographies/Resource Lists

7.191 Asian Women. Berkeley: University of California, 1971. 144 p. $3.50.

A beginning selected bibliography compiled, annotated and edited by Asian American and white women in the Asian Studies women's class. The bibliography focuses on Chinese and Japanese women.[5] [9–12]

7.192 The Chicana: A Comprehensive Bibliographic Study. Roberto Cabello-Argandona and others. 1975. 308 p. Illustrated. (Available from: University of California, Chicano Studies Center, 405 Hilgard Avenue, Los Angeles, CA 90024.)

Includes film serials, books and articles on a variety of subjects; indexed.[4] [7–12]

7.193 Hispanic Women and Education. Women's Educational Equity Communications Network. 17 p. (Available from: Women's Educational Equity Act Program, U.S. Department of Education, Donahoe Building, Room 1105, 400 Maryland Avenue, SW, Washington, DC 20202.)

This publication includes listings of bibliographies, journal articles, statistical profiles and curriculum materials dealing with women of Hispanic origin in the United States. Sections of the bibliography deal with the participation of and influences on the Hispanic woman in education, the labor force and in society. A list of Hispanic organizations and resource groups also is included.[40]

7.194 The Modern Arab Woman: A Bibliography. Michelle Raccagni. Metuchen, NJ: Scarecrow Press, 1978. 272 p. $13.50.

Raccagni has compiled a comprehensive bibliography of some 3,000 books, articles, reports and dissertations dealing with the Arab woman in all matters of religion, marriage and family life, judicial status and feminist issues since the 1890s. The bibliography includes works in Western languages, primarily English and French, as well as Arabic sources. *The Modern Arab Woman* identifies a considerable number of Arabic primary sources as well as important works in English and French that are often bypassed by researchers because they are little known. It is an indispensable tool for anyone seriously interested in researching the past and/or current roles played by the Arab woman in her society.[45]

7.195   New Feminist Scholarship: A Guide to Bibliographies. Jane Williamson. Old Westbury, NY: The Feminist Press. $15.00.

This new, annotated bibliography brings together nearly 400 bibliographies on every aspect of women's lives and history in one indispensable volume. The most comprehensive such volume to date, *New Feminist Scholarship* is organized into 30 subject headings which include anthropology and sociology, art and music, childcare, history, lesbians, psychology, third world countries and work. An essential research tool for student, teacher and general reader.[19] [9–12]

7.196   Raza Women. (Available from: Concilio Mujeres, 2588 Mission Street, Room 237, San Francisco, CA 94100.)

A bibliography of materials dealing with Chicano and Spanish women.[1]

7.197   A Resource Guide on Black Women in the United States. Arlene B. Enabulele and Dionne Jones. Howard University, 1978. 107 p. (Available from: Institute for Urban Affairs and Research, Howard University, 2900 Van Ness Street, NW, Washington, DC 20008. $3.95.)

Contains statistical data, a list of national organizations, special education and employment programs, and a bibliography.[33]

7.198   Rural Women and Education: Annotated Selected References and Resources. Women's Educational Equity Communications Network. (Available from: Women's Educational Equity Act Program, U.S. Department of Education, Donahoe Building, Room 1105, 400 Maryland Avenue, SW, Washington, DC 20202. $2.50.)

Describes books, articles, bibliographies, periodicals and other resources dealing with rural women in history, in the workforce and in education.[17]

7.199   Strong Women: An Annotated Bibliography of Literature for the High School Classroom. Deborah Silverton Rosenfelt. Old Westbury, NY: The Feminist Press, 1976. 56 p. $1.95.

A selective, annotated bibliography for high school teachers and students who want inexpensive supplementary readings by women, which emphasize the strengths and accomplishments of women. The bibliography has organized the materials to include anthologies, autobiography and biography, drama, novels, short stories and poetry. A cross-topical index with the following categories also is provided: adolescence, female sexuality, women in the arts and professions, women and political commitment, third-world women and working class women. [9–12]

7.200   Women's Book of World Records and Achievements. Lois O'Neill. New York: Doubleday, 1979. 798 p. $9.95.

This almanac-style collection of portraits and summaries is full of interesting information and facts regarding the achievements of women.[44] [7–12]

7.201   Women's Studies: A "Core Bibliography." Esther Stineman. (Available from: Libraries Unlimited, Inc., P.O. Box 263, Littleton, CO 80160. $27.50.)

Ms. Stineman, women's studies librarian-at-large for the University of Wisconsin system, has compiled a compendium of most of the works produced by women. This even includes a guide to related pieces appearing in periodicals.[14]

7.202   Women's Studies Abstracts. New York: Rush Publishing Company. $20.00/year (quarterly) for individuals; $25.00 for libraries.

Bibliographic essays, abstracts and bibliographic lists; indexed. A basic source, though its coverage is selective. Black women, for example, are covered well, but Chinese American women are not.[5]

7.203   Women's Studies Bibliography. Massachusetts Institute of Technology (MIT). (Available from: MIT Humanities Library, Room 14S-200, Cambridge, MA 02116. $3.00.)

A list of part of the collection at the Humanities Studies Collection at MIT; including newspaper and journal articles, unpublished theses, and papers and ephemera of the women's movement.[1]

7.204   Women's Studies Film List. University of Michigan Audio-Visual Education Center. (Available from: University of Michigan Audio-Visual Education Center, 416 Fourth Street, Ann Arbor, MI.)

A listing of films available through the center which are appropriate for women's studies courses at all grade levels.

7.205   Women's Studies Sourcebook: A Comprehensive Classified Bibliography. Judith D. King, 1976. 68 p. (Available from: Grand Valley State College Library, College Landing, Allendale, MI 49401. $3.00.)

Bibliography on topics from abortion to women's rights.

7.206   Women's Work and Women's Studies. Kirsten Drake, Dorothy Marks and Mary Wexford. Pittsburgh, PA: KNOW, Inc., 1972. 175 p. $4.50.

Bibliography of the year's scholarly research on women; directory of women's organizations, action projects and communication outlets.[20]

SAMPLE LESSON PLAN: SOCIAL STUDIES
Institutional Sexism in Social Studies Instruction

AUDIENCE:

Secondary 20th century American history students

OBJECTIVE:

To encourage students to become aware of institutional sexism in a "traditional" 20th century history and social studies unit. The project will focus on the Eisenhower and Kennedy period which is particularly important because of the civil rights activities during this era of history.

MATERIALS:

Two texts, *Episodes in American History* (Burns) and *A History of the United States from 1877* (Resjord); three films, "Dwight D. Eisenhower," "Age of Kennedy," and "Martin Luther King"; antidiscrimination law handouts.

LEARNING ACTIVITIES:

1. Have students examine the assigned reading material and films for sex role stereotypes and bias.

2. Have students discuss how traditional history instruction teaches sex role stereotypes and reflects a biased view of the world by omitting contributions of women.

3. Ask students to list ways in which a "male dominated" society is presented through the eyes of male historians in history texts.

4. Provide students with information on antidiscrimination laws and discuss how the laws guarantee rights for students and employees in educational institutions:
   - Title IX of the Education Amendments of 1972
   - Title VI of the Education Amendments of 1972
   - Title VII of the Civil Rights Act of 1964
   - Equal Pay Act, as amended in 1972
   - Vocational Education Act of 1963
   - Executive Orders 11246/11375
   - Rehabilitation Act of 1973
   - Pregnancy Discrimination Act
   - Age Discrimination Act

Adapted from a Sex Equity Action plan developed by Elwood Ostrom (Lakeridge High School, Lake Oswego (Oregon) School District), in a BIAS (Building Instruction Around Sex Equity) inservice training workshop, January 1980.

8.0 Sex Equity Organizations

WOMEN'S EDUCATIONAL EQUITY

8.1   American Federation of Teachers, Women's Rights Committee, 11 Dupont Circle, NW, Washington, DC 20036, (202) 797-4400.

This group has produced a number of pamphlets about women's rights for the teacher.[1]

8.2   Asian Women United, Suite 5A, 170 Park Row, New York, NY 10038.

A grassroots feminist group committed to educating Asian and Pacific American (APA) women and the community at large about issues important to their lives through forums, discussions and workshops.[35]

8.3   Black Women's Educational History Project, Minority Concerns Committee, National Association for Women Deans, Administrators and Counselors (NAWDAC), 1028 Connecticut Avenue, NW, Washington, DC 20036, (202) 659-9330.

Begun in 1978, the project houses tapes and transcripts of NAWDAC panels and interviews relevant to black women.[33]

8.4   Council of Asian American Women, Inc., 3 Pell Street, New York, NY 10013, (212) 349-4417.

One of the organization's primary goals is to establish the first Asian American women resource center in New York.[35]

8.5   Feminist History Research Project, P.O. Box 1156, Topanga, CA 90290, (213) 455-1283.

An excellent slide show about women in history available from this group; other programs about women forthcoming.[1]

8.6   Links, Inc., 1522 K Street, NW, Suite 404, Washington, DC 20005, (202) 783-3888.

Each of the 174 chapters of this black women's organization are involved in educational, cultural and civic activities in their own communities. One focus for 1979 was educational and career counseling for high school girls.[33]

8.7   National Alliance of Black Feminists, 202 South State Street, Suite 1024, Chicago, IL 60604, (312) 939-0107.

Conducts conferences, forums, panels, workshops and speak-outs on issues of concern to black women.[33]

8.8   National Archives for Black Women's History, National Council of Negro Women, 1318 Vermont Avenue, NW, Washington, DC 20005, (202) 332-1233.

Initially begun in 1940 and reactivated in 1977, the archives comprises the largest collection of black women's history.[33]

8.9   National Association for Girls and Women in Sports (NAGWS), 1900 Association Drive, Reston, VA 22091, (703) 476-3450.

This membership organization serves the interests of teachers, coaches, officials, trainers and administrators of women's programs at all levels. It publishes official guides and rulebooks and sponsors conferences.[2]

8.10   National Black Feminist Organization, 14414 Innsbruck Court, Silver Springs, MD 20906, (301) 598-5480.

Established in 1973, ten chapters of black women activists have been set up.[33]

8.11   National Coalition for Sex Equity in Education (NCSEE), P.O. Box 288, Sacramento, CA 95802, (916) 322-7388.

NCSEE was formed in 1980 with the purpose of enhancing, fostering, influencing and expediting the effective infusion of sex equity concepts into existing educational processes. Membership is open to all persons who have official responsibilities for the advancement of sex equity in education.

8.12   National Council of Negro Women, Inc., 1819 H Street, NW, Suite 900, Washington, DC 20006, (202) 293-3902.

This umbrella group of 11 regional organizations and 20 local sections has created 14 human service programs. Their concern include education and career counseling for youths and women and the preservation of black women's history.[33]

8.13 National Hook-Up of Black Women, Inc., 2021 K Street, NW, Suite 305, Washington, DC 20006, (202) 293-2323.

A communications network of black women dedicated to improving the condition of black women and the black community overall. The compilation of a national registry of black women's organizations is planned.[33]

8.14 National Women's History Network, P.O. Box 3716, Santa Rosa, CA 95402, (707) 526-5974.

Beginning with the first observance of Women's History Week, project staff have created an effective network for the promotion of National Women's History Week and the integration of women's history in the curriculum. Serves as a resource center for women's history materials and conducts training sessions. Brochure is available.

8.15 New Directions for Young Women, 376 Stone Avenue, Tucson, AZ 85701, (602) 623-3677.

This organization presents and sponsors workshops for young women and adults; provides consultation services for community agencies and schools and presents workshops on sex role stereotyping, nonsexist curriculum and sex bias for school personnel. The staff has developed a program called the Sex Stereotyping Awareness Tool (SSAT) to increase educators' and counselors' awareness and knowledge of the special vocational needs of young women. SSAT is now being tested and will be available in 1981.[1]

8.16 Organization of Chinese American Women, 956 North Monroe Street, Arlington, VA 22201, (703) 522-6721.

With over 1500 members and 19 chapters throughout the country, this national organization is involved in overcoming barriers to the full participation of Chinese American women in American society. Write for the proceedings from their first national conference on *Chinese American Women in Voluntary Community Service and Leadership* ($2.00).

8.17 Organization of Pan Asian American Women, Inc., 915 15th Street, NW, Washington, DC 20005, (202) 737-1377.

An organization active in facilitating appointment of Asian and Pacific American (APA) women to national advisory committees and councils; educating and promoting public awareness of APA women; developing leadership skills of APA women; and establishing a national communications network among APA women's groups, APA groups and other women's organizations.[35]

8.18 Project on Equal Education Rights (PEER), 1112 13th Street, NW, Washington, DC 20005, (202) 332-7337.

PEER monitors and publicizes enforcement progress and problems of Title IX implementation. It provides information to individuals and organizations via a newsletter, free publications, reprints of articles and information papers. "Cracking the Glass Slipper: PEER's Guide to Ending Sex Bias in Your School" is a kit for parent and citizen action groups who want to check on Title IX progress in their local schools. A publications list is available.[2]

8.19 Project on the Status and Education of Women, Association of American Colleges, 1818 R Street, NW, Washington, DC 20009, (202) 387-1300.

The project develops and distributes free materials which identify and highlight issues and federal policies affecting women's status as students and employees. These materials include a quarterly newsletter; information on Title IX; information on recruiting students, employees and minority women; as well as topical papers on subjects concerning the impact of the 1976 Education Amendments on women and girls in vocational education and working women. A publications list is available.[2]

8.20 CCSSO Resource Center on Sex Equity, Council of Chief State School Officers, 400 North Capitol Street, NW, Suite 379, Washington, DC 20001, (202) 624-7757.

This organization has produced several publications dealing with the elimination of sex discrimination, sex bias and sex stereotyping in education. It publishes a newsletter, *Research/Action Notes,* containing information on activities and resources relating to the alleviation of sexism in elementary and secondary education. Currently, they are developing training materials for vocational educators to eliminate sex role stereotyping in vocational education.[9]

8.21 Women's Educational Equity Act Program (WEE-AP), 400 Maryland Avenue, SW, Washington, DC 20202, (202) 245-2181.

WEEAP is a discretionary grants program supporting numerous activities, including the development, evaluation and dissemination of curricula, textbooks and other educational materials. A limited supply of their annual report is available free on request; it provides a brief description of legislation as well as summaries of awarded grants and contracts.[2]

8.22 Women's Equity Action League (WEAL), 805 15th Street, NW, Suite 822, Washington, DC 20005, (202) 638-1961.

Formed in 1968, WEAL works to promote economic progress for American women by seeking better educational, child care, health, insurance, tax credit and pension opportunities and benefits for women and by fighting in Washington, state capitols and court for full access to all forms of social and economic participation denied to women. WEAL operates SPRINT, the national referral and information network on sex discrimination in sports and publishes the *WEAL Washington Report,* a national legislative publication on all women's issues and *WEAL Informed,* a legislative alert to women activists.

8.23 Women's History Research Center, 2325 Oak, Berkeley, CA 94708, (415) 548-1770.

The Women's History Research Center has collected and organized over a million documents (many on microfilm) relating to the role of women in our society. Their collection includes *History, Women and Health/Mental Health,* and *Women and Law* microfilms which incorporate articles gathered from women's publications, mass and alternative press, professional journals, and unpublished pamphlets and manuscripts from all over the world.

8.24 Women's Sports Foundation, 195 Moulton Street, San Francisco, CA 94123, (415) 563-6266.

National nonprofit organization devoted to the development of sports for women at all levels of endeavor. It provides print and nonprint materials and sponsors seminars and sports activities. Membership includes a subscription to *Women's Sports* magazine.[29]

VOCATIONAL EDUCATION

8.25   American Institute for Research, 1791 Arastradero, P.O. Box 1113, Palo Alto, CA 94302, (415) 493-3550.

This organization conducted the national Vocational Education Equity Study to assess the extent to which sex discrimination and stereotyping exist in all vocational programs and to assess the progress that has been made to reduce the inequities. Products that will be available through the U.S. Department of Education are an interim report analyzing the literature and legislation relating to discrimination and stereotyping in vocational education; a case study report of 15 effective programs and practices which describes useful procedures for a replication handbook and the procedures used in the study; and an executive summary and final report to provide Congress, administrators and other users with the major results of the study.[2]

8.26   The Federal Education Project, Lawyer's Committee for Civil Rights under the Law, Suite 526, 733 15th Street, NW, Washington, DC 20005, (202) 628-6700.

Technical assistance and information is provided to individuals and organizations concerned about equal opportunity in vocational education. The project produces a monthly newsletter containing articles on current developments affecting sex bias in vocational education, especially in the areas of federal legislation, rulemaking and enforcement activities. Future activities include publication of a pamphlet outlining the provisions of the 1976 Vocational Education Act Amendment; a handbook on model programs for eliminating bias and stereotyping; and a report on the quality and content of state five-year plans for vocational education.[9]

8.27   Fink, Kosecoff, Inc., 1535 6th Street, Suite 205, Santa Monica, CA 90401, (213) 394-9791.

This organization has developed staff materials and curriculum materials for secondary students and conducted research and evaluation projects on sex equity. Current projects include developing a communications network for the state of California in vocational education and evaluation of implementation of sex equity in vocational education. A newsletter is available.[2]

8.28   Miranda Associates, Inc., 4340 East West Highway, Suite 906, Bethesda, MD 20814, (301) 656-2208.

This organization implemented a "Business and Management Development Program for Minority Women" to train Hispanic women in management techniques. Their conference report on "Non-Traditional Occupations for Women of the Hemisphere—the U.S. Experience" is prepared in both English and Spanish. As part of the nationwide study of vocational education, the staff prepared a monograph of the concerns of minority women with respect to vocational education.[2]

8.29   The National Center for Research in Vocational Education, The Ohio State University, 1960 Kenny Road, Columbus, OH 43210, (800) 848-4815 or (614) 486-3655.

The National Center staff continues to progress in the area of sex equity and welcomes inquiries about their efforts as well as information about endeavors at other agencies. The National Center for

Research in Vocational Education has available over 20 publications on sex fairness in career guidance, career development and vocational education which are useful to teachers, counselors, administrators and parents. Projects have spanned basic research, curriculum development, technical assistance to state and local agencies, the development of bibliographies and other resources, and the dissemination of the results of these studies.[2]

8.30   Women's Bureau, Office of the Secretary, U.S. Department of Labor, Washington, DC 20210, (202) 523-6611.

The bureau has produced many reports on the status of women in the labor force: booklets, pamphlets and handbooks for women, educators and employers, and project reports on women and training. A publication list is available.

PUBLICATIONS/MEDIA

8.31   Canadian Women's Educational Press, 280 Bloor Street West, Suite 313, Toronto, Ontario, Canada, M5S 1W1, (416) 922-9447.

A nonprofit collective strongly committed to presenting material of importance from the women's movement.

8.32   Council on Interracial Books for Children, Room 300, 1841 Broadway at 60th Street, New York, NY 10023, (212) 757-5339.

The council was founded in 1966 by writers, editors, illustrators, teachers and parents committed to promote learning materials that embody the principles of cultural pluralism in their publications. Their Racism and Sexism Resource Center for Educators collects, adapts and publishes books, pamphlets, lesson plans and teaching strategies to develop pluralism in education. A catalogue listing materials and services will be sent on request.

8.33   The Feminist Press, Box 334, Old Westbury, NY 11568, (516) 997-7660.

The Feminist Press is a nonprofit, tax-exempt, educational and publishing organization working in many different ways to change learning. The Press works to eliminate sex role stereotypes in books and schools by providing a new literature with a broad vision of human potential. Their books—high quality paperbacks—include reprints of important or "lost" women writers, feminist biographies of women and nonsexist children's books. Curricular materials, bibliographies, directories and the *Women's Studies Newsletter* provide information and support for women's studies at every educational level. A complete description of more than 40 books and curricular materials is available in their publications catalogue.

8.34   Kelsey Street Press, P.O. Box 9235, Berkeley, CA 94709, (415) 841-4506.

A nonprofit alternative publishing association that has been producing books since 1975.

8.35   Kids Can Press, 585½ Bloor Street West, Toronto, Canada, M6G 1K5, (416) 534-3141.

Publisher of picture books based on folklore from around the world for children age 6–10.

8.36 KNOW, Inc., Box 86031, Pittsburgh, PA 15221, (412) 241-4844.

An alternative publisher of distinctly feminist publications.

8.37 Learn Me Bookstore, 642 Grand Avenue, St. Paul, MN 55105, (612) 291-7888.

A bookstore and resource center with learning materials free of stereotypes by sex, race, age or class for children, parents and teachers. All materials are screened for stereotypes and include positive, alternative, realistic images and text. Call or write for a catalogue.

8.38 Lollipop Power, Box 1171, Chapel Hill, NC 27514, (919) 929-4857.

Publishes nonsexist and nonracist children's books.

8.39 New Day Films, P.O. Box 315, Franklin Lakes, NJ 07417, (201) 891-8240.

New Day Films was formed in 1972 as a distribution cooperative for feminist films. Their films explore the lives of both women and men and offer a fresh perspective on a broad range of subjects: marriage, growing up in America, masculinity, sexism, women as workers, women as mothers, women as creators, living alone, families, aging, history and societal values.

8.40 New Seed Press, 1665 Euclid Avenue, Berkeley, CA 94709.

New Seed Press publishes children's books free from stereotyping; books that portray all kinds of people, living in all kinds of ways; and books that encourage thinking about how the world could be different and how to change it.

8.41 Over the Rainbow Press, P.O. Box 7072, Berkeley, CA 94707, (415) 525-4020.

Over the Rainbow Press is dedicated to publishing children's books with positive images of both girls and boys.

8.42 Women's Educational Equity Act Publishing Center, Education Development Center, 55 Chapel Street, Newton, MA 02160. Toll free (800) 225-3088, MA residents (617) 969-7100.

The Dissemination Center is a collaborative effort by the Education Development Center and the Wellesley College Center for Research on Women in Higher Education and the Professions for the review, production and dissemination of materials and programs developed through projects funded by the Women's Educational Equity Act program, (WEEAP). Materials include print, nonprint, and mixed-media packages. Contact the dissemination coordinator for information about specific products, programs, services and costs.[2]

SEX DESEGREGATION CENTERS

8.43 Sex Desegregation Assistance Center (Service Area I), Leslie Hergert, Director, New England Center for Equity Assistance, 290 South Main, Andover, MA 01810, (617) 470-1080.

Funded under Title IV of the Civil Rights Act of 1964, this desegregation assistance center for sex discrimination serves the states of Connecticut, Massachusetts, Maine, New Hampshire, Rhode Island and Vermont.

8.44 Sex Desegregation Assistance Center (Service Area II), Rebecca Lubetkin, Consortium for Educational Equity, Federation Hall-Douglass Campus, New Brunswick, NJ 08903, (201) 932-9808.

Funded under Title IV of the Civil Rights Act of 1964, this desegregation assistance center for sex discrimination serves the states of New Jersey, New York, Puerto Rico and Virginia.

8.45 Sex Desegregation Assistance Center (Service Area III), David Sadker, Director, Mid-Atlantic Sex Desegregation Assistance Center, The American University, Foxhall Square Building, Suite 224, 3301 New Mexico Avenue, NW, Washington, DC 20016, (202) 686-3511.

Funded under Title IV of the Civil Rights Act of 1964, this desegregation assistance center for sex discrimination serves the states of Delaware, Maryland, Pennsylvania, Virginia, Washington, DC and West Virginia.

8.46 Sex Desegregation Assistance Center (Service Area IV), Gordon Foster, Director, Southeast Sex Desegregation Assistance Center, University of Miami, School of Education, P.O. Box 248065, Coral Gables, FL 33124, (305) 284-5324.

Funded under Title IV of the Civil Rights Act of 1964, this desegregation assistance center for sex discrimination serves the states of Alabama, Florida, Georgia, Kentucky, Mississippi, North Carolina, South Carolina and Tennessee.

8.47 Sex Desegregation Assistance Center (Service Area V), Dr. Charles D. Moody, Director, The Great Lakes Sex Desegregation Assistance Center, 3951 North Meridian, Indianapolis, IN 46208, (313) 763-9910 or (800) 428-2165.

Funded under Title IV of the Civil Rights Act of 1964, this desegregation assistance center for sex discrimination serves the states of Illinois, Indiana, Michigan, Minnesota, Ohio and Wisconsin.

8.48 Sex Desegregation Assistance Center (Service Area VI), Dr. Bennat Mullen, Director, Sex Desegregation Assistance Center of the Southwest, Stephen F. Austin State University, Box 13010A, Nacogdoches, TX 75962, (713) 569-5307.

Funded under Title IV of the Civil Rights Act of 1964, this desegregation assistance center for sex discrimination serves the states of Arkansas, Louisiana, New Mexico, Oklahoma and Texas.

8.49 Sex Desegregation Assistance Center (Service Area VII), Dr. Charles Rankin, Director, Kansas State University, College of Education—Holton Hall, Department of Administration and Foundation, Manhattan, KS 66505, (913) 532-6408.

Funded under Title IV of the Civil Rights Act of 1964, this desegregation assistance center for sex discrimination serves the states of Iowa, Kansas, Nebraska and Missouri.

8.50 Sex Desegregation Assistance Center (Service Area VIII), Richard Thomas, Director, Mountain West Sex Desegregation Assistance Center, Weber State College—1101, Ogden, UT 84408, (801) 626-6650.

Funded under Title IV of the Civil Rights Act of 1964, this desegregation assistance center for sex discrimination serves the states of Colorado, Montana, North Dakota, South Dakota, Utah and Wyoming.

8.51 Sex Desegregation Assistance Center (Service Area IX), Dr. Barbara A. Peterson, Sex Desegregation Assistance Center, Education Classroom Building, Room 327, California State University—Fullerton, Fullerton, CA 92634, (714) 870-3141 or 870-3811.

Funded under Title IV of the Civil Rights Act of 1964, this desegregation assistance center for sex discrimination serves the states of Arizona, California, and Nevada.

8.52 Sex Desegration Assistance Center (Service Area X), Lisa Hunter, Director, Sex Desegregation Assistance Center—the Pacific, Far West Laboratory for Education, Research and Development, 1855 Folsom, San Francisco, CA 94103, (415) 565-3110.

Funded under Title IV of the Civil Rights Act of 1964, this desegregation assistance center for sex discrimination serves Hawaii, Guam, American Samoa, the Territory of the Pacific Islands, and the Commonwealth of the Northern Mariana Islands.

8.53 Sex Desegregation Assistance Center (Service Area XI and XII), Barbara Hutchison, Director, Center for Sex Equity, Northwest Regional Educational Laboratory, 300 SW Sixth Avenue, Portland, OR 97204, (503) 295-0220 or (800) 547-6339.

Funded under Title IV of the Civil Rights Act of 1964, these desegregation assistance centers for sex discrimination serve the states of Alaska, Idaho, Oregon and Washington.

Appendix 1: Subject Definitions

The guide contains citations for nonsexist teaching activities organized into the subject areas that follow.

1.0 GENERAL AWARENESS

Resources designed to increase student awareness of sex role stereotyping and to provide teachers with strategies and materials for increasing equity in the classroom and the educational process.

Sex Role Stereotyping

Materials to increase student awareness of sex role stereotypes and sex bias, including the implications for their personal lives and how they view the world and themselves.

Women's Educational Equity

Resources and strategies focusing on alleviating sex-biased classroom instruction and increasing equity for girls and women in the educational process.

Male Sex Role Stereotyping

Materials focusing on the deleterious effects of sex role stereotypes on boys and men.

Nonsexist Materials

Materials focusing on the issue of the sex bias in student books and supplementary materials; resources for locating and adapting nonsexist compensatory materials.

0 COUNSELING AND CAREER GUIDANCE

Resources designed to aid counselors and vocational educators in providing students with nonsexist counseling and career guidance.

Counseling

Nonsexist counseling resources for students making decisions about their lives and confronting problems such as family breakups, abortion, rape and changing lifestyles.

Career Guidance

Materials using a nonbiased approach to increase student awareness of options and opportunities available to them when making career choices, including information on nontraditional careers and vocational education.

3.0 FINE ARTS

Resources designed to help teachers increase student awareness of the contributions of women to the fine arts.

Art

Materials focusing on the contributions of women in painting, drawing, sculpture, photography and film.

Dance

Materials focusing on the contributions of women to the choreography and performance of dance, including modern, jazz and classical forms.

Music

Materials focusing on the contributions of women musicians, composers, conductors and singers; lyrics, music and songs about women's issues and history.

4.0 HEALTH AND PHYSICAL EDUCATION

Resources designed to provide health and physical education teachers and coaches with strategies and resources to provide nonbiased instruction in health and equitable opportunities for the participation of women and girls in physical education classes and sports.

Health

Materials focusing on individual health care, sex education and family living.

PE/Sports

Resources and strategies for providing equitable opportunities for the participation of women and girls in sports and athletic events; guidelines for implementing programs in compliance with Title IX.

5.0 LANGUAGE ARTS

Resources to aid teachers in providing language arts instruction which focuses on the contributions of women authors, the images of women and girls in literature, and writing in an unbiased manner.

Literature/Children's Books

Materials focusing on literary works, including poetry, prose and drama, by women authors; materials focusing on how women are portrayed in literature.

Women Writers

Materials focusing on the lives and contributions of women authors.

Writing/Language

Materials to increase student awareness of biased language and words, including alternatives for how to write in a nonbiased manner.

6.0 MATH AND SCIENCE

Resources and materials designed to help students recognize the contributions of women to the fields of math and science as well as strategies to help alleviate the special problems many girls and women have with math and science because of society's role expectations.

Math

Materials about women mathematicians and career opportunities in the area of mathematics.

Science

Materials to provide students with information on (1) the contributions of women in the field of science, including biology, chemistry and physics; (2) the rela-

tionship of women to science and society; and (3) opportunities in the fields of science and technology.

7.0 SOCIAL STUDIES

Resources to aid teachers in providing equitable instruction in history and social studies classes, as well as interdisciplinary materials focusing on the study of women.

History

Nonsexist and compensatory resources recognizing the contributions of women throughout history, particularly famous women in American history.

Social Studies

Nonsexist and compensatory materials focusing on the behavioral sciences, including anthropology, psychology, sociology and political systems.

Women's Studies

Materials about the modern day women's movement and "feminist" issues; materials focusing on the contributions of women viewed from a variety of educational disciplines; materials about the lives of everyday women.

8.0 SEX EQUITY ORGANIZATIONS

Organizations focusing on women's educational equity and vocational education; publishers and film distributors; and sex desegregation centers which provide resources for implementing educational equity in the schools.

Women's Educational Equity

Organizations conducting research, developing programs or providing resources focused on increasing educational equity for women and girls.

Vocational Education

Organizations developing programs or resources aimed at providing equitable opportunities for girls and boys in vocational education.

Publications/Media

Publishers and film distributors of nonsexist and compensatory student and instructional print and nonprint resources.

Sex Desegregation Centers

Regional desegregation assistance centers for sex discrimination funded under Title IV of the Civil Rights Act of 1964, designed to assist school districts in providing resources to facilitate the implementation of sex equity in the school.

Appendix 2: Footnote Sources

1. Olin, Ferris. *Fair Play, A Bibliography of Non-Stereotyped Materials (Volume I)*. New Brunswick, NJ: Training Institute for Sex Desegregation of the Public Schools, June 1976.
2. The National Center for Research in Vocational Education. *Resource Update: 1979 Sex Equity in Vocational Education*. Columbus, OH: The Ohio State University, 1979.
3. *Advisory List of Instructional Media for Reduction of Sex Bias*. North Carolina State Department of Education, 1979. ED 149 755.
4. Hulme, Marilyn. *Fair Play, A Bibliography of Non-Stereotyped Materials (Volume II)*. New Brunswick, NJ: Training Institute for Sex Desegregation of Public Schools, September 1977.
5. Rosenfelt, Deborah Silverton. *Strong Women: An Annotated Bibliography of Literature for the High School Classroom*. Old Westbury, NY: The Feminist Press, 1976.
6. Geisler, Harlynne. *A Bibliography of Non-Sexist Books for Junior and Senior High Readers*. Champaign, IL: NOW, 1973.
7. "Heresies: A Feminist Publication on Art and Politics." New York: Heresies. (Publication brochure).
8. Sadker, Myra and David. *Beyond Pictures and Pronouns: Sexism in Teacher Education Textbooks*. Women's Educational Equity Act Program, DHEW, Office of Education. (Unpublished work).
9. *Resources on Eliminating Sex Role Stereotyping in Vocational Education*. Columbus, OH: The Center for Vocational Education, 1977.
10. *1978-1979 Catalog: Racism and Sexism Resource Center for Educators*. New York: Council on Interracial Books for Children and the Foundation for Change, 1978.
11. *Midwest Sex Desegregation Assistance Center Resource Library Annotated Bibliography*. Manhattan, KS: Midwest Sex Desegregation Assistance Center, June 1979.
12. *TABS: Aids for Ending Sexism in School*, Vol. 2, No. 3 (Spring 1979).
13. *Newsnotes*, No. 8 (Spring 1979). Old Westbury, NY: The Feminist Press.
14. *Network News and Notes*. San Francisco, CA: Women's Educational Equity Communications Network, Far West Laboratory for Educational Research and Development, Fall 1979.
15. The National Center for Research in Vocational Education. *Centergram*, Vol. 16, No. 2 (February 1979). Columbus, OH: The Ohio State University.
16. Training Institute for Sex Desegregation. *List of Media*. New Brunswick, NJ: Rutgers University, October 1978.
17. "WEECN Publications." San Francisco, CA: Women's Educational Equity Communications Network, Far West Laboratory for Educational Research and Development. (Brochure).
18. The National Center for Research in Vocational Education. "RBS Mini List: Resources for K–12 Instructional Materials on Women's Educational Equity." Columbus, OH: The Ohio State University, 1978. (Brochure).
19. "Women's Studies for All Ages: New Books from The Feminist Press." Old Westbury, NY: The Feminist Press, Fall 1979. (Brochure).
20. *Catalogue*. Pittsburgh, PA: KNOW, Inc., April 1979.
21. Matomatsu, Nancy R. *A Selected Bibliography of Bias Free Materials: Grades 1-12*. Olympia, WA: Washington Office of the State Superintendent of Public Instruction, November 1977.
22. *Choices*, Vol. 1, No. 2 (April 1979). Manhattan, KS: Midwest Sex Desegregation Assistance Center.
23. Golden, Glora; Hunter, Lisa; and Morine, Grets. *The Process of Change: A Handbook for Teachers on the Concept of Changing Sex Role Stereotypes*. Oakland Unified School District and Far West Laboratory for Educational Research and Development, 1974. (Draft copy).
24. Martin, Wanda and Terry, Arthur F. *Sex Equity Guidelines for Teacher Educators*. Salem, OR: Marion County Education Service District, Interinstitutional Consortium for Career Education, August 1979.

25. Johnson, Laurie Olson. *Non-Sexist Curricular Materials for Elementary Schools.* Old Westbury, NY: The Feminist Press, 1974.

26. *Resources for Ending Sex Bias in Schools.* PEER, Washington, DC. (Revised July 1978).

27. *TABS: Aids for Ending Sexism in School,* Vol. 2, No. 4 (Summer 1979).

28. Training Institute for Sex Desegregation of the Public Schools. *List of Media.* New Brunswick, NJ: Rutgers University, July 1980.

29. *Resource Roundup: Girls and Women in Sports.* San Francisco, CA: Women's Educational Equity Communications Network, Far West Laboratory, February 1979.

30. *Network News and Notes.* San Francisco, CA: Women's Educational Equity Communications Network, Far West Laboratory, Summer 1979.

31. *Resource Roundup: Disabled Women and Equal Opportunity.* San Francisco, CA: Women's Educational Equity Communications Network, Far West Laboratory, April 1979.

32. Allman, Joanna, et al. *Understanding Sex Roles and Moving Beyond: A Learning Teaching Guide.* Model Sex-Fair Training Program in Educational Psychology and Guidance, University of Tennessee, 1979.

33. *Resource Roundup: Black Women and Education.* San Francisco, CA: Women's Educational Equity Communications Network, Far West Laboratory, April 1979.

34. *MSDAC Resource Library Annotated Bibliography.* Manhattan, KS: Midwest Sex Desegregation Assistance Center, Kansas State University, January 1980.

35. *Resource Roundup: Asian/Pacific Women in America.* San Francisco, CA: Women's Educational Equity Communications Network, Far West Laboratory, May 1980.

36. *Network News and Notes.* San Francisco, CA: Women's Educational Equity Communications Network, Far West Laboratory, Spring 1980.

37. *Publications List.* Washington, DC: National Alliance for Optional Parenthood, July 1980.

38. *Michigan Career Education Resource Materials.* East Lansing, MI: Michigan State University.

39. *10 Years Publishing Women: 1970-1980.* Old Westbury, NY: The Feminist Press. (Catalogue).

40. "WEECN Announces Series of Annotated Bibliographies on Women and Education." San Francisco, CA: Women's Educational Equity Communications Network, Far West Laboratory. (Undated press release).

41. *Sex Equity and Vocational Education: Some Recent WEECN Publications.* San Francisco, CA: Women's Educational Equity Communications Network, Far West Laboratory.

42. *180 Plus: A Framework for Non-Stereotyped Human Roles in Elementary Media Center Materials.* Kalamazoo, MI: Kalamazoo Public Schools, July 1976.

43. *Network News and Notes.* San Francisco, CA: Women's Educational Equity Communications Network, Far West Laboratory, Spring 1979.

44. *Project Equity: $500.00 Sex Equity Model Materials Collection.* Fullerton, CA: California State University, Sex Desegregation Assistance Center.

45. *Resource for Women's Studies Collections.* Metuchen, NJ: Scarecrow Press, 1980. (Catalogue).

46. *Counseling Resources 1980: American Personnel and Guidance Association.* Falls Church, VA: American Personnel and Guidance Assocation, 1979.

47. Training Institute for Sex Desegregation of the Public Schools. *Strategies for Equality: Mathematics/Science.* New Brunswick, NJ: Rutgers University, July 1980.

48. Training Institute for Sex Desegregation of the Public Schools. *Lists of Games and Simulations.* New Brunswick, NJ: Rutgers University, 1980.

49. Training Institute for Sex Desegregation of the Public Schools. *Strategies for Equality: Vocational Education, Including Home Economics and Industrial Arts.* New Brunswick, NJ: Rutgers University, August 1979.

Appendix 3: How to Obtain Materials Listed in the Guide

The items listed in the guide may be obtained from a variety of sources. You may order the materials directly by writing to the publisher or distributor noted in the citation. Or, you may wish to investigate local and regional sources which often have many of the items available on loan or for rental.

Among the sources you may wish to consult for assistance in locating the materials you need for yur classroom are:

- School librarians
- School district curriculum and resource specialists
- School district media centers
- State systems of higher education
- University film libraries
- Regional Title IV sex desegregation assistance centers/institutes
- City, county and state libraries

To locate the address of publishers noted in the citations, please refer to the 1978–79 *Books in Print* (R. R. Bowker).

Prices indicated were taken from a secondary source and should be considered only as approximations.

Several items listed in the guide can be found in ERIC, a nationwide information system established to help educators stay informed about developments in education. This system acquires, selects, abstracts, indexes, stores, retrieves and disseminates significant and timely education information related to research, instruction and personnel preparation at all levels and in all educational institutions. Items found in ERIC may be ordered from EDRS (ERIC Document Reproduction Service) and are available on microfiche (MF) and sometimes in paper or hard copy (HC).

Although the citations note prices for hard copy and microfiche, the price per document is based on the number of pages and is subject to change over time. An ERIC price codes schedule is included in this appendix and will allow you to convert all price codes to actual dollar amounts. Also included is a sample form you may wish to copy to use in ordering ERIC documents from EDRS.

HOW TO ORDER ERIC DOCUMENTS

ERIC® DOCUMENT REPRODUCTION SERVICE
P.O. Box 190 ARLINGTON VIRGINIA 22210 • (703) 841-1212   **EDRS**
OPERATED BY   COMPUTER MICROFILM INTERNATIONAL CORP.

ORDER FORM

IMPORTANT INSTRUCTIONS

SHIP TO: _____

- **ORDER BY ED NO.** (6 digits)
  See Resources in Education
  (RIE)

- **SPECIFY EITHER:**
  Microfiche (MF)
  or
  Paper Copy (PC)

- **ENTER UNIT PRICE**
  (See Below)

- **INCLUDE SHIPPING CHARGES**
  (See Charts Below)

- **ENCLOSE CHECK OR MONEY ORDER**
  Payable to EDRS in U.S.
  Funds. Check must indicate
  the U.S. transit number of your
  banks agency.

- **OR ENCLOSE AUTHORIZED ORIGINAL PURCHASE ORDER**

- **COMPLETE AND SIGN BELOW**

BILL TO: _____

Date _____

Signature _____

Title _____

ED NUMBER	NO. OF PAGES	NO. OF COPIES		UNIT PRICE	TOTAL
		MF	PC		

UNIT PRICE SCHEDULE

MICROFICHE (MF)

NUMBER FICHE EACH ED #	PRICE CODE	Price
1 to 5 (up to 480 pages)	MF01	$ .91
6 (481-576 pages)	MF02	1.10
7 (577-672 pages)	MF03	1.29
8 (673-768 pages)	MF04	1.48
Each additional microfiche (additional 96 pages)		.19

PAPER COPY (PC)

NUMBER PAGES EACH ED #	PRICE CODE	Price
1 to 25	PC01	$2.00
26 to 50	PC02	3.65
51 to 75	PC03	5.30
76 to 100	PC04	6.95
Each additional 25 pages		1.65

TOTAL NO. OF PAGES		SUBTOTAL	
TAX EXEMPT NO. _____		VA RESIDENTS ADD 4% SALES TAX	
		SHIPPING	
DEPOSIT ACCT. NO. _____		TOTAL	

CHARTS FOR DETERMINING SHIPPING CHARGES

1st CLASS POSTAGE FOR

1-3 Microfiche ONLY	4-8 Microfiche ONLY	9-14 Microfiche ONLY	15-18 Microfiche ONLY	19-21 Microfiche ONLY	22-27 Microfiche ONLY	28-32 Microfiche ONLY
$.18	$.35	$.52	$.69	$.86	$1.03	$1.20

U.P.S. CHARGES FOR

1 lb 33-75 MF or 1-75 PC PAGES Not to Exceed $1.40	2 lbs 76-150 MF or PC PAGES Not to Exceed $1.75	3 lbs 151-225 MF or PC PAGES Not to Exceed $2.11	4 lbs 226-300 MF or PC PAGES Not to Exceed $2.46	5 lbs 301-375 MF or PC PAGES Not to Exceed $2.81	6 lbs 376-450 MF or PC PAGES Not to Exceed $3.16	7 lbs 451-525 MF or PC PAGES Not to Exceed $3.52	8 to 20 lbs. 526-1500 MF or PC PAGES Not to Exceed $3.87-$8.09

NOTE — Orders for 33 or more microfiche and all orders for paper copies (PC) will be shipped via United Parcel Service unless otherwise instructed

Revised January 1981

PLEASE DO NOT REMOVE.
THIS FORM MAY BE PHOTOCOPIED OR ADDITIONAL COPIES OBTAINED FROM EDRS.

Prices subject to change without notification.

ERIC PRICE CODES

PAPER COPY/HARD COPY

PRICE CODE	PAGINATION	PRICE
PC 01	1 - 25	$2.00
PC 02	26 - 50	3.65
PC 03	51 - 75	5.30
PC 04	76 - 100	6.95
PC 05	101 - 125	8.60
PC 06	126 - 150	10.25
PC 07	151 - 175	11.90
PC 08	176 - 200	13.55
PC 09	201 - 225	15.20
PC 10	226 - 250	16.85
PC 11	251 - 275	18.50
PC 12	276 - 300	20.15
PC 13	301 - 325	21.80
PC 14	326 - 350	23.45
PC 15	351 - 375	25.10
PC 16	376 - 400	26.75
PC 17	401 - 425	28.40
PC 18	426 - 450	30.05
PC 19	451 - 475	31.70
PC 20	476 - 500	33.35

ADD $1.65 FOR EACH ADDITIONAL 25 PAGES, OR FRACTION THEREOF

MICROFICHE

PRICE CODE	PAGINATION	NUMBER OF FICHE	PRICE
MF 01	1 - 480	1 - 5	$ .91
MF 02	481 - 576	6	1.10
MF 03	577 - 672	7	1.29
MF 04	673 - 768	8	1.48
MF 05	769 - 864	9	1.67
MF 06	865 - 960	10	1.86

ADD $0.19 FOR EACH ADDITIONAL MICROFICHE (1 - 96 PAGES)

From: Resources in Education. Washington, DC: National Institute of Education, U.S. Department of Education, July 1981, Vol. 16, No. 7, p. 351.

Appendix 4: Model for Developing Nonsexist Lesson Plans

The following is a model for developing lesson plans. There are two areas of focus: (1) the content to be presented and (2) equity education related to the content.

CONTENT PLANNING	EQUITY PLANNING
STEP I: IDENTIFYING OBJECTIVES	
Assessing Needs, Identifying Objectives (example: addition skills; students will be able to add two-digit numbers)	Identifying Student Equity Needs (example: students think math is for boys—awareness level needs about sexism)
STEP II: IDENTIFYING MATERIALS TO SUPPORT INSTRUCTION	
Finding Appropriate Texts, Books, etc.	Evaluating Materials for Bias (biased, equitable or compensatory)
STEP III: PLANNING INSTRUCTIONAL ACTIVITIES	
Sequencing Events (presentations, discussions, work assignments)	Planning Ways to Work with Materials in Nonsexist Manner
INTERFACING MATERIALS AND STRATEGIES WITH EQUITY PLANS	
STEP IV: CARRYING OUT INSTRUCTION	
STEP V: ASSESSING THE RESULTS*	
Administering Cognitive Test (or other way to gather data on student understanding/skill)	Assessing Student Change in Terms of Equity

*Data from assessment is recycled into Step I: Identifying Goals.

Developed by Janice Druian, Northwest Regional Educational Laboratory, for BIAS inservice training workshops.

Appendix 5: Lesson Planning Activity Sheet

OBJECTIVE(S)	
MATERIALS	
PROCEDURES Monday	
Tuesday	
Wednesday	
Thursday	
Friday	
ASSESSMENT (procedures for measuring whether objectives were met)	

Developed by Janice Druian, Northwest Regional Educational Laboratory, for BIAS inservice training workshops.

Appendix 6: Guidelines for Developing Nonbiased Instruction

The following guidelines are adapted from some generated at a National Conference on Nonsexist Early Childhood Education. While they were originally intended for publishers of educational materials and professional journals, we feel they have meaning for the classroom teacher who often develops materials. In addition to using these guidelines to develop new materials, you can also use them to assess or modify existing materials.

DOES YOUR MATERIAL:

1. Reflect an accurate and broad view of the world
   - represent various groups according to race, culture, age, physical and mental disability, economic status, creed, religion, political ideology, sex
   - reflect the world as populated equally by men and women

2. Emphasize positive role models
   - competent humans who have a sense of self worth and dignity
   - characters displaying the following traits:
     —problem solving
     —respect for others and self
     —concern for well-being of others and self
     —physical and emotional strength

   This does not mean that stories dealing with antisocial behavior should be eliminated; rather, when presented, they need to be presented with a clear emphasis on the consequences of behavior.

3. Help children understand their real capabilities

   Stories that emphasize unusual strength, magical powers, super human skill or improbable solutions to problems do not help children identify their own skill and strength.

   There needs to be a balance between fantasy and created worlds and materials that give examples of real people doing real things. It is especially important for young boys to understand that there are other values as important as or more important than being a super hero.

4. Have accurate visuals

   It is important that visual images accurately depict physical images, life styles, cultural traditions and surroundings when portraying children from different racial/ethnic backgrounds. It is not enough to simply change skin color or names.

5. Reflect teaming relationships

   - cooperative action between girls and boys
   - real friendships between girls and boys

   Stories that emphasize excessive conflicts or excessive competition between girls and boys do not promote non sexist attitudes.

It is highly unlikely that all these guidelines can be attended to in one story or one set of materials. However, within the context of a unit of study, these things need to be considered.

Adapted from: "Guidelines for the Development and Evaluation of Unbiased Educational Materials," prepared by Felicia R. George, Project Administrator, NON-SEXIST CHILD DEVELOPMENT PROJECT, January 1978. Non-Sexist Child Development Project, Women's Action Alliance, Inc., 370 Lexington Avenue, New York, NY 10017.

Title Index